ıal Readers   ان &
                 Students

DUE FOR RETUR

Essays in Nineteenth Century Economic
History: The Old Northwest

Essays in

NINETEENTH CENTURY
ECONOMIC HISTORY

The Old Northwest

Edited by
David C. Klingaman
and Richard K. Vedder

OHIO UNIVERSITY PRESS: ATHENS

PREFACE

The editors are indebted to several people for both encouragement and financial support during the preparation of this book. Dean John M. Peterson of the Ohio University College of Business Administration offered support and encouragement during the entire process from idea to actuality. Burton W. DeVeau, Chairman of the Economics Department, deserves our many thanks. Our colleagues, Lowell Gallaway and Lee Soltow, were instrumental in our planning the volume.

We wish also to acknowledge the financial support given us by the Earhart Foundation during the time this volume was being planned and the editors' papers written. Richard Vedder also benefited from the generosity of Edwin and Ruth Kennedy, who furnished a John C. Baker grant.

The authors appreciate the work of Patricia Fitch and Holly Mitchell of the Ohio University Press, who competently assumed the task of converting our manuscript into print.

Special thanks are given to Marie Frontera, our Economics Department secretary, who provided her high-quality secretarial services "above and beyond the call of duty."

Most important, we acknowledge the work done by the authors of the papers whose research, writing, and courteous cooperation was vital to the publication of this book.

CONTENTS

CONTENTS

EDITORS' INTRODUCTION

This is a book of essays on nineteenth century American economic history. Several essays encompass the whole economy, yet the theme of the book is midwest America. Perhaps the unique feature of the volume is its focus on a relatively neglected region, the Old Northwest. Why a collection of essays stressing the economic development of the Old Northwest during the nineteenth century? What is there about the region that would justify the existence of this volume? At least a partial answer to these questions is contained in the simple table (labeled Table 1) that follows. Annual growth rates in per capita income are presented by region for the period 1840-1900 (where available). From the entries in Table 1, it is clear that what is conventionally called the Old Northwest (i.e., the present East North Central States) showed the most rapid rate of per capita economic growth of any region of the United States during the period of the nineteenth century for which we have data. Consequently, this portion of the United States can be viewed as being perhaps the most significant single region from the standpoint of understanding the nature of economic growth in the United States during the nineteenth century. This strongly suggests that a detailed study of patterns of economic development in this region is of more than merely parochial interest. Rather, it is at the heart of the national experience of this

Table 1

Per Capita Growth Rates in Income, by Region,
United States, 1840-1900

Region	Per Capita Income ($) 1840	Per Capita Income ($) 1880	Per Capita Income ($) 1900	Annual Growth Rate[a]
New England	83	130	147	0.96%
Middle Atlantic	77	116	139	0.99
East North Central (Old Northwest)	46	102	120	1.61
West North Central	51	90	120	1.43
South Atlantic	55	51	61	0.17
East South Central	55	57	64	0.25
West South Central	104	63	77	-0.50
Mountain	-	170	178	0.23
Pacific	-	182	176	-0.17

Source: Easterlin, Richard A., "Interregional Differences in Per Capita Income, Population, and Total Income, 1850-1950," in *Trends in the American Economy in the Nineteenth Century, Studies in Income and Wealth*, Volume 24, National Bureau of Economic Research, Princeton University Press, Princeton, 1960, pp. 73-140.

[a]Growth rates are calculated for the period 1840 to 1900 except for the Mountain and Pacific states where the period is from 1880 to 1900.

period, namely, the beginnings of the movement towards sustained growth in per capita levels of national income.

In the broadest and simplest sense, per capita economic growth can be viewed as occurring for one of two reasons: (1) increases in per capita levels of factor inputs into the process of producing goods and services or (2) rising levels of productivity of the factor inputs that are employed. The first of these may occur because of rising levels of labor force participation among the population, a more extensive per capita utilization of available land resources, or capital goods formation that takes place at a more rapid rate than the population is growing. Thus, what is basically involved here is the manner in which people make the decisions as to how and when to sell the productive services (either human or non-human) they possess.

The second aspect of economic growth, increasing resource productivity, is an exceedingly complex issue. A variety of potential sources of this phenomenon exist. First, there is the possibility that qualitative improvements in factor inputs occur that are not taken into account in the way in which these inputs are measured. For example, land of higher fertility may be brought into cultivation, particularly if there is room for geographic expansion of the limits of settlement. Or, the character of the labor force may change. This may especially be the case if there is a general increase in the quantity of education being provided to individuals in the society. Finally, it is possible that the quality of capital goods will be improved through technological changes which enhance their productivity. However, much of this ought to be captured in the conventional measure of capital stock, which is in value terms.

An additional source of enhancement of the productivity of factor inputs is investment in various forms of what may be thought of as "social overhead" capital. Examples of this type investment abound, but some of the most common ones involve the developing of transportation facilities, such as highways, railroads, and canals. These are an integral part of what is frequently called the "infra-structure" of an economy and have a tendency to produce economic benefits beyond those implicit in the actual value of the transportation services that are provided. The "external" benefits of this type of economic activity frequently take the form of higher levels of factor productivity in other industries (brought about by the more efficient combinations of resources that better transportation facilities permit). External benefits may also involve higher levels of per capita factor supply, usually in the form of a greater per head investment in capital goods that follows from certain technological possibilities becoming economically feasible given the presence of improvements in transportation.

A final possible source of increases in factor productivity is the general set of institutional arrangements created by society to facilitate the implementing of economic decisions of all kinds. These encompass a wide range of matters, such as legal codes, social attitudes towards economic activity, and the like. In short, they make up what can be viewed as the broad "environment" within which such prosaically technical phenomena as levels of factor inputs and optimum factor combinations are determined. The nature of this "environment" can be a critical determinant of the extent to which efficient resource combinations actually occur. For example, a social milieu which discourages attitudes that would lead resource owners to being responsive to economic differentials in disposing of the services of their resources will not produce as high a level of economic activity as one that is congenial to resource owners maximizing their economic advantage.

In order to explore the wide range of possible sources of economic growth during the nineteenth century, we have assembled eleven essays dealing with various aspects of economic life in the midwest. These essays have been contributed by both prominent and less well known scholars in the field of American economic history. Methodologically, the essays represent a variety of approaches to dealing with historical processes, ranging from highly esoteric forms of the "new" economic history which employ econometric techniques and emphasize quantitative measurement to more traditional and literary treatments of the subject. Put succinctly, we have made no attempt to collect a set of essays that are consistently of either the "new" or "old" economic history variety. Instead, the emphasis has been placed on competent scholarship and ability to contribute to our knowledge of the nature of economic development in nineteenth century America.

To organize the essays we have chosen to concentrate on the traditional division of productive agents into land, labor, and capital. In order to provide a broad overview of the economic life of the area and its relation to the remainder of the American economy, William Parker's essay, "From Northwest to Midwest: Social Bases of a Regional History," is presented initially. This is then followed by three essays dealing with various aspects of land use. First, Robert Gallman treats the general question of growth in agricultural output in the United States during the nineteenth century. Given the generally agricultural character of the midwest at this time, the conclusions from this essay set the stage for a good deal of the ensuing material. Following Gallman's essay, Richard Easterlin moves to a more disaggregated level and focuses on patterns of agricultural production and income by region as of mid-nineteenth century. Gallman and Easterlin go beyond the Old Northwest, though the region is very much a part of their work, and extend their analysis to the more general level of economic development in the United States before 1850. An essay by Edward Rastatter assesses the controversial role of the land speculator in agricultural development with particular emphasis on Ohio during the period 1820-40.

The following group of essays emphasizes the human inputs into the productive process. First, Don Leet explores the relationship between agricultural economic opportunity and the natural rate of population increase in Ohio over the period 1810-60. This is followed by an essay by Richard Vedder and Lowell Gallaway which discusses population migration into the Old Northwest with a special emphasis on pre-1860 migration into the states of Ohio, Indiana, and Illinois. A picture of individual wealth in Ohio in 1860 is provided by David Klingaman. And last, Lee Soltow offers a rather detailed description of the impact of economic development on the human factor in production in the form of income and wealth distribution patterns in the state of Ohio from its early beginnings down to the present day.

The third group of essays concerns itself with developments in the area of capital formation, particularly of the social overhead type. Donald Adams has contributed a study of the role of commercial banking institutions in the economic development of the Old Northwest. Adams reviews the literature and the problems of interpretation and considers some interesting capital and credit problems. This is followed by Roger Ransom's analysis of the impact of public investment in canals on economic life in the region. The volume closes with a lengthy essay by Jeffrey Williamson on the role of railroads in late nineteenth century economic development in the midwest and offers a striking reinterpretation of midwest economic growth. However, beyond this it also presents another overview of the economy of the region we are considering, one that complements Parker's in two fundamental respects. First, it employs quite explicitly the methodology of the "new" economic history, and second, it is concerned more with the end of the century whereas Parker's essay deals primarily with earlier economic developments in the Old Northwest.

The contrast between the Parker and Williamson essays serves to highlight the essential character of economic development in the Old Northwest. That development had its inception in the first seepings of population through the chinks in the Appalachian mountain barrier. Once over the crest of the mountain obstacle, the rivers of the Mississippi basin became the pathways of even further migration, and the Old Northwest ceased to be the preserve of the Indian tribes and hunters and trappers. Now the process of "taming the wilderness" (to use a cliché) began in earnest. Of necessity, the early economic life that developed was agrarian in nature, and at the time at which we pick up the story it remains just that. However, the thrust throughout the nineteenth century is in the direction of moving away from the agrarian mold and toward the highly complex and interdependent industrial type of society that will characterize American life in the twentieth century. Essentially this is the story of American economic development, and during the nineteenth century the territory known as the Old Northwest moved dramatically in that direction. This set of essays attempts to provide some insight into the processes which gave rise to this pattern of economic development. Hopefully, we have made some contribution in this respect.

ESSAYS IN NINETEENTH
CENTURY ECONOMIC
HISTORY

I

FROM NORTHWEST TO MIDWEST

Social Bases of a Regional History

William N. Parker

Yale University

I

History books tell us that the United States in 1860 was divided into three parts: South, Northeast, and West. The South had in turn three sub-regions: the border states, the southeast and the "old southwest"; the Northeast included New England and what had been the Middle Colonies. The Far West had hardly entered into American economic history, except as a land of mining excitements. A new and arid Southwest lay beyond Texas. A new Northwest on the Pacific was replacing the "old Northwest". The latter had hardly become "old"; its settlement and culture patterns were still vigorously penetrating across into Kansas and Iowa heading into the Great Plains. In each of these three sections—South, Northeast, and Northwest—the population had developed a characteristic social organization and with it a characteristic culture, which the sub-regions exemplified with minor variations.

At a century's distance, and with the record of the War in retrospect, the South appears indeed as a nation, a monolith whose economy, politics, society and morality were dominated by the class of slave-owning planters. Slave owners made up only 3 1/2 per cent of the South's population (5 1/2 per cent of the population excluding slaves), and the "planters" with ten or more slaves, whose holdings accounted for three-quarters of the slaves and at least three-quarters of the cotton grown, numbered only about 100,000 individuals out of a Southern population of about four million slaves and 7,200,000 free persons.[1] One hardly knows whether to marvel more at the politics or at the economics of this vast region. Among other peoples and soils, a small aristocracy had ruled over a large area, restricting its economy along lines compatible with its social dominance. One thinks of the eighteenth century English aristocracy, or more aptly, of the Prussian Junkers and other East European landed groups. But those noble classes ordinarily possessed a degree of local sovereignty, legal control of local justice, and even force, and they dominated the values of a population committed deeply to the principle of social organization through subordination. The achievement of the Southern planters was the more remarkable in that it was carried off in a nineteenth century nation-state, where democracy and free markets had received their supreme expression. To understand the planters' power, one must no doubt look to a system and traditions of local government founded on seventeenth and eighteenth century English landed precedent.[2]

The free North presents no such clear picture of class organization and dominance.[3] Along the Eastern seaboard from Baltimore to Boston and on to the shipping towns of Maine, the mercantile activity of colonial times, after its crisis from 1808 to 1818, had restored itself by the 1830's. It drew on the cotton trade, whaling, and the speed of clipper ships, and increasingly on the connections with the interior by the canals and railroad, the growing exchange of Western grain and meat against European manufactures, and the growing manufactures in Southern New England and around New York and Philadelphia. The location, wealth, working population, and financial institutions of the seaboard cities had gathered to them not only shipping, transshipping, warehousing and packaging of the stream of goods, but also the activities of selling, financing and promoting the trade, and with that the job of modifying through manufacture the form and qualities of the goods in transit.[4] Their strength as commercial and mercantile centers had been early supported by the scatter of small crafts and rural industry over the countryside, using skills and idle labor of the farm and village population. Even in the late eighteenth century, the shippers and craft shops of the coastal towns were imitating their counterparts in northeastern Europe, organizing rural labor in variants of the putting-out system. From the 1820's to the 1850's, they extended the bases of their wealth to include the organization of shipping, the fur trade, the ventures of Western development, and the new factories along the fall line of the nearby rivers, utilizing an influx of native rural—and mostly female—labor. By the 1840's, their cities were beginning that immense absorption of European immigrant labor that was to continue to 1914.[5] The factories, located near water power or conveniently to the import of coal, added another layer to the complex economic life of the seaboard. And around and within this industrial net had collected the industries and trades which made the life of sailors, merchants, railroad men, factory workers possible and endurable—construction workers, tradesmen, domestics, and the purveyors of entertainment, government, and gossip. Like some complex sea organism, the society of the Northeast had grown older and even more structured, piling up layer upon layer of occupations and social groups, adding function to function through complex and interdependent internal markets and contractual arrangements.[6]

Such a growth, through the utilization of a succession of economic opportunities, required strong and adaptable economic forms and sturdy institutions of local government. The development of these forms, the modification of laws and practices of private ownership, contract, social control, and democratic local government which made room for an urban laboring class, powerful financial interests, the practices and influence of the Catholic church, the power of political bosses, and much else unimagined by Locke, Bentham or Jefferson—all this constitutes the institutional history of the eastern seaboard. The manner and order in which this institutional structure utilized the opportunities for increasing income and wealth, the distribution made of the result, the examples of skill and efficiency, the stories of fraud and waste—these constitute its economic history. Both are embedded in the area's social history—the history of homes, families, neighborhoods, and other institutions in which the size and characteristics of the populations were regulated and reproduced.

By 1860, then, the North was like a long animal whose head rested in the Eastern urban region; its body, including factories, shops and commercial farms stretched from fifty to one hundred miles inland and a little like the Cheshire cat, faded back into the woods, hills and flat lands of the West, half dissolved and uncertain in outline. Despite home gardens and domestic livestock in the cities, the seaboard's food needs, including hay for workstock, were mainly supplied from a vast farming area which had begun organizing itself for two decades into cropping regions on a continental scale. The rural out-migration from upper New England and central Pennsylvania and New York had been in two directions: toward the coastal cities and to the West. Much of the Westward migration was in part the transfer of a commercial farming activity to a more suitable region—the movement of grain and meat producers into the Ohio Valley and thence across to the Mississippi,

6

the spread of New York dairying to Wisconsin.[7] These market-directed movements were guided by the prices for land in various locations and strongly affected by the opening of new land and the availability of credit. The degree of spread of a single commerical economy is indicated by the repercussions of the banking crisis of 1819, 1837, 1842, and 1857 producing bursts of bankruptcies and unemployment even in young Western towns.[8]

The lands between the Ohio and the Mississippi were connected then in 1860 to the seaboard through the market for their farm products—that "surplus" to which the transport improvements had given vent.[9] In this respect their position did not differ from that of the South, except that their product was a bit more varied and their position in foreign markets much less prominent or secure. Like the South, the West received back from the East manufactures —textiles and iron ware and a thousand miscellaneous items. Both West and South were collections of local economies, of semi-self-sufficient families or neighborhoods which formed economic and political regions not because of an internal interdependence, but because of a common link to Eastern and European markets and suppliers. But the West's connection to the East had grown far closer than the cotton South's in more vital and intimate ways—in the movement of loans for land holding, railroad and minerals development, and in the movement of men from the same farms and stock as those from which men had moved into seaboard cities.[10] Westward movement both regions had enjoyed, but the Old Southwest was settled from *its* East, where the procession of planters, slaves, and yeomen farmers moved out to reproduce the same social and economic system on new and more fertile soil. The old Northwest received free small farmers from the border South and the Northeast, and placed them in a social structure looser than the South's and an economic structure more varied and more complex. In

7

1860 this broad and populous farming region stood on the eve of an industrial development whose end is even today not yet in sight. From a congeries of local economies, of farm families and small village centers, the native population of the midwest was to furnish food, fuel, metals, and transport together with the skills, drives, savings, steadfast work, sheer human energy, and much of the manual labor that transformed the area into the rich and sometimes alarming industrial society called—with its eastern, southern and far west extensions—the United States of America.

II

To make some rough assessment of a regional character type and to link it to the response made in following decades to opportunities for acquisition of wealth in industry and commerce is a notoriously risky enterprise. For one thing, it is necessary to sketch and to evaluate those opportunities. A huge study would be required to sketch their sheer magnitude, derivable from physical production advantage—in agricultural productivity, cheap minerals, and easy transport. A physical advantage so well suited to the techniques and markets of the late nineteenth century could hardly have been missed by any population with reasonable access to a knowledge of those techniques and to the means of finance. Furthermore, a single "history" of the response of a population, without specifying a standard of comparison, is not a mode of explanation acceptable to a skeptical modern mind. One ought at least to find a similar opportunity in this period which a population did *not* utilize. The history of Southern industrial development, for example, might provide such a comparison, although there the opportunity, at least in heavy industry, is obviously not as great. But certainly industrialization can occur—and could occur in the late nineteenth century—in a variety of social settings. The examples of the Northwest European industrial belt from Dortmund to Liège, of the Saar-

8

Lorraine areas, of Japan and North Italy after the 1870's come to mind. The experience of England and New England must be examined for an earlier period and under a rather different condition of technology and markets.[11]

At the outset of such an effort, one must face the famous "frontier hypothesis" about the American (i.e., Midwestern) character. A mere economic historian cannot well assess Turner's hypothesis, its development and use by "his school", and the controversy and revisions it has survived.[12] Some direct impressions from the materials of agricultural and business history may be more to the point.

The rural society of the old Northwest was peculiarly well adapted, it might be argued, to what a Marxist would call its "historic role" in the mid-nineteenth century. Taken across the whole area from central New York and Pennsylvania to the Plains, conditions were remarkably homogeneous. The land, cut up by the rectangular survey and offered at auction sales, had undergone settlement between 1800 and 1860 under rather steady or regularly recurrent conditions of population growth and credit availability. Land auctions, the knowledge of insiders, the pressure of squatters, the homemade banking institutions, the presence of eastern speculators—all of these had left each tier of counties settled in turn in a pattern of free farms, clustering in size between eighty and 160 acres, enough to occupy a family labor force, with some help at harvest, and perhaps some surplus land for speculative sale. Unlike the European or early New England pattern, settlement was not in villages, but in the isolated farmstead, set in the middle of a large, consolidated holding, with no common lands and very little fragmentation. Except for mortgaging, landownership was absolute; speculators, early ranchers, states, and railroads who had large holdings held them to sell, not to farm with tenants. Within this monotonously repetitive pattern of rural settlement supplementing and drawing on the versatility of the settlers, a marked specialization of economic function early appeared. Speculators, ranchers, mixed farmers, dairymen, even frontier bankers on occasion, moved West as the comparative advantage of a county shifted with growing density of settlement. The comparison to the movement of an Army is more exact than is often realized, for the body of settlers was divided to a degree into corps—cavalry of ranchers, an infantry of woodsmen, quartermaster, ordnance and signal corps of suppliers of commercial services and contacts. For this reason settlement proceeded rapidly and with a high degree of efficiency.[13]

The homogeneity of the population and of its fortunes was of course not absolute. In the scramble for settlement, families were sucked in from the South as well as the East—from Kentucky and Western Virginia, as well as Central Pennsylvania, New York and the back countries of New England. The Ohio River, geographical boundary between slavery and freedom, was overlapped by a zone of Southern border settlement extending into the Southern half of Illinois, far up into Indiana and cutting off the Southeastern hill country of Ohio. The outlawry of slavery by the Ordinance of 1787 was an absolutely decisive fact in the social development of this region: it meant that the Southern stock of settlers—whatever habits of mind and sympathy they evinced—was formed of the non-slave-owning class, the yeomen farmers of Owsley's history[14]— or the drifters and footloose population of the back country and hills. Their attitude both to the blacks and to their beleaguered homeland in the War was an ambivalent one, as evidenced by the cautious approach to emancipation by the most famous of their number, Abraham Lincoln. Their attitudes to commercial farming may have been less wholehearted than those of their Northern neighbors and their location and terrain less suited to it. These divisions of mind may have made the Southern-derived population of the Old Northwest less effective in charting the direction and influencing the tone of the region than their numbers would have justified. They formed—with many exceptions—the laboring and poor-farmer stratum of the population, achieving sometimes a better adaptation to Middlewest conditions than the New Englanders, but taking risks and pursuing rationality in money-making less ardently perhaps than the Yankees.

New Englanders came early into the territory from the settlements of Connecticut veterans on the so-called Western Reserve, and a steady stream moved from Massachusetts and Vermont after 1830 as those farming regions shifted cropping patterns under the joint pressure of the pull of labor to the mills and the market competition of Western grain and meat. Spreading across northern Ohio,[15] eastern Michigan, where Boston money had always been involved, and down from the lake into central Illinois, Yankee farmers and villagers settled quickly into all the money-making activities that were to be found—activities which included farming but were by no means limited to it.

Between Southerners and Yankees, the migrants from Pennsylvania and New York shared with the German and the later Scandinavian migrants to Wisconsin and beyond a certain peasant-like competence in the agricultural arts. Their origins did not lie in the uplands of Appalachia but generally in flat and fertile farming areas, where careful tillage and husbandry had long been rewarded by good yields, where stable family and village structures had made for a solid, conservative and dependable style of farming and of living—a style which could take root quickly and flourish abundantly on good soils under good market opportunities.[16]

Any reconstruction of a regional character must be partly imaginary, particularly at a hundred years' distance, and a tracing of its origins must involve a degree of plausible myth. Yet it is hard to feel that the Midwestern character as it shows itself in farming, business, and politics after the Civil War does not owe something to this

11

mix of rural backgrounds of the region's native population. The three groups shifted West initially in rather fixed geographical strata: the Yankees moved into the belt of ultimately greater financial opportunity around and below the lower lakes; settlers from the Middle colonies and rural immigrants from Europe moved in above and below them; New Yorkers, Germans and Swedes into Wisconsin after the 1850's; and Pennsylvanians and Germans across the middle counties of Ohio and down the Miami River. The Southern hill people settling at the bottom of the area occupied a great Southern belt across to the Mississippi.[17] As transportation improved and markets shifted, these groups mixed and mingled, facing a rather uniform natural environment, similar economic experiences, and enjoying easy mobility within a loose and democratic social structure. As they did so, a middle-western character was formed. Is it too fanciful to see in its upper reaches the drives, acuity, shrewdness and hardness of the Yankee combined with the animal energy, competence and sturdiness of the German peasant, and among its common people an emotionality, tempered by a sophistication about human suffering, that must have belonged to a people that grew up among the moral and human ambiguities of Southern slavery?

These distinctions among the population, nebulous as they are, based on its points of ancestral origin, were accompanied by, and not completely correlated with, distinctions based on wealth. How these arose and were reinforced by economic activity is an interesting matter for speculation. It would indeed have been surprising if, despite the rather considerable uniformity in land distribution—at least among the large share of the population that got land—the distribution of wealth or income had been exactly equal. There were some differences in the resources that settlers brought in with them, and considerable difference in their luck at the land sale and in their access to credit. Whatever their source, differences were to a degree reinforced by early ventures in farming or business. Now the shape of wealth distribution in a rural area has important consequences for the area's later industrial development. A very skewed distribution favors saving and capital accumulation but provides only restricted markets particularly for factory products; an equal distribution has the reverse effect. Obviously, as in most economic problems, there is an optimum level of spending and accumulation which combines these two contradictory effects to an optimal degree for rapid economic growth. Our concern here, however, is with the relation of wealth distribution to the structure of society. Quite obviously, too, as many observers of American manners have pointed out, in a society so new, so democratic and homogeneous in most respects, such differences in wealth stood out, as almost the only mark of individual or familial distinction and prestige. The worship of wealth appeared where so little else existed on which men could exercise the impulse to make distinctions or establish a standard by which to define and imitate success.

Beneath the surface of homogeneity and equality in 1860 in the Northwest lay elements of social differentiation based on family origin and especially on wealth. In social organization too, one sees a similar blending of opposites: the opposition of a family-centered individualism and a community-centered corporate spirit. The frontiersman, it is said, was an individualist—with, at the extreme, an almost psychotic hatred of human society: one who cleared his patch in the wilderness and moved on as soon as he saw the smoke from a neighbor's cabin. Added to this is the stereotype of the nineteenth century competitive entrepreneur in whose breast all human social bonds had been dissolved and metamorphosed into the selfish drive for money and through money for control over men. The Midwest was wide and rich enough to sustain and encourage numbers of such entrepreneurs, and it called their achievements success.

13

Mixed with such figures is the figure of the insecure, grasping, land-hungry peasant familiar in European history. And since men cannot survive, procreate, and produce a history utterly alone, they were set in the Northwest in the so-called "nuclear" family of a long North European lineage. Midwestern individualism, as it showed itself in farming and in business achievement, was rooted in the family organization brought into the region and reinforced by the conditions of rural settlement on isolated farmsteads, growing crops initially only for themselves, then for sale in anonymous competition with neighbors for distant markets. A direct physical sharing of crops—the dominant mode of distribution in tribal and village societies from time immemorial in the world's agriculture, the basis on which Egyptian, Oriental, and Medieval lords, dynasties and ecclesiastical organizations were supported and their populations tied to the soil—was wholly unknown, undreamed of by the original rural population of the Middle West. Some exceptions to this stark, small-family individualism appeared among immigrant groups and among Southerners or among adherents to a sectarian religion like the Mennonites[18] where settlement in larger family or community groups occurred. But these are notable as exceptions, and their cohesiveness was often short-lived under the corrosive influence of the markets for crops and land and the ready mobility of a second or third generation.

And yet—and yet, that is surely not quite the whole story. If it had been, midwestern society could never have survived. In European villages, the peasant household had been incorporated within a village structure. The European peasant of the nineteenth century may have revealed a narrow selfishness when village and feudal organization was dissolved. Then unrelated households were nakedly exposed in all their anarchy, like worms under a suddenly lifted rock. But the earlier agrarian culture of northern Europe added to its nuclear families a certain organization of public

14

cooperation and responsibility. This was evident particularly in the German and Scandinavian groups, but it existed also among native Americans whose culture derived from the England or Scotland of the seventeenth or early eighteenth century.

To this basis for cooperation were added also the effects of common dangers, common tasks, and common abundance in the early western environment. Perhaps loneliness and the desire to escape it is an innate characteristic of the human mind, an inextricable element in the human condition. But the premium on news must have been high in the darkness and uncertainties of a frontier, and settlers longed not only for the sound of a voice, but for what a voice might say—about Indians, neighbors, politicians, and other potential intruders on their lives. Together with information gained through social contact, community projects—for defense and later for the creation of public goods—yielded high returns to community self-help. The federal government was remote, and, through constitutional theory and the strength of Southerners in Congress, it remained weak. State governments financed and organized canals and railroad projects and established a basic framework of control and law. But they were large, and much of their sovereign powers devolved on the locality—the county, the township, the school district. Taxes, roads, fire, police and schools were all largely local matters; the division of the land into regular townships with surveys contemplated a close local organization of those who purchased their land at a single land office. The abundance of land in new areas, the prodigality of nature in crude necessities—food and lumber—made it easy to welcome the stranger and to incorporate his strength in community tasks. The rural neighborhood with schools, churches, and politics added then to the family life an indispensible element of social organization. Midwesterners were individualistic on their farms and in their productive activities, but

15

they were generous to neighbors and combined readily in community projects. Clubs, churches, circles, lodges, societies flourished in the midwest soil—the more so because their members felt themselves to be free and equal individuals. And certainly there were some who found in such association the means to respect and status that seemed so hard to achieve in a near egalitarian society, except, as we have noted, through lucky and successful economic activity. Of all the puzzles in the frontier character, the paradox of individualistic neighborliness is the most striking and potently pregnant with promise of strength for the industrial culture that was to come.

The society of the old Northwest in 1860 is to be viewed, in short, as a variant of the peasant society of Protestant Europe from which it derived all those intimate values and ethical norms expressed in religion and family structure, and much even of what was expressed in community life. But the conditions of formation of this society differed from those in Europe in two respects—each obvious when taken by itself, but producing together an interaction that might not have been predicted. On the one hand, these farmers and villagers were placed in an economic framework of pure market capitalism and given the means of maintaining independent fortunes and positions. No titles, no feudal dues, no tenancies, no village obligations existed in law or memory to restrain their utter economic freedom. On the other hand, the settlers were placed, as the colonists had been in the first coastal settlements, in a new, unknown, and often menacing natural environment, whose rich returns would be yielded only to individual effort sustained and helped by considerable community organization. The counterpart of individual freedom was the danger of social isolation—no established church, no landlord, no clustered village, and hardly a state. These could be compensated for by hard work only up to a point; beyond

that, the performance of their functions required organization.

To what extent did this transforming experience differ from that of the New Englanders or the Virginians two centuries before? The Puritan, more often a townsman than a peasant, brought to the wilderness a firm corporate spirit and a strict hierarchy; he was to see both dissolve under the corrosive influence of free land, money, markets, and trade. The Virginian brought a venturesome individualism, which was transformed along the seaboard, under the opportunities of profit and power, into a caste system. The Westerners in both regions from the eighteenth century on, form the prototypes of the midwestern spirit and society. A hundred years of semi-self-sufficiency in farmsteads and rude settlements across the Appalachians was the immediate forerunner of midwestern settlement, mixed after 1830 with movement from the already commercialized farms of up-country New England and the middle states. What was truly new to the nineteenth century was the growing commercial opportunity for "western" crops—an opportunity which was apparent with the first shipments on rafts down the Ohio and the Mississippi and the driving of animals through the Cumberland Gap, which built up to the intense demand for internal improvements in the 1820's and 1830's, and reached a climax in the opening up of European markets after 1850. It was in response to these opportunities before 1860, and for several decades thereafter, that the Western character and rural society was to achieve its fixed and final form.

III

The opportunity which settlers faced in the Northwest comprised both the peasant's opportunity for a home and the gambler's opportunity for a fortune. Between these extremes lay the whole range of economic opportunities

for men who felt themselves freed from eastern or European society and able partly to determine their own eco
nomic destiny. The mix of risk and security, flutuating
income and steady yields, market orientation and self-
sufficiency, mobility and steadfast local residence, varied
with choice and circumstance. Nor could any objective be
pursued by a man in isolation from some of the institutions
of settled society, from the shade of their protection and
the shadows of their unwanted intrusions.

At first glance, the gambler and the peasant as ideal types
appear to have much in common. Both wanted to separate
themselves in the Northwest from the common experience
of the race—the one by lucky windfalls, reaping where
he had not sown, the other by the complete security of his
own holding. Each might hold more land than he could
use—the gambler in hopes of a "killing" on resale, the
peasant as a means of saving and later distribution to his
family. Both in the new country depended on the institutions of organized government. Their needs from government and from the region's resources, however, were of
quite different sorts. The peasant-minded settler needed
the rudimentary services of government—notably, physical
protection against the Indian and the legal protection to
insure security of tenure. The fly-by-night gatherer of
wealth needed some of the apparatus of money and markets,
so that his winnings could be put into a liquid and transportable form, and he needed above all communication—
ideally, private news of opportunities and rapid means of
moving to take advantage of them. Corresponding to these
types of ambitions would come two contrasting geographical
patterns in the opening up of the country. The gambler's
strategy was to move out—ahead of the herd, taking risks
to penetrate deeply inland, to establish early claims, to
find fur or minerals, to produce salable surpluses of
transportable crops early. At the extreme opposite was
the almost mindless steady expansion of an agricultural

18

population like a glacial sheet—the joining of field to field in contiguous and riskless settlement.

History would be simple if these two "ideal" character types corresponded to the pioneers of specific seaboard regional or European material stock. But, of course, no such identification is possible at so distant a date; no one knows just where the Yankee, the Southerner, or the Pennsylvania German modal personalities fell along the spectrum. Perhaps individual differences over the range of human nature were more decisive than background. It is clear that both types existed and complemented one another in the rapid development of the region. It would be simple too, if the gamut of economic opportunities--as they succeeded one another in the region's development--utilized first the gambler, then moved slowly toward the peasant. To some degree, as Turner averred, this was the case. The opportunities—as sketched below—moved from those demanding physical endurance and prowess to those demanding social skills and from the more to the less risky. So the "waves" of Turner's frontiers--trapper, trader, surveyor, land clearer, rancher, farmer--succeed one another at each location, but with many exceptions and variations. There were gentle, settled spirits even among the first settlers--among the Ipswich, Massachusetts, families that moved to Marietta to occupy the Ohio Company's claim.[19] New Englanders and Pennsylvanians came early from settled villages to establish their lives and fortunes anew. Nor was the freebooting frontier gambler a phenomenon simply of the early stages of settlement; he was a character-type continually recreated in Western society, on hand in copper discoveries in Michigan in the 1840's, or iron discoveries in Minnesota in the 1880's, or in the episodes of transcontinental railroad building and finance. Within the limits of region and period, the riskiness, speed, and efficiency of settlement in the different states and localities depended very strongly upon the general state of organization, of civilization, of technology in the region, as a whole, *at the time* that a specific locality was settled and connected with society to the East. The pioneers into Indiana and Illinois from Ohio or Kentucky in the 1820's and 1830's brought a different experience with them than those into Ohio from New England or Virginia in the 1800's. They came out of an economy connected with the South and the East, possessing techniques of manufacturing, transport, and even of farming and pioneering not known three decades earlier.

Utilizing this array of character types, opportunities unrolled over time and space in the Old Northwest prior to the Civil War. The ventures of fur trapping and Indian trading, organized formally under the Federal system of outposts or factories in 1796, were economic activities indeed, but ones more important for the information they yielded about terrain and Indians than for any direct product. The first important economic activity in or over the area was the land grab for the Ohio country just after the Revolution. It took two forms: (1) speculation in the military warrants, entitlements to land issued to veterans by Virginia and by the Continental Congress, and (2) lobbying by groups of ex-generals and other influential citizens to obtain grants of the lands from Congress for resale under favorable terms.[20] What seems a corrupt and privileged system in retrospect did not in fact seem so to contemporaries. Ample precedent existed in the colonial grants of the crown and in the example of the Holland Land Company which had acquired the land management and sale of most of western New York. A similar arrangement seemed not amiss in encouraging movement into the Ohio country.

One may observe in the early organization of both the Indian trade and land settlement an effort to work under the dying shadow of eighteenth century mercantilist policies. The system of posts and regulated trade conformed to British precedent in Canada, without the intermediary of a joint stock company. The Ohio and Scioto companies were indeed joint ventures on the model of the company by which Virginia was first settled, but with a clearer title to land and a more single-minded dedication to its profitable settlement and sale. They assumed no political powers, and contemplated holding the land only long enough to make a profit of suitable size. Yet it proved impossible at any point to maintain a large para-governmental organization, except for the Army and the Federal land offices in the area. Even before the Indian danger abated, the federal factories were ignored and the peculiarly American organization of the Indian and fur trade, by small capitalists working on individual account, with no accountability to the government or other claimant of ownership or sovereignty, asserted itself. The gamblers and high risk-takers took over and swept across the Midwest to the Missouri country and on into the Rockies, until at last, in the 1830's, when --with knowledge more certain and risks reduced-- Astor's American Fur Company could take over and the big capitalist could gobble up the little ones. In land settlement, too, large private organizations rapidly proved themselves incompetent. The Scioto Company failed rather quickly; the Ohio Company and J. C. Symmes rather rapidly divested themselves of their grants. Settlement in the Virginia Military District was small-scale, even when the warrants had been bought up in blocks, and the settlement into the Connecticut Reserve came in small groups from various towns in the state. The small party of twenty-five to fifty persons from a New England town was the largest unit; the settlers moving over the border from Pennsylvania, squatters in advance of surveys, and the Kentuckians and Virginians moved individually or in small family groups. By 1800, then, the Act of 1796 was in full operation, with surveys of the ranges of townships, land offices, auction sales, reserved school lands, and state lands. Settlers,

21

ranchers, small-scale speculators, successful and well located farmers, the developers of a town, a county, or a river valley, were firmly in control of the territorial government and brought Ohio to statehood as early as 1803. In Indiana and Illinois, the same organization of settlement proceeded without the eighteenth century over-hang of land companies.

IV

A huge net of opportunity then unfolded over the North-west as one tier of counties after another was opened up. But land values could rise with settlement only as farming grew more productive of value; that in turn depended both on the growth of a local economy, with trade and specialized production, and on the possibility of export. Settlement, initially and persistently, was not simply to plant home-steads or villages to reproduce a traditional agrarian society in a colonial setting. Settlement brought value to the land, and it did so by realizing on internal or external markets the value of the land's economic potential; the "economic surplus" was a concept well known to readers of Niles' Register long before it was used by Marxists. And of these opportunities, it would seem clear that to realize on exports from the region was a faster way to wealth than to wait for a thickening settlement to produce internal markets. For the latter to occur, the development of im-port-substituting manufactures was required as well as effective local overland transport. Both of these were to occur along with the growth of exports, and indeed their satisfactory response to the stimulus of the incomes earned in exports is largely responsible for the region's growth; it meant that the "multiplier" (in old-fashioned Keynesian language) applied to the "accelerator" of rising exports was high, and induced further investment and more internal acceleration within the region. But clearly before 1830, the lower and eastern Midwest still looked like an agricultural export region, whose fertile soils and favorable terrain were set too remotely into the American land mass to assure easy access to the markets of the South, the East, and Europe.

The period before 1830 was also one of a decided Southern orientation of the Northwest's economy—toward the Ohio and Mississippi valleys. Exact figures on the trade must be viewed with suspicion, but Kohlmeier's search in state and federal documents showed that nearly all the corn and corn products (hogs and whiskey) and over 70 per cent of the wheaten flour exported from the Northwest in 1835 went downriver either for consumption or for transshipment from New Orleans, and that nearly half the region's imports, by weight, came up that route.[21] This trade was great enough to create Cincinnati as a city of four thousand by 1814 and six thousand by 1816. It was confirmed and intensified by the steamboat in the 1820's.[22] The canals into the Ohio marked the route even plainer, and as settlement extended to the southern counties of Indiana and Illinois, the advantage of trade over this route was even more marked. Until the 1840's, the lower Northwest settlement was an extension of the upper South, without slaves, but with mostly Southern and border people, with crop mix and farming patterns characteristic of Kentucky and Tennessee. This was the Democratic-Northwest—of Jacksonian persuasion, eager to chase Indians, to grab land, to float produce to New Orleans, yet retaining strong distrust of banks and credit and Northern ways of doing business. And on top of this stratum was a small business class, merchants and bankers, the Western Whigs, followers of Clay and Harrison, without strong feelings about sectional alliances, as ready to combine with Southern Whigs as with the party's New England wing— but eager for Union and the "American System," for tariffs to develop home markets and for internal improvements to link the West to them. Thus far had the population of the Old Northwest stratified itself by the election of 1840.

The weakness in the Southern orientation lay in the urge to expand to markets in whatever direction. By improved canals, a canal around the Falls of the Ohio at Louisville, and steamboats on the up-river journey, the link of the Ohio River Valley was made via New Orleans with the world. But the canals ran both ways, and steamboats were indifferent as to what region they traversed. Two sorts of events before 1850—one immediate and major, the other, less prominent at first, but later quite decisive—began to cause the region around the lower edge of the Lakes to grow and to be linked within itself and to the East. They were events that were to be repeated with increasing strength over the nineteenth century.

First, of course, were the transport improvements: the National Road opened in 1818 to Wheeling and by 1833 to Columbus, the Erie and Ohio Canals, the clumsy Pennsylvania canal and road system. These for the first time gave shippers in Eastern Ohio the chance to play rival routes off against one another, and against the great natural route to the South. The timing of these and their economic effects have been often described, or assumed, but never thoroughly analyzed and measured. We may cite several such effects, some directly observed in the record of settlement and shipment, others coming under the head of effects which economic theory tells us must have taken place. First, there was an undeniable speed-up in the rate of immigration from the Northeast, the more rapid because it could move into a region where northerners already predominated. But much of the economic efficiency of a new agricultural region depends on the mass of settlement; even without external trade a large enough population can generate its own industrial civilization. Second, the existing farm population—in particular the wheat growers who had already entered from Pennsylvania—enjoyed a market advantage, and the development of eastern Ohio in wheat soon followed. Third, the impact of Eastern manufactures

24

must have had the same effect as that observed along the Erie Canal itself: the disappearance of home industry and a shift of farm labor to farming tasks, notably dairying, or to village manufactures where the small-scale shop still had a place. Finally, it should be emphasized that the East-West improvements were not confined to northeastern and central Ohio. The whole southern shore of Lake Erie was affected by the canal links at Cleveland and Toledo to Western Ohio and Indiana. The Illinois-Michigan canal joined Chicago to the Mississippi; and the Soo canal, opened in 1855, brought surpluses from Northern Illinois and the early farms of Eastern Wisconsin in reach of the Great Lakes trade. But already by the late 1840's, the lake trade was a flourishing, mercantile enterprise, developing all the institutions of markets, credit, and competition with which Boston, New York, and Cincinnati had long been familiar.

Apart from the water transportation improvements, a second stimulus to wealth accumulation and commercial enterprise with an eastern orientation appeared in the 1840's: the minerals rush into Michigan copper. The rush, coming in the wake of the geological reports of Houghton in 1843, reached a climax in May, 1846, when about one thousand permits for exploration were issued in a single month. By 1847 the bubble had burst, but the beginnings of an orderly exploitation and of continued disorderly exploration into the mineral resources of the upper Lakes had been laid.[23] The form of the episode was followed closely in the rush into Pennsylvania oil in 1856. The impetus both for the rush and for the continued exploitation in these two cases came partly from the surrounding areas—from lower Michigan and from Western Pennsylvania—and partly from New England. In Michigan in particular, Boston financial control of the major mines was established as regular exploitation began in the early 1860's. More important than the ore discovered and the dividends paid out was the stimulus given to further exploration in the upper peninsula of Michigan and to the improvement of navigation of Sault Ste. Marie. The south shore of Lake Superior—the farthest reach of the Great Lakes system—was joined to the developing agricultural and industrial region of northern Ohio. The way was prepared for the movement into Minnesota wheat and more significantly into Menominee and Mesabi iron.

V

By the late 1840's, the lines of connection of Northwest and Northeast were well laid. Two great forces in that decade and the one following were to rivet the two regions together: the railroad and the struggle over slavery.

It is idle, but intriguing, to speculate on the Northwest's development path if the railroad had been technically and financially practicable just after the War of 1812. Might it have been used to develop Cincinnati's southern connections to Richmond or Charleston? One recalls Hayne's unsuccessful project for this purpose in Charleston in the 1830's. Lincoln is supposed to have said that had it been carried out, the War might never have occured! But Calhoun did not favor it, and looked instead for the rails to join together the parts of the cotton kingdom. The Cincinnati investors, too, dragged their feet, preferring—Kohlmeier supposes—the greater benefits to be derived from building roads within Ohio and attracting immigration from the East.[24] And in the East, the rails followed rapidly upon the canals. The Baltimore and Ohio stretched toward the West in the 1830's, the rivalry of the three mid-Atlantic ports pushed the whole system West, and by the early 1850's local lines in Ohio could be joined to the east at three points with only small extensions of track.[25] In choice of terrain, in mode of finance, in the assembly of construction gangs, in leading settlement and agriculture along lines into which rail traffic could flow—the canals were a test-run of the railroads along many of the main routes. And the rails, with their wider choice of terrain, their all-year operation and their speed, and with the technical and engineering skills they used and diffused, were decisive instruments of industrial development—no matter how arithmeticians may calculate, under restrictive assumptions and with self-corroborating data, their exact contribution to the national product in a given year.

The 1850's saw railroad development in the Midwest at two levels: (1) a penetration from the East of lines joining to the great and new trunk systems: the Baltimore and Ohio, the Pennsylvania, the Erie, and the New York Central, and with this (2) a great thickening of the connections in the interior, especially from North to South. The development of the 1840's had connected only a few obvious points, in such a way as to leave the region's orientation still ambiguous. A rail line across Southern Michigan effectively gave access from Lake Michigan to Detroit. Indianapolis was joined to the Ohio River, and the Ohio lines followed the Miami valley from Cincinnati north, meeting Lake Erie at Sandusky and at Cleveland. Obviously traffic on such lines could move both ways—to the Ohio-Mississippi valley or to the Great Lakes water system. But the movement of the trunk lines from the East across to Chicago and St. Louis effectively settled the outcome. Then local lines became feeders to the North and East, and the days of the downstream river-oriented economy, even in the southern midwest, were virtually over. The Illinois Central came too late to tie the state into an economic union with Mississippi and the Southwest. Instead, all that Douglas's efforts could do was to direct the produce of the central Illinois prairies north to Chicago—as Douglas himself realized when he invested in Chicago real estate.[26] Paul Gates gives the following telling quotation about the Illinois Central, from the *New York Evening Post* of September 22, 1858 (as cited in the Sparks edition of the Lincoln-Douglas debates):[27]

Jonesboro is a mile and a half from the railroad. The station is called "Anna" and is as large as the town itself. The station is Republican; the town is democratic. The land sales of the Illinois Central Railroad, by opening the country to the advent of settlers, have introduced the men of the East, who bring certain uncomfortable and antagonistical political maxims and thus the time-honored darkness of Egypt (i.e., Southern Illinois) is made to fade away before the approach of middle state and New England ideas. Let these land sales go on and a change will take place in the political physiognomy of Southern Illinois. All things suffer a "sea change" and already the alternative influence of these new ideas is insensibly felt in this section.

The second source of the connection with the Northeast —the joint struggle against slavery and for the Union—was a more complex affair. American history of the antebellum decade is inevitably directed toward an understanding of the decade's tragic outcome. An economic historian in particular must contribute an answer to at least two questions: first, to what degree did the economic links among the regions in 1860 condition their alignment in the struggle, and second, to what degree did these regional economic interests require of the struggle so violent a course? The first of these questions may be answered by an economist immediately; the second, being impossible, takes a little longer.

If war was inevitable in 1860—which no historian should admit—and if the Northwest had to choose sides, then economics makes clear where its interests lay. The breakup of a political union is chiefly important for the opportunity it gives the constituent regions to conduct their own economic policies. In the mid-nineteenth century, this meant mainly tariffs. But a tariff between Northeast and Northwest in 1860 was unthinkable; all the economic policies and development of six decades had been directed to stimulating trade, lowering transport costs, increasing interdependence. Industrial growth in neither the Midwest nor the South had been sufficient to make the economies of those two regions complementary. The South, indeed, was itself more closely bound to New York, Philadelphia, and the New England mills than to Ohio or the upper Mississippi Valley.

But why then should not the North—east and west—simply have let the South secede? Such a question draws the economist far, far from home. Certainly the "mind" of the Northwest—if one may permit one's self such a construct—as late as the mid-1850's was still divided. Economically, the Southern orientation of the region's lower half was far from extinguished. The boom in the Southwest continued to pull trade down the Mississippi; Kohlmeier's figures, shaky but indispensable, show that the transport watershed for the traditional staples—corn and hogs—still ran straight along the line of the National Road from Wheeling and Columbus on west to the Mississippi.[28] What had happened in the previous decade was that the settlement, farming, and light manufactures in the area north of that line, tributary to the Great Lakes, had sprung into life. Paradoxically, then it was the interest most involved in the Southern route that was most intent that New Orleans should not be controlled by a foreign power. If Southern Ohio, Indiana, and Illinois could not secede with the South, then the South should remain in the Union with them. The American system was a living fact in most minds, and its definitions encompassed the vision of the back country along the whole length of the Mississippi, as well as the East-West connections.[29] Yet the Northeast could probably have taken over the surplus produce of this lower region directly at very slight increase in transport cost. Most of the produce found its way back up the Atlantic Coast anyway, and the Mississippi route was clearly heading for obsolescence. So one must move to more intangible fears and passions to explain the war.

Here, no doubt, mere economic historians should retire gracefully, murmuring a *Nunc Dimittis*. But the question is too intriguing to abandon. Two points may be made.

29

First, it is clear that all the politicians in 1860--including Lincoln--underestimated the idealism and radicalism of the Republican creed, and the popular strength of the power structure that supported it. That creed, echoing and repeating the slogans of the French Revolution and the Declaration of Independence, was implicit in the more cautious and materialistic Whiggery of Webster and Clay. Democracy, as represented by the Democratic Party in 1856, had lost much of its idealism; it had become a loose congeries of interests, dominated by professional compromisers. Freedom, material welfare, and property were the goals that could draw far enough down into the population to command a political predominance. Across the North, in towns and rural neighborhoods a structure of income and wealth, of economic ambition and respectability lay, strong as a net,[30] waiting to be drawn together in a cause. The anti-slavery crusade was not quite such a cause, but when sharpened by the danger of dissolution of the Union, the fusion of the Republican Party could occur. Then a Northern unity and anger appeared that moved from the mere defense of freedom where it existed or might be extended into a crusading aggressive action against the slave owning class itself. That many Northwesterners came from slave states made some of them ambivalent, but made others the more engaged to free the South from class domination. The Civil War was a radical Republican crusade for the Union. That Union's heart and soul was in the free commercial farmers and small businessmen of the Northwest who most appreciated its value and its glory.

Finally, one must ask whether the Republicans' zeal in the 1860's was activated in any degree by foreknowledge of what would lie ahead for the American economy and policy after a Northern victory. Across the Northwest from the start had grown up a substantial stratum of local industry. This is not surprising, yet it is often forgotten in focussing on the area's huge agricultural expansion and the central place of construction and transportation projects. Many industrial skills had come in from the Northeast or middle South with the settlers--iron working, leather working, and a wood working that encompassed carpentry and the making of wooden machinery. Rural neighborhoods had organized themselves readily to produce jobs for specialized craftsmen--a blacksmith, a miller, a harness maker, a teacher--quite soon. The rapid growth of small towns--and of central market cities--with good supply of urban services is a testimony to this. The respect for schooling and a real interest in the practical arts is everywhere present in the rather thick layer of middle class "culture" that lay on top of the canal men, laborers, and roughnecks. Wherever an industrial opportunity appeared, the skills, enterprise, and institutions needed to utilize it were present. The differences in this respect from the civilization of the middle South are very sharp indeed.

So around Pittsburgh, as early as 1800, around Cincinnati and the Miami and Scioto Valley by the 1830's, along the Lakes, at Cleveland, Chicago, and Detroit after 1840, and in a great grid across the whole area where farmers could get out produce for sale, small-scale commercial manufactures arose. The growth was helped by the very lack of water power which encouraged not only canal building but the making of steam engines. It utilized native materials--flax, wool, wood--to produce for local or regional markets on a large enough scale to maintain competition against imported goods.

The importance of such a grid, and of the business and political institutions accompanying it, for the industry of the upper Midwest after 1860 is obvious. No doubt in retrospect the South, as part of the Federal Union, was not essential either as a market or as a materials source for the industry of the Midwest. But the instinct of the small business civilization of the Northwest in 1860 was profound and passionate. A national union, protecting free

31

labor, the free ownership of property, and the integrity and expansion of its own territorial markets, was an economic ideal for American society under which the Republican class of the Northwest could dominate and prosper.[31] The political correctness of the instinct that led the Northwest into the Civil War was even more apparent than its economics: in the great Republican era from Grant to Taft, every elected President of the United States, except one, was to call his native state, either Ohio, or someplace within one hundred miles of her borders.

1. Census of 1860, *Agriculture*, p. 247. G. Wright calculates that on the basis of a Census sample the top twenty per cent of slaveholders (i.e. about 75,000 individuals) held 77.7 per cent of the slaves and that the top twenty per cent of cotton growers grew 77.4 per cent of cotton produced in 1860. These are almost certainly nearly wholly overlapping classifications. G. Wright, "The Economics of Cotton in the Antebellum South," unpublished dissertation, Yale University, 1969, 102.

2. Concerning the "oligarchical principle" and influence of the property qualification on English local government, see Sidney and Beatrice Webb, *The Development of English Local Government 1689-1835* (London: Oxford University Press, 1963) Part I. (First published as Chapter V of Volume IV of *English Local Government*, London 1922.)

The extensions of these principles in Virginia are alluded to by Wertenbaker. T. J. Wertenbaker, *Patrician and Plebian in Virginia* (Charlottesville: Michie Co., 1910), 33-34, 39, 57-58.

3. William B. Weeden, *Economic and Social History of New England 1620-1789*, Volume II (Boston: Houghton, 1891), 786-815, 840-876. Kenneth Lockridge, "Land, Population and the Evolution of New England Society 1630-1790," *Past and Present* 39 (April 1968), 62-80. See also Robert E. and B. Katherine Brown, *Virginia 1705-1786: Democracy or Aristocracy?* (East Lansing: Michigan State University Press, 1964).

4. G. R. Taylor, *The Transportation Revolution 1815-1860* (New York: Rhinehart & Co., 1951), 207-249 describes the transition from household to factory organization in manufactures. See also R. M. Tryon, *Household Manufactures in the United States, 1640-1860* (Chicago: University of Chicago Press, 1917), 242-303.

5. Oscar Handlin, *Boston's Immigrants: A Study in Acculturation*, revised edition (Cambridge, Mass.: Harvard University Press, Belknap Press, 1959), Ch. VII, VIII.

6. Stuart Bruchey, *The Roots of American Economic Growth 1607-1861: An Essay in Social Causation* (New York: Harper and Row, 1965), 193-207, analyzes the nineteenth Century social structure of New England. See also, Blanche Hazard,

The Organization of the Boot and Shoe Industry in Massachussets Before 1875, Harvard Economic Studies XXIII (Cambridge, Mass.: Harvard University Press, 1921).

7. Lewis D. Stillwell, "Migration from Vermont (1766-1860)," in *Proceedings of the Vermont Historical Society* V 2 (1937), 135, 185-96, 214, 215.

8. Richard C. Wade, *The Urban Frontier: The Rise of Western Cities, 1790-1830* (Cambridge, Mass.: Harvard University Press, 1959), 161-202. See also the extended discussion of Western cycles in Thomas S. Berry, *Western Prices before 1861* (Cambridge, Mass.: Harvard University Press, 1943), Ch. XII-XVI.

9. This development is recognized by G. S. Callender in his discussion of western settlement in *Selections from the Economic History of the United States 1765-1860* (Boston: Ginn and Co., 1909), 600-601.

For a discussion of the "surplus" concept in the south and west, see R. A. Billington, *Westward Expansion, A History of the American Frontier* (New York: Macmillan, 1949).

10. Douglass C. North, "Interregional Capital Flows and the Development of the American West," and Douglas F. Dowd, "A Comparative Analysis of Economic Development in the American West and South," *Journal of Economic History* XVI 4 (1956), 493-505, 558-74; James S. Duesenberry, "Some Aspects of the Theory of Economic Development," *Explorations in Entrepreneurial History* III 2 (December 1950), 97-102.

11. The only scheme for organizing these experiences is that offered by Gerschenkron's 'relative backwardness' hypothesis. It suffers from three flaws: (1) it attributes to relative backwardness some phenomena of later nineteenth century industrialization (e.g. greater importance of heavy industry, the greater role of banks) which may be due to the course of the technological and institutional change in the nineteenth century; (2) its applicability to non-European cases (Japan, U.S.A.) has not been made manifest; (3) it fails to specify the mechanism by which a nation's relative backwardness produces 'tensions' within the national society. Alexander Gerschenkron, *Economic Backwardness in Historial Perspective* (Cambridge, Mass.: Harvard University Press, Belknap Press, 1962), 5-30, 353-64.

12. The most interesting current work done on the subjects that absorbed Turner is by Allen G. Bogue. See especially his early article, "Social Theory and the Pioneer," *Agricultural History* XXIV (January 1960), 21-34, and his synthesis of much of his work in *From Prairie to Corn Belt* (Chicago: University of Chicago Press, 1963), especially Ch. 1, 2.

13. For a treatment of midwest settlement in a Turnerian mode see Billington, *Westward Expansion*, 246-67, 290-309.

14. Frank Lawrence Owsley, *Plain Folk in the Old South* (Baton Rouge: Louisiana State University, 1949), Ch. II.

15. A. L. Kohlmeier, *The Old Northwest as the Keystone in the Arch of American Federal Union* (Bloomington, Indiana: Principia Press, 1938), 209-211.

Carl Wittke, ed., *History of the State of Ohio*, Vol. II (by F. P. Weisenburger), (Columbus, Ohio: Ohio State Archaeological Society, 1941), 47.

16. Wittke, ed., *History of the State of Ohio*, Vol. II (by F. P. Weisenburger), 48-52.

17. Wittke, ed., *History of the State of Ohio*, Vol. [88], 47.

18. For accounts of Mennonite religious and community life in Illinois see Harry Franklin Weber, *Centennial History of the Mennonites of Illinois 1829-1929* (Goshen, Indiana: Mennonite Historical Society, 1931); in Indiana and Michigan, see John Christian Wenger, *The Mennonites of Indiana and Michigan* (Scottdale, Pennsylvania: Herald Press, 1961); and in Ohio, see William I. Schreiber, *Our Amish Neighbours* (Chicago: University of Chicago Press, 1962).

19. "Seldom have people migrated with less hardship than the New Englanders who moved west with the Ohio Co." Ray A. Billington, *Westward Expansion*, 218. However, this easy transplant was the exception and not the rule. Even those who migrated under the shelter of one of the companies often found they had gambled more than they reckoned. The French settlers who migrated to the Scioto Company's grant, for example, expected a full-scale city, but found only Gallipolis, Ohio, in a very early stage of construction and not enough land to go around.

20. Payson J. Treat, *The National Land System, 1785-1820* (New York: E. G. Treat & Co., 1910), 15-20, 45-64.

21. A. L. Kohlmeier, *The Old Northwest*, 20-21.

22. R. C. Wade, *The Urban Frontier*, 54.

23. W. B. Gates, Jr., *Michigan Copper and Boston Dollars* (Cambridge, Mass.: Harvard University Press, 1951), 12-22.

24. A. L. Kohlmeier, *The Old Northwest*, 22-29.

25. R. A. Billington, *Westward Expansion*, 294; G. R. Taylor, *The Transportation Revolution*, 45-48, and recent fine study by Harry N. Scheiber, *Ohio Canal Era: A Case Study of Government and the Economy, 1820-1861* (Athens, Ohio: Ohio University Press, 1969).

26. G. M. Capers, *Stephen A. Douglas, Defender of the Union*, ed. by Oscar Handlin (Boston: Little Brown and Co., 1959), 16.

27. Paul W. Gates, *The Illinois Central Railroad and Its Colonization Work* (Cambridge, Mass.: Harvard University Press, 1934), 244.

28. A. L. Kohlmeier, *The Old Northwest*, 202-205.

29. Douglas as late as October, 1860, was defining the role and interests of the Northwest as mediate between Northeast and South. At a speech in Dubuque on October 11, 1860, he said, "Bordering upon the Mississippi and upon the Great Lakes; with commerce floating Southward and Eastward, we have an equal interest in the North and in the South. ("That's so" and applause.) We can never consent to any arrangement that would deprive us of our Eastern trade. Nor can we ever permit a toll gate to be established on the Miss. R., that would prevent our free navigation to the gulf and upon the ocean." Text from R. Carey, *The First Campaigner: Stephen A. Douglas* (New York: Vantage Press, 1964), 86.

30. See Clarence Danhof, *Change in Agriculture; the Northern United States, 1820-1870* (Cambridge, Mass.: Harvard University Press, 1967).

31. An abundant historical literature examines these questions. See, for example, the very interesting treatment by Eric Fonor, *Free Soil, Free Labor, Free Men: The Ideology of the Republican Party before the Civil War* (New York: Oxford University Press, 1970).

II

THE AGRICULTURAL SECTOR AND THE PACE OF ECONOMIC GROWTH: U. S. EXPERIENCE IN THE NINETEENTH CENTURY

Robert E. Gallman

University of North Carolina

I

The importance of the agricultural sector in determining the pace of U. S. growth in the nineteenth century can scarcely be denied. As the century opened, almost 85 per cent of the American work force was affiliated with agriculture, according to the most influential extant estimate. Aggregate productivity change in the economy as a whole in the succeeding decades must have been deeply influenced by developments in agriculture, if only because of the weight the sector bore, not to mention its impacts on other sectors.[1] The topic of productivity in agriculture would therefore seem to be of considerable importance and work on the subject of wide interest. Yet in recent years a fundamental re-interpretation of the course of productivity growth has entered the literature, almost without remark and certainly with very little expressed opposition.

It has been widely believed that agricultural productivity increased moderately (if at all), in the first several

35

decades of the nineteenth century, and that the rate of change then experienced a gradual acceleration.[2] This opinion has been challenged as a result of two independent lines of work, resulting in quantitative series on agricultural output and agricultural labor force.[3] When these independently-created series are combined, they show that the growth of labor productivity did not experience an acceleration; indeed, across the first four decades of the century, the average annual percentage gain was somewhat larger than across the last six decades, according to these measurements. The introduction of other factors of production into the analysis tends to accentuate these results: total factor productivity growth appears to have been greater in the early part of the century than subsequently, if one is to believe the testimony of the aggregative series.[4]

Paul David has made an ingenious use of fragmentary data of various kinds to test and defend the recent findings, as they bear on labor productivity gains before 1840.[5] Since the average annual rate of improvement across the full century does not appear to be in serious question, David's work lends support to the notion that there was no acceleration of productivity increase. Yet it is difficult to accept this idea. It runs counter to the burden of the narrative histories of the period, and surely the quantitative work of Parker and Klein on the grains implies that productivity change in the later stages of the century went forward at an accelerated pace.[6] Furthermore, there are features of the new aggregative evidence that suggest possible inconsistencies, both internal and external, that may make the series unreliable guides to productivity improvement. Two of these features are worthy of remark.

The number of hours of agricultural work conducted in any given year can be thought of as a function of the volume and composition of agricultural output and of the labor time required, per unit, to produce each type of output. Now the agricultural output series—the work of Towne and Rasmussen—rests on detailed data on output at decade intervals across the nineteenth century, and these details were reported by Towne and Rasmussen. The literature contains various pieces of evidence concerning nineteenth-century labor requirements and a very complete statement for the early twentieth century. I have combined the output and labor requirements data to estimate the aggregate number of man hours consumed in agricultural work in 1800, 1850, and 1900 (see Appendix.) Since I was obliged to make some use of twentieth-century requirements data, the estimates are probably biased downward, the bias perhaps being somewhat the more serious for the earlier years. Nonetheless, the estimates at least permit a rough check on the consistency of the output and labor force series.

When the figures on man hours worked are compared with the aggregate farm labor force series, they suggest

Table 1

Structure of the U.S. Labor Force and Population, 1800-1900

	(1) Share of Agric. Labor Force in Total Labor Force	(2) △	(3) Share of Rural Pop. in Total Pop.	(4) △
1800	82.6		93.9	
1810	83.7	+1.1	92.7	−1.2
1820	78.9	−4.8	92.8	+.1
1830	70.6	−8.3	91.3	−1.5
1840	63.4	−7.2	89.2	−2.1
1850	54.8	−8.6	84.7	−4.5
1860	53.2	−1.6	80.2	−4.5
1870	52.5	−.7	74.3	−5.9
1880	51.3	−1.2	71.8	−2.5
1890	42.7	−8.6	64.7	−7.1
1900	40.2	−2.5	60.3	−4.4

Sources:
Col. (1): Derived from David, *op. cit.*, p. 196, revised series.
Col. (3): U.S. Bureau of the Census, *Historical Statistics of the United States, Colonial Times to 1957*, Washington, D.C., 1960, Series A 195 and 206.
Col. (2) & (4): Derived from Col. (1) and (3), respectively.

that hours worked in agriculture per member of the agricultural work force increased by 28-35 per cent between 1800 and 1850, and declined by between 13 and 29 per cent between 1850 and 1900. These results are very suspicious, since there is no good reason for believing that average hours worked per laborer did, in fact, rise and fall in this way and to this extent.[7] Since the known biases of the requirements data cannot account for these results, one must suppose that the output and labor force series are inconsistent. Either the labor force series describes too low a rate of change across the first half of the century, and too high a rate across the second half, or else the output series errs in a precisely contrary way.

A second line of evidence suggests that the former interpretation is the more plausible. One would expect to find that changes in the distribution of the labor force between agricultural and non-agricultural activities would roughly parallel changes in the distribution of the population between rural and urban places. The two distributions could not be expected to be identical at any given time—while few farmers live in cities, quite a few artisans, professional people, industrial workers, etc., live in the countryside. The fraction of the population living in rural places could therefore be expected to exceed the fraction of the work force engaged in agricultural pursuits. But one would expect temporal *changes* in the two distributions to move roughly in step. However, the shifts in the structure of the U.S. labor force series—the Lebergott-David series—are *not* similar to the changes shown by population series. According to the labor force series, the agricultural share of the work force fell by 28 percentage points between 1800 and 1850, at a time when the share of the rural population in total population was declining by only 9 points (see Table 1). Over the next three decades, the Lebergott series shows a decline of only 3.5 points, the population series 12.9 points; while over the last half of the century the figures are 14.6 and 24.4, respectively.

The two series appear to be inconsistent[8], and since the population series rests on the more robust empirical basis, the fault would seem to lie with the labor force figures. The total labor force series is less likely to be in error than are the component parts of the series, which suggests that if the structural characteristics of the total are wrong, the fault must lie with the agricultural component. Taken together with the results of the first test, the second test suggests that the agricultural labor force series describes too *low* a rate of growth across the first half of the century and too *high* a rate of growth across the second.

The two tests I have described are not conclusive, of course, and both are subject to interpretations different from those I have given them. Nonetheless, they do raise the suspicion that the Lebergott-David agricultural work force series may misstate the pattern of change of the number of agricultural workers during the course of the century. It takes only a little thought to appreciate that, if this is the case, the pattern of productivity change derived from the labor force and aggregate output series is also in error. In view of the importance of the issue—the bearing it has on the interpretation of economic change across the nineteenth century—it would seem to be desirable to pursue the question further and to attempt to assemble alternative, independent measures of productivity change. That there are data adaptable to such a purpose has already been suggested, in the previous treatment of the estimates of labor time consumed in agricultural activities.

The rest of this paper describes an attempt to produce direct measures of productivity change, appraises the results, and assesses their significance. The evidence is flimsy, indeed, but the findings appear to be plausible and lead to conclusions of some interest.

II

Total factor productivity rises when:
(1) there is an improvement in the quality of inputs; and/ or

(2)   there is an increase in the intensity of use of inputs; and/ or

(3)   there is an improvement in the allocation of factors of production among types of production; and/ or

(4)   there is an improvement in the techniques of production in use.

Given sufficient information it should be possible to identify changes falling under each of these headings during the relevant time periods and to compute the effects of these changes on productivity. For example, we know that the quality of land varied from one region to another and that quality differences were reflected in yield differences. The effect of the regional redistribution of production on average yield per acre is subject to calculation, given appropriate data on yields and the regional distribution of land under crops. Similarly, we know something about the effects of technical changes on the productivity of labor in the production of various crops. While the calculations are subject to familiar index number problems, labor productivity change estimates, by crop, can be aggregated to give estimates of total labor productivity change. In the same way, the effects of shifts in the composition of output on productivity can be computed. Finally, direct estimates of partial productivity change (i.e. land productivity change, labor productivity change, etc.) can be aggregated, following procedures similar to those developed by Denison.[9]

The spirit of the model proposed is precisely the spirit of the model used by David to generate estimates of the rate of change of per capita Gross Domestic Product across the period 1800-1840. And I can do no better than to quote David on that subject:[10]

"We must be primarily concerned with problems of acceptable prediction rather than attempts at a thorough explanation and analysis of known events . . . Simple assumptions fail to do justice to the complexities of long-run economic change, and naive, highly aggregated models may not carry us far toward a satisfactory understanding of the way in which the behavior of producers and consumers meshed together to yield the historical course of events observed in a market economy. Yet, when it comes to predicting or simulating aggregate phenomena, it is frequently found that an admixture of näiveté and aggregation is not necessarily bad."

While the set of calculations described above could be made, given sufficient evidence, in fact certain important pieces of evidence are lacking and we must make do in other instances with data that are quite defective. The chief deficiencies of the evidence are as follows:

(1) It would be desirable to break the record at several points in time and to make calculations for several periods of the century. But at present it is possible to establish breaks only at 1800, 1850, and 1900.

(2) The available evidence relates only to the grains and cotton, not all agricultural activity. These crops were important, accounting for over half of the value of agricultural output. (see Appendix.) But one would clearly like to be able to deal with a wider range of activity.

(3) So far as the effects of technical change on labor productivity are concerned, the firm evidence with respect to grains is restricted to the second half of the century.

(4) There are no very useful quantitative data that bear on the quality of the work force and the effects of changes in quality on productivity.

(5) I have been unable to assemble data by which direct estimates of the productivity change of capital can be made. The calculations are thus restricted to labor and land productivity.

(6) I have also been able to assemble no evidence by which changes in the intensity of factor use can be computed directly and the effects of such changes assessed.

Given the fragmentary nature of the evidence, it is obviously important to devise a test of the ultimate results,

41

in order that we may know the general order of importance of the components of productivity change that I have been forced to neglect. Now a fairly strong test of the ultimate results is, in fact, available. There appears to be no good reason to believe that the estimates of productivity change across the *full* century that have been derived from the aggregate output and input series (hereafter referred to as the "indirect estimates of productivity change") are seriously in error. The only question at issue is the question of shifts in the trend of productivity change *within* the century. That being the case, the indirect estimate of productivity change across the full century is an appropriate testing value. Total factor productivity change, so measured, comes to about .56 per cent per year for the full century. The new, direct estimate described in this paper, is a little less than .50 per cent per year.

That seems a reasonable enough result. It is likely that most of the nineteenth-century gains in productivity were achieved in cropping, and that they were derived mainly from improvements in land and labor productivity in the grains and cotton, improvements captured by the direct estimate of productivity change.[11] There were improvements in animal husbandry, but insofar as they affected productivity, they probably involved savings of capital—a larger output of animal products per animal in inventory —purchased in part by a larger input of land—in the form of more and better feed—and labor.[12] Any remaining gains in farm productivity must have come chiefly from improvements in the allocation of resources among types of output, not all of which are captured in the direct measure of productivity change. On the whole, the sources of improvement outside grains and cotton do not appear to have been of enormous significance, and therefore the direct, and incomplete, measure of productivity change for the full century seems not inconsistent with the indirect and comprehensive measure. Furthermore, in view of the fact that the direct measure appears to account for the chief components of productivity change, it would seem to be an appropriate means for exploring shifts in the trend of productivity change across the century.

I turn, then, to the detailed direct estimates of productivity change, treating the two halves of the century separately and, insofar as possible, distinguishing sources of productivity change.

III

Let me begin with land productivity, for which there are reasonably comprehensive data. Improvements in land productivity can be regarded as a consequence of (1) shifts in the locus of production from low yield to high yield areas; (2) shifts in the composition of output, crops yielding a high value per acre increasing an importance relative to crops yielding a low value per acre; (3) increases in the relative importance of double (multiple) cropping; (4) increases in yields per acre, due to the use of improved techniques and seeds and/or the application of larger amounts of other factors per acre. We have no data by which the effects of the third factor may be judged, but I doubt that it was an important source of productivity change.

We have data on yield, by state and by crop, for the beginning, middle, and end of the century. The yields for the beginning of the century are supposed to be "common" yields, while those for the middle are supposed to be "good." The data for the end of the century refer to crop year 1899, which was probably somewhat above the average year for that period, but not much above average.[13] Assuming that these crop year characterizations are accurate, then the direct measurements of land productivity change made from these data will probably overstate actual gains in the first half of the century and understate those in the second half. In fact, it is doubtful that this source of bias is very serious.

We also know the distribution of output among crops in 1800, and among crops and states, in 1850 and 1900 (crop years 1799, 1849, 1899) and I have estimated the distribution of outputs among states in 1800, based on data for 1850 (for states in existence in 1800).

Finally, we have data on the prices of farm crops.

With these three sets of data it is possible to make measurements of changes in land productivity and also to distribute the responsibility for change among three factors:

(1)   changes in the quality of land occasioned by the westward movement;

(2)   changes in the composition of output;

(3)   changes in yields within old areas of production. The third factor presumably reflects several component elements: (a) changes in technology affecting yields; (b) changes in factor proportions; (c) short-term influences on yields (to the extent that the measures of yield deviate from "trend" values); (d) changes in the average quality of land occasioned by, e.g., the expansion of production into new areas in the old states, the withdrawal of some land therein from production, and land exhaustion. The effects of these four separate influences cannot be distinguished with the data and model being discussed here, but the effects of the second are presumably eliminated when land and labor productivity change estimates are aggregated and the effects of the third are believed to be modest.

The calculations are subject to the usual index number problems, but these turn out to be relatively insignificant, with one exception, taken up in the appropriate place, below.

What findings can one derive from the calculations? First, the data suggest that grain yields in the old areas of settlement—that is, the states in production in 1800— changed very little between 1800 and 1850 and between 1850 and 1900 (Appendix Tables). The yields of individual grains did shift somewhat, but when one values grains and aggregates across crops (holding the composition of output fixed), one finds that the value yield did not change much. The price base selected matters little. One gets about the same results whether prices of 1800, 1850, or 1900 are used to value crops.

Second, the data show that the shift of production between 1800 and 1850 into new areas of production raised yields by about 13 per cent. Notice that this could have been occasioned by: (1) a change in output mix associated with the westward movement; (2) higher yields in the West; or (3) some combination of the two. In fact, the result was due almost exclusively to higher yields in the West and, once again, the results are not altered much by a shift in the valuation base.

Third, the persistent shift of output into states that were "new areas of production" in 1850 continued to raise yields between 1850 and 1900, accounting for a substantial part of the total yield gain in the fifty-year period. The expansion of cultivation into states that came into production between 1850 and 1900 apparently had limited effect.

Finally, the increase in cotton cultivation had a major impact on value yield changes before 1850, but not thereafter. Here for the first time the price base selected has significance for the measurements. Using a price base of 1850 or 1900, one finds that the shift into cotton raised the value yield about 12 per cent between 1800 and 1850, while using the base 1800, the figure rises to 37 per cent! The reason is clear enough. In 1800, cotton production was negligible and cotton prices were high. Using the price base of 1800, one appraises the results of the shift into cotton in terms of the high 1800 price. But the expansion of cotton cultivation took place chiefly in the presence of much lower cotton prices—indeed, by 1810 the price had already fallen by about 60 per cent—and should be appraised in these terms. Furthermore, since we are interested in testing the indirect measures of productivity change, which are based on output figures valued in late year prices, the 1850 price base appears to be the more reasonable one to select.

In toto, the gains in land productivity were approximately the same in both halves of the century, about 26 per cent for each fifty-year period. The responsibility for the improvement in the first half-century was shared almost equally between the effects of the westward movement on grain yields and the shift in the composition of output favoring cotton, while in the second half the improvement in grain yields due to the westward movement was chiefly responsible. The direct measurements suggest that land productivity went up by something under one-half of 1 per cent per year across each half of the century.

The preceding discussion treats partial productivity measures. But fundamentally we are interested in total factor productivity measures. How far did improvements in land productivity affect total factor productivity? The answer appears to be, not very far. The contribution of gains in land productivity to total factor productivity depends upon the size of the gains and the relative importance of land in the production process. Presumably the latter must be judged, for present purposes, by the share of land in total agricultural income, which is Denison's method.[14] On average, income to land accounted for only about 14 per cent of total agricultural income in the nineteenth century.[15] Furthermore, as noted previously, the crops figuring in the calculations of this paper accounted for only about half of total agricultural income. Presumably, then, the contribution of measured gains in land productivity to improvements in total factor productivity should be calculated as the product of the income share of land (.14), the fraction of total income comprehended by the measurements (.50), and the rate of gain of land productivity (.46 per cent). Based on these calculations, the contributions of improvements in land productivity in grains and cotton to total factor productivity were very modest in both halves of the century: .14 × .50 × .0046 = .00032 or .032 per cent per year.[16]

IV

The measurements of labor productivity change are restricted in two ways. First, I am able to deal only with cotton and three grains, corn, wheat, and oats, and for the period 1800-1850 I am only able to measure the effects of changes in the regional distribution of production, yield improvements, and shifts in the composition of output on labor productivity in grains. (That is, I am unable to deal with the effects of technical changes on labor productivity in grains, although I am able to deal with this phenomenon in cotton production.)

These restrictions are not quite so serious as they seem. Corn, wheat, and oats account for most of the land under grains and most of the value of output of grains. The measurement of the effects of the three factors on labor productivity, 1800-1850, exhausts the estimate of labor productivity advance in corn, 1800-1840, prepared by Cooper, Barton, and Brodell, and accounts for about 40 per cent of the gain in wheat. If the Cooper, Barton, Brodell estimates are intended to cover all sources of labor productivity advance, then the suggestion is that technical change was not an exceptionally important source of change, at least between 1800 and 1840.[17]

The results of our calculations show that in the first half of the century labor productivity in the three grains and cotton went up by about .30 per cent per year, while in the second half it rose by 2.05 per cent per year. For the full century, labor productivity rose about 1.17 per cent per year.

Labor income accounted for about 76 per cent of total agricultural income[18], and income from the grains and cot-

47

ton was about half of total income. Following the same methods of calculation as used above for land, gains in labor productivity contributed about .11 per cent to annual total factor productivity advance before 1850, .78 per cent after 1850, and .45 per cent for the full century, 1800-1900. Combining the effects of improvements in land and labor productivity, we can account for a gain in total factor productivity of about .14 per cent per year, 1800-1850, just over .80 per cent per year, 1850-1900, and almost .50 per cent per year across the full century.

V

What can one make of these results? Are they at all plausible? Do they tell us anything significant about the major substantive issues raised at the beginning of this paper?

First, it is worth noticing that the direct measure for the full century—a little less than .50 per cent per year— is fairly close to the value of the indirect measure—about .56 per cent per year, a point mentioned previously and one that testifies to the plausibility of the direct measure.

The distribution of improvements between the two halves of the century differs markedly between the two measures, however. The indirect measure suggests that the pace of change did not vary much between the first and second halves of the century, whereas the direct measure indicates that the gains were very much more pronounced in the second half than in the first. The data for the pre-1850 period underlying the direct measure are incomplete, of course, containing no evidence of the effects of technical changes on labor productivity in grains. But the figures for the post-1850 years rest on a fairly solid foundation, notably the careful work of Parker and Klein on grains.[19] Given the very high values for productivity improvements after 1850 and the reasonably good reconciliation of the direct and indirect estimates across the full century, there does not appear to be much reason to suppose that a fuller account of the factors influencing productivity change before 1850 would alter very much the picture presented above.

Other tests of plausibility can also be made. In the first section of this paper it was argued that the extant agricultural labor force series—the Lebergott-David series—may misstate the course of labor force change across the century, and two tests of this proposition were made. At issue was the rate of growth of the labor force in the first half of the century, relative to the rate of growth in the second half. It will simplify matters if we stipulate, for the sake of argument, that of the three labor force estimates under discussion—the estimates for 1800, 1850, and 1900 —the first and third are probably of the right order of magnitude, and that any error in the series is likely to be located in the figure for 1850. Now given this stipulation, it is possible to derive a new labor force figure for 1850, based on estimates developed in this paper, and to submit it to the same tests to which the Lebergott-David estimate was subjected. These tests amount to indirect tests of the new productivity estimates.

If we accept the Lebergott-David figure of the labor force in 1800, then all we need to know in order to derive a new estimate for 1850 is the rate of growth of the labor force between 1800 and 1850. This rate of growth can be approximated by subtracting the rate of growth of labor productivity from the rate of growth of output. The latter is available, of course, from David's work with the Towne-Rasmussen series. As to the former, we have the direct estimate (section IV, above) of productivity change in cotton and the grains, and we know that across the full century productivity improvement in these activities probably accounted for about four-fifths of total agricultural labor force productivity advance.[20] How the remaining one-fifth was distributed across the century, we do not know. But for the sake of the tests, I assume that it was distributed equally between the two halves of the century; that is, that productivity advance in activities omitted by the direct measure had the same effect on aggregate agricultural labor productivity improvement in each half of the century.

With this assumption, it is possible to recompute the labor force figure for 1850. The results suggest that the Lebergott-David estimate is short by about 12 per cent, or roughly six hundred thousand workers. The estimate does not appear to be unduly sensitive to the assumption concerning the components of productivity advance omitted by the direct measure. For example, even if we assume that *all* of this productivity improvement was concentrated in the first half of the century—surely an extreme and unwarranted assumption—the Lebergott-David figure is shown to be short, and by a substantial amount, roughly three hundred thousand workers.

I have adjusted the Lebergott-David figure for 1850 by the amount of six hundred thousand and have re-run the tests conducted in the first section of this paper. The results appear in Table 2. There it will be seen that the pattern of change in the labor force, implied by the direct estimates of productivity improvement, is somewhat more plausible than the pattern described by the Lebergott-David series. The number of hours worked per laborer is more stable across time,[21] and the changes in the structure of the work force seem more consistent with the evidence on the rural-urban distribution of the population. The two indirect tests, therefore, lend some support to the direct estimates of agricultural productivity advance. The data suggest that if I have erred, the error has been in the direction of *under-estimating* the degree of acceleration of productivity advance.

A final test, less demanding than the ones described above, but nonetheless of some interest, can be made. Paul David has constructed estimates of Gross Domestic Product

Table 2

Tests of the Lebergott-David and the Revised Labor Force Series

Panel A: *Changes in Implicit Hours of Work per Agricultural Worker*

	1800-1850	1850-1900
(1) Lebergott-David Series	+28 to +35%	-13 to -29%
(2) Revised series	+11 to 18%	0 to -19%

Panel B; *Changes in the Percentage Share of the Total Population in Rural Places and in the Share of Total Labor Force Affiliated with Agriculture*

	1800-1850	1850-1900
(1) Population	-9.2	-24.4
(2) Labor Force		
(a) Lebergott-David	-27.9	-14.6
(b) Revised	-20.3	-22.2

Sources: See text and notes to Table.
See Appendix, Part D.
The revised, conjectural estimate of agricultural labor force in 1850 is 5,150,000.

in 1800, based importantly on the Lebergott labor force series and the Towne and Rasmussen agricultural output series (both adjusted, in some measure, by David.) These estimates have been criticized on the ground that their structural characteristics (derivable internally and from independent data) are implausible. Specifically, it has been argued that the implicit share of perishables in final product flows is too large, and it may also be argued that the share of agricultural output in total output is too large.[22]

Given the revised agricultural labor force estimate for 1850, it is possible to re-work David's estimates for 1800. I have done so, following David's procedures in every respect, except that I have made the 1800 estimates by projection from 1850 (David projects from 1840) and I have used the revised 1850 agricultural labor force estimate for that date. (See notes to Table 3). The new figures for 1800 should bear the characterization "conjectural", the characterization David gives his figures. Indeed, the even weaker term, "illustrative", might be preferable, since the figures are intended to illustrate the implications of the finding that agricultural productivity growth accelerated during the nineteenth century.

The structural features of the revised 1800 figures are compared, in Table 3, with the implicit structural features of the David estimates. It will be seen that substitution of the new labor force estimate into the David estimating structure produces gross product estimates at 1800 that allow for relatively larger amounts of non-agricultural product and non-perishable final flows. The deviations from David's original figures therefore appear to be at least in the right direction, although the test tells us little more than this.

The tests described above appear to suggest that the direct estimates of agricultural productivity change are more plausible than are the indirect estimates previously available. I turn, then, to the third question raised at the beginning of this section: Do the new productivity estimates tell us anything significant about the major substantive issues raised at the beginning of this paper?

VI

This question has already been answered, in part. The new estimates tell us that the rate of advance of agricultural productivity—both labor productivity and total factor productivity—experienced a fairly pronounced acceleration during the nineteenth century. The account of agricultural change that antedates the recent quantitative, aggregative exploration of this issue appears to be generally validated. Unfortunately, the direct estimates do not permit one to date the acceleration; all that can be said is that the pace

Table 3

Structural Characteristics of the David and the Revised GDP Estimates, 1800, Prices of 1840

Shares in Total Product (%)

	(1) David Estimates	(2) Revised Estimates
A - Variant I*		
1 - Agricultural Output	64	60
2 - All Other Output	36	40
Total	100	100
3 - Perishable Goods	76	71
4 - All Other Goods	24	29
Total	100	100
B - Variant II*		
1 - Agricultural Output	61	56
2 - All Other Output	39	44
Total	100	100
3 - Perishable Goods	72	66
4 - All Other Goods	28	34
Total	100	100

* The definitions of the two variants are David's.

Sources:

Col (1): lines A 1 and 2, B 1 and 2, derived from David, *op. cit.* Tables 3, 5, 6, 8.

Col (1): lines A 3 and 4, B 3 and 4, derived from Gallman, "The Statistical Approcah . . .", *op. cit.*, Table 4.

Col (2): Estimates of agricultural output and flows of perishables were derived as above (David, Tables 5 and 8; Gallman, Table 4.)

Estimates of GDP were derived following David's procedure, as described in the text. The details are as follows: Estimates of Gross Farm Product and Gross Domestic Product in 1840 (David, Table 5) were extrapolated to 1850 (David, Tables 2 and 3 and Towne and Rasmussen, p. 266, line 8). The resulting values (prices of 1840) are (mil $):

	GFP	GDP
Variant A	791.0	2,320.7
Variant B	1,032.5	2,636.5

These values, together with the revised labor force figures for 1850 (agriculture: 5,150,000; all other: 3,100,000), David's labor force values for 1800 (David, p. 196) and David's implicit estimates of GFP at the same date (Variant A: $187.9 mil; Variant B: $245.3 mil) were used to estimates GDP in 1800. David's assumption that productivity change in non-agricultural activities proceeded at the same rate as productivity change in agriculture was also accepted. David believes that, in fact, the former went forward at a faster pace than the latter, which implies that his implicit estimate of non-agricultural output in 1800 is an *upper bound* estimate. However, these judgments appear doubtful (See text. See, also, Gallman, "The Statistical Approach . . .", p. 84).

of change was more rapid in the second half of the century than in the first.

Since agriculture bore such a heavy weight in the economy, one would suppose that the pattern of agricultural change would be somehow reflected in aggregate economic growth. The "conjectural" or "illustrative" estimates of Gross Domestic Product in 1800, described above, throw some light, admittedly murky, on this question. According to these estimates, GDP per capita increased at a rate of roughly 1 per cent per year, between 1800 and 1840. A fairly wide margin for error must be allowed, but we can be sure that the correct value is well below the average rate of gain experienced after 1840, which was about 1.5 per cent per year.[23] While the rate of change varied from decade to decade after 1840, there does not appear to be any alteration in the trend rate of growth; a straight line trend appears to fit the post-1840 observations quite well. Thus the "illustrative" estimates for 1800, taken together with the post-1840 data, appear to suggest an acceleration in the rate of growth during the nineteenth century, although, once again, the timing cannot be precisely established.

The preceding comments refer to the growth of per capita gross real product, conventionally defined. Presumably, one would prefer *net* measures, and the experiments that have been made along these lines indicate that the rate of change of per capita net product experienced continuous acceleration after 1840.[24] But more important than this is the fact that during the nineteenth century the mix of marketed and non-marketed product was changing, perhaps importantly. The conventional measures capture only part of non-marketed output (agricultural output and the shelter value of owner-occupied houses). It is well-known that the omission of the remaining components of non-marketed output tends to bias conventional measures of output growth in an upward direction, and one calculation

54

shows that the bias in the per capita measure for the U.S. for the period 1840-1900 amounts to about .3 per cent per year, or roughly one-fifth of the measured growth rate.[25]

All of these considerations suggest that U.S. per capita product, comprehensively measured on a net basis, would describe an accelerating rate of growth across the entire nineteenth and early twentieth centuries and that the acceleration would be pronounced, in the sense that the trend rate might well double during this period. One final consideration suggests that the increase over the longer term, appropriately measured, might be even greater than this.

One of the most striking features of American growth in the present century is that it has been accompanied by a pronounced reduction in the average work year. Kuznets has argued that the leisure time obtained is part of the product of growth, and that ideally we would place a value on it and incorporate it in the national product. According to illustrative calculations he made, proper account of the value of increased leisure might increase the American rate of growth between the late nineteenth century and mid-twentieth century by as much as one-fifth.[26]

While twentieth-century growth rates should perhaps be adjusted upward to allow for the value of increased leisure, it seems probable that similar adjustments for the nineteenth century would result in a *downward* adjustment in the rate of growth. The reason is that the shift from agricultural to non-agricultural work may well have *increased* the average number of hours of labor per year engaged in by the typical worker.

According to the calculations described earlier in this paper (Section I; see, also, the Appendix), the amount of labor consumed in agriculture per agricultural worker came to about one thousand hours per year in the nineteenth century. The estimate is biased downward for three reasons: it omits labor performed in the production of about 20 per cent of agricultural output, it excludes tasks of

55

management, and it makes no allowance for time consumed in moving from one task to another.[27] But proper adjustment of the estimates for these omissions would surely not raise the figure above two thousand hours per year. Now two thousand hours is approximately the work year in manufacturing today. In the nineteenth century, the manufacturing work day ranged from ten to twelve hours, and the work week was six days. Even making large allowances for sick time and unemployment, the work year was unlikely to have been much less than three thousand hours. The question immediately arises as to why the work year was so much lower in agriculture.

No doubt part of the explanation is that the agricultural workers also participated in other sectors—they engaged in home manufacturing, forest work, road building, hauling and other activities during slack times.[28] Perhaps in these activities they raised their work year to the level experienced in the non-agricultural sectors of the economy. But it seems more reasonable to suppose that the typical agricultural worker—slaves apart—was unable (and perhaps unwilling) to fill his year with work. The seasonal pattern of agricultural labor—certainly in the North, in places distant from urban centers—produced twelve- or fourteen-hour days and six- or seven-day weeks at active times of the year, but substantial leisure at other times.

If this interpretation is correct, then the structural changes of the American economy during the nineteenth century produced an increase in the average number of hours of work per year performed by the typical worker. Per capita income growth was purchased, in part, at the cost of more work per laborer. Proper allowance for lost leisure would show that the real income gains achieved during the nineteenth century were smaller than the standard income measures suggest. Viewed in the most comprehensive way, then, the pace of American growth since 1800 would describe a pronounced and persistent acceleration, very modest net gains in the early nineteenth century being succeeded by gradually increasing improvements.

This account of things also helps to explain the wide disparities in per worker output levels between the agricultural and non-agricultural sectors. The disparities may be explained in part by the fact that agricultural workers helped to produce non-agricultural output, and in part by the fact that the work year was shorter inside agriculture than outside the sector. The nature of the problem of off-season slack time surely varied from region to region and time to time, reflecting differences in institutions, crop mixes, crop routines, degrees of mechanization, and the development of village and town life. The differing nature of the labor force interactions between agriculture and the other sectors in these settings is a subject clearly worthy of intensive study. While it has not been neglected, the lessons it has to teach about the process of American economic growth—and economic growth generally—have not yet been fully learned. The learning promises to be rewarding.

APPENDIX

A. *Land Productivity*

1. *Yield Data*

The grain yield data for 1800 were taken from Samuel Blodget (*Economica, A Statistical Manual for the United States of America*, 1806, reprint ed., New York: Augustus M. Kelley, 1964, p. 97); for 1850, from the compendium of the seventh census (Washington: Beverly Tucker, Senate Printer, 1854, p. 178); and for 1900, from the census of agriculture for 1900. The Blodget data are described and appraised in Gallman, "Changes . . . ," *op. cit.* Briefly, they were gathered in 1791 by correspondence with observers throughout the country, who were asked to supply estimates of "common" and "good" yields. Tests suggest that the estimates of "common" yields are consistent with Blodget's estimates of land under crops in 1800, on the one hand, and the Towne and Rasmussen estimates of agricultural output—which, in the cases of the grains, refer to average performance at the turn of the century—on the other. The Towne and Rasmussen series (Marvin W. Towne and Wayne D. Rasmussen, "Farm Gross Product and Gross Investment in the Nineteenth Century," in William N. Parker (ed.), *Trends in the American Economy* . . . , *op. cit.*) is the one used by David and the one underlying the indirect measures of total factor productivity described in the text of this paper. I therefore decided to use the common yield estimates to represent the level of productivity at the turn of the century.

The data in the compendium of the seventh census were gathered by census enumerators and were supposed to represent "good" yields for the period. Whether in fact they represent good yields is arguable. Tests of consistency among the yield estimates and the census returns of output and improved land are difficult to conduct and interpret, but the tests we carried out suggest that the yields returned by the enumerators are at least as good as the yields realized in the census year, a year described by Thorp as an "excellent" crop year, although apparently the wheat crop was short (Gallman, "Changes . . . ," p. 208 and sources cited therein. See, also, DeBow's efforts to reconcile the yield and output returns of the census, Compendium of the Seventh Census, *op. cit.*, p. 176.) On the other hand, the average nationwide grain yields we derived from the census evidence are very close to the figures used by Parker and Klein to represent average yields for the period 1840-60. Furthermore, the 1850 grain yields in the territory that was in production in 1800 are close to Blodget's "common" yield figures for 1800. Unless soil exhaustion was a serious problem, the suggestion is that the 1850 data are probably representative of average experience. I assumed that they are. If the assumption is contrary to fact, then my estimates of land productivity change between 1800 and 1850 probably overstate true productivity gains, which tends to make the ultimate conclusions of the paper more secure.

The data for 1900 represent actual experience in crop year 1899, as returned by the census. According to Thorp (Willard Long Thorp, *Business Annals*, New York: National Bureau of Economic Research, Inc., 1926, p. 138) 1899 was a year of "large crops." But the yield figures are not far different from values derived from the census for crop year 1889, a year of mixed experience, and are somewhat higher, but close to, the yields used by Parker and Klein to represent average experience, 1900-1910. I assumed therefore, that the 1900 data do not deviate from trend values in a different direction from, or by markedly larger margins than, the data for 1800 and 1850.

2. *Land Under Crops*

As will appear, estimates of land under crops were necessary for purposes of weighting, and these were derived from yield estimates and data on output. For 1850 and 1900 we used census data on output, since they are available at the state level. It should be noted that some of the census figures of national output deviate slightly from the values implicit in the Towne and Rasmussen estimates. However, the effects of these deviations on my ultimate results are slight.

3. *Calculations of Productivity Change, 1800-1850*

Blodget provides estimates of land yields in wheat, rye, barley, oats, Indian corn, and buckwheat for New England, "Carolina" (presumably the Carolinas, combined), "Western Territory," New York, Pennsylvania, New Jersey, Delaware, and Virginia, but no estimates for Maryland and Georgia and no separate estimates for Tennessee and Kentucky, presumably included in "Western Territory". We made no use of the "Western Territory" figures. Had we treated them as representative of experience in Tennessee and Kentucky—a reasonable choice—the direct measure of land productivity change, 1800-1850, would have been somewhat smaller than it is. That is, the procedure selected tended to bias my results against the conclusions ultimately reached in this paper.

The first step in the calculations was to compute the volume of land under each grain in each state in 1850, New England and the Carolinas being treated as single states for these purposes. The required figures were arrived at by dividing census output data by the 1850 yield estimates. (In a few unimportant instances state yield figures had to be derived from evidence for neighboring states.) The figures on land under crops were used as weights in the calculation of average nationwide yields in 1800. Similar average yields were derived for 1850, the averages referring to the nation as constituted in 1800, exclusive of Maryland, Georgia, Tennessee, and Kentucky. The averages for the individual grains at each date were then valued and aggregated into (weighted) estimates of the average value of grain output per acre devoted to grain production. Two sets of values were calculated for each date, one expressed in prices of 1800, the other, in prices of 1850, the prices being taken from Towne and Rasmussen. The values were then converted into index numbers (base 1800), which were intended to express the relative levels of the real value of output per acre at the two dates, given no changes across time in the distribution of output among states and among crops. That is, the only variables allowed to change between the two dates were the individual state yield estimates. The index numbers therefore are intended to show the effects of yield changes within the states that were in production in 1800 (exclusive of Maryland, Georgia, Tennessee, and

Kentucky), hereafter referred to as the "old area of production." The index numbers, given below, have exactly the same form as fixed weight price index numbers. The results suggest that, on average, yields changed little within the "old area" between 1800 and 1850:

(a) Value of output per acre expressed in: *1800   1850*

      Prices of 1800   100   99
      Prices of 1850   100   99

In the second calculation, the distribution of output among types of grains was also allowed to change. That is, the weights were allowed to shift. The relevant weights in 1800 were derived by dividing output figures for 1800 by the average yield estimates relevant to that date. (See Gallman "Changes . . . ," p. 199.) The procedure amounts to the assumption that average yields in the "old area" are representative of average yields in the old area plus Maryland, Georgia, Tennessee, and Kentucky—hereafter referred to as "the old area plus four." (The evidence for 1850 suggests that the assumption is fair enough.) The 1850 averages were also adjusted to take into account performance at that date in Maryland, Georgia, Tennessee, and Kentucky. New index numbers were then computed from these estimates. They describe the effects of yield changes and the effects of changes in the composition of output within the "old area plus four" on land productivity. (Unfortunately, no system for allowing changes in the distribution of output among states could be devised.) The index numbers suggest that the combined effects of these two sets of changes were slight:

(b) Value of output per acre expressed in: *1800 1850*

      Prices of 1800   100   101
      Prices of 1850   100   101

Next the 1850 averages were adjusted to take into account performance in states that were in production in

1850, but not in 1800. Two sets of calculations were made, one in which the mix of output was held fixed, and the other in which the mix was allowed to change as it did historically. The results of the two sets of calculations were identical:

(c) Value of output per acre, expressed in: *1800 1850*

Prices of 1800	100	113
Prices of 1850	100	113

These three sets of calculations underlie the text statements that: (1) the change in land productivity in grains between 1800 and 1850 amounted to 13 per cent, that (2) the westward movement was chiefly responsible for the increase in productivity and that (3) these conclusions emerge whether one computes output in prices of 1800 or in prices of 1850.

The next step was to incorporate cotton into the calculations. We accepted Whartenby's yield estimate for 1800 (Franklee Whartenby, "Land and Labor Productivity in United States Cotton Production, 1800-1840" Ph.D. dissertation, University of North Carolina, 1963, p. 54, the lower of the two yields) and calculated a figure for 1850 by weighting regional estimates, derived from Whartenby (for 1840), with 1850 land weights. The land weights were produced by dividing regional output data—from the census —by regionally specific land yields. Price weights were again taken from Towne and Rasmussen.

Introducing cotton into the calculations produces the following results:

(d) Value of output per acre, expressed in: *1800 1850*

Prices of 1800	100	155
Prices of 1850	100	126

The index numbers for 1850 are significantly raised by the incorporation of cotton into the computations. Holding all other factors constant and allowing only cotton to affect the results we obtain the following index numbers:

(e)	Value of output per acre, expressed in:	*1800*	*1850*
	Prices of 1800	100	137
	Prices of 1850	100	112

Comparing the index numbers given above under (c) and (e) one obtains the conclusions that (1) productivity gains arose chiefly from the effects of the westward movement on grain yields and (2) from the expansion of cotton cultivation and that (3) if valuations are expressed in 1850 prices, these two developments were of roughly equal importance.

4. *Calculations of Productivity Change, 1850-1900*

Indexes of land productivity change in grains were also calculated for the period 1850 to 1900. The following set of indexes is equivalent to the set listed in section (c) above:

(f)	Value of output per acre, expressed in:	*1850*	*1900*
	Prices of 1850	100	126
	Prices of 1900	100	121

The shift in the price base from 1850 to 1900 is modestly, but perceptibly, reflected in a decline in the value of the index number for 1900, suggesting that the composition of output shifted somewhat across the last fifty years of the period. In fact, the composition of output altered very little in the "old", "old plus four", and "new" areas, but the states that came into production after 1850—hereafter called the "west"—produced considerably more wheat and less corn and oats, in relative terms, than did the other areas and this is the source of the compositional change. Land under cotton also increased in relative terms, not through development of the "west", but in the "new" area, and when cotton is brought into the index (using census data for 1900) the effect is to compensate for the other compositional changes:

(g)   Value of output per acre, expressed in: *1850* *1900*

Prices of 1850	100	127
Prices of 1900	100	126

Altogether, the effect of cotton in the second period is quite modest, however.

Putting all calculations on the price base 1900, which is perhaps the most reasonable system, since the indirect estimates of productivity change depend upon an output series valued in prices of 1910-14 (the Towne and Rasmussen series), the direct measures of productivity change in grains and cotton show a gain of about 25 points, 1800-1850, and 26 points, 1850-1900, a difference too slight to warrant attention.

Returning to the grains, in the second half of the century the rate of change of the value of output per acre is affected very little by the inclusion or exclusion of the "west". The indexes for the "old plus four" and "new" areas, combined, are:

(h)   Value of output per acre, expressed in: *1850* *1900*

Prices of 1850	100	125
Prices of 1900	100	124

Since the distribution of land among the grains in these areas (individually and combined) changed little between 1850 and 1900, the rise in the indexes must be attributed to improvements in average yields within the areas. The sources of these improvements were the continuing shift of production into the "new" area, in which yields were relatively high, and increases in average yields within the "new" area, perhaps partly due to a change in the distribution of output among states in that section of the country. Thus within the "old plus four" area, the value of output per acre rose by only about 2 per cent, while within the "new" area, it went up by between 16 and 17 per cent. The growing relative importance of the "new" area, therefore, played an important role in the increase of the average value of output per acre.

B. Labor Productivity

1. Procedure

The estimating procedure followed was very similar to the procedure used to obtain the indexes of changes in the value of output per acre. The total volume of labor required to produce each crop was calculated by multiplying man hours required per unit of output by the total volume of output. Man hours were then summed across crops and the total divided through the value of the output of these crops, to yield the value of output per man hour. The output and price data used were the data described in section A of this appendix.

The number of man hours required per unit of output sometimes depends upon yields and therefore we required yield data. The yield data used are described in section A of this appendix.

Once again, computations were made by region, although the form of the data—which did not altogether fit my regional scheme—required us to attribute to individual states the average labor productivity characteristics of the region in which they were situated. Tests of the results are therefore important and are conducted in the following section.

2. Labor Productivity Changes in Corn, Wheat, and Oats, 1800 to 1850 to 1900

Data on labor productivity by crop and region circa 1850 and 1900 were obtained from Parker and Klein. Also available are figures for corn and wheat derived by Cooper, Barton, and Brodell (op. cit.) for 1800, 1840, and 1900, although the Parker and Klein estimates are the more re-

65

cent, involved a much larger scholarly effort, and clearly constitute a more reliable guide to changes in the second half of the century. Parker also estimated the effects of regional shifts between 1800 and the middle of the century on productivity in the three grains. (W. N. Parker, "Sources of Agricultural Productivity . . .", *op. cit.*)

We used the work of Parker and of Cooper, Barton, and Brodell to test our results.

As it turns out, our results with respect to changes in labor productivity from all sources are very similar to the ones we would have obtained had we used the work of Parker and Klein without modification—i.e., had we used their regional distributions, yields, and output data. The estimates obtained by applying value weights to the un-revised Parker and Klein figures show a very slightly higher rate of gain for the second half of the century and a very slightly lower gain for the first than do the revised figures. This can be demonstrated most easily by re-cording the average annual rates of change computed from the two sets of estimates:

	1800-1850	1850-1900	1800-1900
Prices of 1800			
Unrevised series	.2%	2.9%	1.6%
Revised series	.3	2.7	1.5
Prices of 1850			
Unrevised series	.3%	2.8%	1.5%
Revised series	.4	2.7	1.5
Prices of 1900			
Unrevised series	.3%	2.8%	1.5%
Revised series	.4	2.7	1.5

Restricting the analysis to corn and wheat it is possible to compare the unrevised and revised series with estimates based on the work of Cooper, Barton, and Brodell.

	1800-1850	1850-1900	1800-1900
Prices of 1850			
Unrevised series	.3%	2.8%	1.5%
Revised series	.4	2.6	1.5
Series based on			
Cooper *et al.*	.7	1.0	.9

(The rates of change based on Cooper, Barton, and Brodell refer, of course, to the periods 1800-1840 and 1840-1900.) All three series show that the rate of change of productivity was higher in the second part of the century than in the first, although the temporal disparity is much smaller in the case of the third series than of the first two. The assertions in the text of this paper depend upon calculations with the revised series, which is also the series used in the rest of this appendix.

3. *Labor Productivity Changes in Cotton, 1800 to 1850 to 1900*

The data on cotton productivity are less substantial and less apposite, but are probably adequate. We had to depend upon the work of Cooper, Barton, and Brodell, which, in the case of the grains, has been shown to be inconsistent with the more recent work of Parker and Klein. If we may infer from the record with respect to the grains, Cooper *et al.* may have understated the pace of productivity change across the last half of the century. Our use of the Cooper *et al.* data on cotton productivity may therefore bias downward our final estimates of productivity change in the second half of the century.

We used the Cooper *et al.* estimates of man hours required per acre in cotton and converted them into requirements per pound of cotton by use of the yield estimates described in section A of this appendix. (Had we used the yield estimates provided by Cooper *et al.* the results would not have been far different.) Unfortunately, it was necessary to use the Cooper *et al.* labor productivity

67

figure for 1840 as an approximation to the 1850 level. Whether labor requirements per acre rose or fell across the decade of the 1840's is by no means clear, so that we cannot venture a judgment as to the direction of bias imparted to the ultimate productivity change measures by this feature of the evidence. The 1840's was not a decade of pronounced expansion in cotton production, and one may suppose that the bias—whatever its direction—is not very large.

The estimates of changes in labor productivity in grains and cotton combined are as follows:

	1800-1850	1850-1900	1800-1900
In prices of 1800	.7	2.1	1.4
In prices of 1850	.3	2.1	1.2
In prices of 1900	.3	2.1	1.2

Regardless of the price base chosen, the rate of change across the last half of the century is substantially greater than across the first half. The results of the calculations on the price bases 1850 and 1900 are similar, whereas the series expressed in the 1800 prices describes a somewhat higher rate of gain across the first half of the century and also between 1800 and 1900, for reasons explored in the text of this paper.

The underlying data are in a form to permit a partitioning of productivity change among sources, along the lines explored in section A of this appendix, but the necessary computations have not yet been completed.

C. Weighting Schemes

1. Combining Measures of Factor Productivity

In order to combine individual factor productivity change estimates, it is necessary to weight them. As the text of this paper indicates, we chose income weights, following Denison. Denison uses his procedure to combine rates of change of factor supplies, but it is easily demonstrated that the method is equally applicable to the problem at hand, so long as income shares exhaust income.

Let o, k, n, and t refer to rates of change of output, capital, labor and land and x, y, and z, the shares of income earned by capital, labor, and land, respectively. Then my proposed estimate of total factor productivity change can be described as follows:

(1) $(o-k)x + (o-n)y + (o-t)z$

which can also be expressed as:

(2) $ox - kx + oy - ny + oz - tz$

or:

(3) $ox + oy + oz - kx - ny - tz$

Then if $x + y + z = 1$, we get:

(4) $o - (kx + ny + tz)$,

which is Denison's formulation. Therefore, if we can assume that economies or diseconomies of scale are absent, or negligible, my procedure amounts to a variant of Denison's. (I am grateful to my colleague, Vincent Tarascio, for suggesting this form of proof.) Furthermore, since the Denison procedure was also used to derive the indirect estimates of total factor productivity change described in this paper (Gallman, "Changes . . . ,"), the proof demonstrates that the methodologies followed in the construction of the direct and indirect measures are consistent, which validates the comparisons drawn in this paper between the results of the two studies.

2. Income Weights

The income shares required are the shares in income earned in the activities treated in this paper—grain and cotton production. In the absence of the required data, I used evidence relating to the entire agricultural sector (see the text of this paper). Since grain and cotton production are relatively labor intensive, as compared with the chief agricultural activities neglected in this paper—for example, animal husbandry—one would suppose that the labor share appropriate to this study should be somewhat larger than the sectoral average, and the land share somewhat smaller. Were an appropriate adjustment of this type within my power and were I to make it, it would have a negligible impact on my estimate of total factor productivity change across the first half of the century—since the land and labor productivity change estimates are so nearly at the same level— but it would raise the estimate across the second half of the century. That is, with appropriate income share data, the conclusions of this paper would be made somewhat more secure.

3. The Relative Importance of Productivity Change in Grains and Cotton

The direct measures of productivity change assembled in this paper refer to only part of total agricultural activity. In order to know how important the productivity changes were it is necessary to put them into the context of the full sector. My method of doing so is to attempt to answer the question: how great would the gain in total agricultural productivity have been had there been no other sources of gain or loss, apart from those explored in this paper? To answer the question, one needs to know the way in which productive resources were distributed between the activities covered by the paper, on the one hand, and those ignored, on the other. The appropriate measure is of exactly the same character as the measure discussed in section C1, above. That is, the share of agricultural resources devoted to grain and cotton production is measured by the ratio of the value of grain and cotton output (expressed in current prices) to the income earned by the agricultural sector.

I used the Towne and Rasmussen data to calculate the appropriate measure. Towne and Rasmussen introduce the grains into their estimates, net of seed and feed allowances. So far as the feed allowances are concerned, the procedure amounts to attributing part of the value of output of the grain industry to the husbandry industry. But for present purposes it is clear that the value of feeds (apart from feeds going to work animals employed in grain and cotton production) should be attributed to the grain industry. We therefore adjusted the Towne and Rasmussen estimates of the value of grain production, changing them from a net to a gross basis by use of coefficients published by Towne and Rasmussen. Unfortunately, it was impossible to distinguish between feed and seed allowances and, among feeds, between feeds going to work animals in grain and cotton production, on the one hand, and all other feeds, on the other. Our estimates of the share of grains and cotton in total agricultural income are therefore somewhat too large. Furthermore, the general weighting procedure involves the distribution of resources among crop-specific activities, making no allowance for general tasks of management. This also results in too heavy a weight for productivity changes in the grains and cotton. We rounded the estimates downward, to take these biases into account. The estimates are as follows:

		1800	*1850*	*1900*
1.	Ratio of the value of output of corn, wheat, oats, and cotton to total agricultural income	.540	.546	.505
2.	Ratio of the value of output of all grains and cotton to total agricultural income	.584	.566	.519

We rounded these estimates downward to .50, to account for the upward biases in the estimates discussed above.

D. *Estimates of Hours Worked in Agriculture*

To estimate the hours of labor implicit in agricultural output, we first converted the Towne and Rasmussen output estimates to a gross basis—i.e., output inclusive of seeds and feeds. We then computed labor requirements in the production of corn, wheat, oats, and cotton at each date from the output data and the labor productivity estimates described in section B of this appendix. For rye,

71

buckwheat, barley, Irish potatoes, sweet potatoes, dairy products, pork, beef, and mutton we used the Towne and Rasmussen output data and estimates of labor productivity *circa* 1910 contained in John A. Hopkins, *Changing Technology and Employment in Agriculture*, U.S. Department of Agriculture, Bureau of Agricultural Economics, May 1941.

We prepared two sets of estimates of labor used in the improvement of farms: clearing and breaking land, fencing, constructing buildings. The first was derived directly from the work of Towne and Rasmussen, who estimated the value of improvements at each date. Their procedure consisted of valuing the labor content of improvements, and they published sufficient information (pp. 267, 269, 270) to permit one to reconstruct the underlying labor input series.

The second set of estimates depends upon the subsequent, and more intensive, efforts of Martin Primack. ("Farm Capital Formation as a Use of Farm Labor in the United States, 1850-1910," *The Journal of Economic History*, Vol. XXVI, No. 3, September 1966, p. 35). Primack estimated the average annual volume of labor used in farm improvements in the decades 1850-59 and 1890-99. We estimated the hours per worker taken by farm improvements at the middle of the century as the ratio of Primack's annual average value, 1850-59, to the mean of the labor force in 1850 and 1860. We followed the same procedure for the estimate at the end of the century. We derived the volume of labor consumed in improvements in 1800 by extrapolating Primack's average for 1850-59 to 1800 on the Towne and Rasmussen estimates of the real value of improvements.

Our estimates of the percentage changes in the annual hours of work per worker are as follows, Variant A incorporating the Towne and Rasmussen improvements data, Variant B, the Primack data:

	1800-1850	1850-1900
Exclusive of improvements	+35%	-13%
Inclusive of improvements		
Variant A	+28%	-19%
Variant B	+28%	-29%

Labor requirements estimates based on twentieth-century evidence account for between one-fifth and one-fourth of the number of hours of work in both 1800 and 1850. That is, the aggregate estimates of hours of work at these dates depend chiefly on productivity evidence relating to the nineteenth century, not the twentieth century.

The products represented in the labor hours estimates were very important, of course. Their gross value accounting for the following fractions of the gross value (i.e., gross of feed and seed production) of farm output:

	1800	1850	1900
Exclusive of farm improvements:			
Current prices	.80	.79	.79
Prices of 1910-14	.75	.79	.77
Inclusive of farm improvements:			
Current prices	.82	.83	.80
Prices of 1910-14	.81	.83	.79

*This paper continues work begun in two earlier papers: R. Gallman, "The Statistical Approach: Fundamental Concepts as Applied to History", in George Rogers Taylor and Lucius F. Ellsworth (eds.), *Approaches to American Economic History*, Charlottesville, Virginia: University of Virginia Press, 1971, and "Changes in Total U.S. Agricultural Factor Productivity in the 19th Century", *Agricultural History*, Vol. XLVI, No. 1, January 1972. Some of the data used in this paper and the preceding one were originally gathered in connection with a project funded by the National Science Foundation, and tests of data and calculations were financed by the same grant. Kenneth Pauwels carred out many of the computations, for which I am grateful. A draft of the paper was prepared while I was a Guggenheim Fellow. William N. Parker kindly read an earlier draft and offered his criticisms, although he should be absolved of all responsibility for errors of fact or interpretation that may appear in the finished product.

1. Paul David, "The Growth of Real Product in the United States before 1840: New Evidence and Controlled Conjectures," *The Journal of Economic History*, Vol. XXVII, No. 2, June 1967, pp. 171-173, 196.

2. See, for example, William N. Parker and Franklee Whartenby, "The Growth of Output before 1840", in William N. Parker (ed.), *Trends in the American Economy in the 19th Century*, Studies in Income and Wealth, Volume 24, by the Conference on Research in Income and Wealth, A Report of the National Bureau of Economic Research, Princeton, New Jersey: Princeton University Press, 1960, pp. 207-208 and Parker's treatment of the topic in L. E. Davis, R. A. Easterlin, W. N. Parker, et. al., *American Economic Growth, An Economist's History of the United States*, New York, Evanston, San Francisco, London: Harper and Row, 1972, pp. 370-372. See, also, the last two sources cited in footnote 6.

3. Marvin W. Towne and Wayne D. Rasmussen, "Farm Gross Product and Gross Investment in the 19th Century", in W. N. Parker (ed.), *Trends in the American Economy, op. cit.* and Stanley Lebergott, "Labor Force and Employment, 1800-1960", in Dorothy S. Brady (ed.), *Output, Employment, and Productivity in the United States after 1800*, Studies in Income and Wealth Volume 30, by the Conference on Research in Income and Wealth, New York and London: National Bureau of Economic Research and Columbia University Press, 1966.

David (*op. cit.*) has made revisions and adjustments to both series and in what follows I use David's versions of the two series.

4. See Stanley Engerman, "Discussion", *American Economic Review*, Vol. LVII, No. 2, May 1967, p. 308 and Gallman, "Changes in Total Agricultural Factor Productivity . . .", *op. cit.*, pp. 207-210.

5. David, *op. cit.*, pp. 174-86.

6. William N. Parker and Judith L. V. Klein, "Productivity Growth in Grain Production in the United States, 1840-60 and 1900-10" in Brady, *op. cit.*, and William N. Parker, "Sources of Agricultural Productivity in the 19th Century," *Journal of Farm Economics*, Vol. 49, No. 5, Dec. 1967, pp. 1455-68. See, also, the discussion of the Parker paper by Gordon A. MacEachern, same journal and issue, pp. 1469-72.

7. The increase between 1800 and 1850 may be due, in some measure, to biases in the labor requirements data, discussed in the text (above) and the Appendix. But it is unlikely that these biases are fully, or even chiefly, responsible, as will appear. (See also, the Appendix.) It may be thought that the decrease between 1850 and 1900 reflects the termination of the slave system, an event that no doubt diminished the intensity of work of one component of the work force. But the effects of the change are reflected in the *labor force series*, which treats slave women and children as members of the work force, but not freed women and children. Thus the effect of emancipation on the ratio: "hours worked to members of the work force" is to reduce the *denominator*. No doubt the numerator was also reduced—men, women and children probably worked fewer hours per year in freedom than they did under slavery. But since women and children continued to do some farm work, in freedom, the decline in the numerator is likely to have been smaller than the decline in the denominator. Consequently, one would expect that the effect of emancipation on the *measures being discussed here* might be to *increase* the hours worked per member of the work force, not decrease them. Additionally, activities associated with the harvest of the corn plant (fodder), as distinct from the corn grain, and the shelling of corn are omitted. These are activities of some importance. A partially offsetting bias is that free women and

children, who contributed in some measure to agricultural work, are not counted as members of the agricultural work force.

8. This point is also made by Engerman (*op. cit.*)

9. Edward F. Denison, *The Sources of Economic Growth in the United States*, New York: Committee for Economic Development, 1962, Ch. 4. Denison combines rates of change of individual factor inputs into a rate of change of total factor inputs. His system is to weight the rate of change of each factor input by the share of total income earned by the factor. Precisely the same weighting scheme can be used to combine rates of change of partial productivity measures. See the Appendix.

10. *op. cit.*, pp. 158, 159, 161.

11. Some of these gains reflected the substitution of capital for labor, so that a comprehensive total factor productivity change estimate for these crops might be slightly lower then the value given in the text. The indirect measure of the change in partial productivity of capital in agriculture, 1800-1900, is minus .26 per cent per year (Gallman, "Changes . . . ," p. 206, Table 6, Col. (3) line (1) minus line (4).) Weighting this value by the share of capital in income produces a value of minus .03 per cent per year, which is the effect on total factor productivity of changes in capital productivity, according to the indirect measure of the latter. However, this calculation refers to the effect of changes in capital productivity on the agricultural sector as a whole, not just in the grains and cotton.

12. See, for example, Fred Bateman, "Improvement in American Dairy Farming, 1850-1910: A Quantitative Analysis," *The Journal of Economic History*, Vol. XXVIII, No. 2, June 1968, p. 271.

13. See the Appendix for a documentation of these statements and similar statements made in the rest of this section. The Appendix also contains the estimates and detailed notes on estimating procedures.

14. See footnote 9 and the Appendix.

15. Gallman, "Changes . . . ," *op. cit.*, p. 205.

16. This statement leaves out of account the effects of changes in land productivity on changes in labor productivity, which are captured in the measures of the latter. Clearly, factor productivity changes are interrelated and efforts to distangle them risk a simplistic account of historic change. See the discussion of this point in Section II, above.

17. M. R. Cooper, C. T. Barton, A. P. Brodell, *Progress of Farm Mechanization*, U. S. Department of Agriculture, Miscellaneous Publication 630, October 1947. See the Appendix for a discussion of these estimates. See also, the reconciliation of the direct and indirect estimates of productivity change (Section II, above), which gives a stronger basis for the belief that the pre-1850 direct estimates are adequate.

18. Gallman, "Changes . . . ," *op. cit.*, p. 205.

19. Parker and Klein, *op. cit.*

20. According to the indirect measure (Gallman "Changes . . . " *op. cit.*), agricultural labor productivity improved at an annual rate of about .735 per cent per year between 1800 and 1900. The direct measurements derived in section IV, above, account for a rate of advance of about .585 per cent per year, (1.17 per cent per year in the grains and cotton, multiplied by .50, the share of the grains and cotton in total output), or about four-fifths of the rate computed indirectly,

which I take to be a reasonable approximation of the true average rate of change for the century.

21. It may appear that this would be true, almost by definition, since both the estimates of hours worked and the revised labor force figures depend upon direct estimates of labor productivity. However, the range of activities covered is much wider in the case of the former estimates than in the case of the latter, so that there is a degree of independence between the two sets of estimates.

22. Gallman, "The Statistical Approach . . .", pp. 66-79.

23. Computed from data underlying Table 2 in Robert E. Gallman, "Gross National Product, 1834-1909", in Brady, *op. cit.*, p. 9.

24. See Davis, Easterlin, Parker *et. al., op. cit.*, p. 41.

25. *Ibid.*, pp. 44, 45.

26. Simon Kuznets, "Long Term Changes in the National Product of the United States of American since 1870", in International Association for Research in Income and Wealth, *Income and Wealth of the United States: Trends and Structure* (Income and Wealth Series 2) (Cambridge, England: Bowes and Bowes, 1952), pp. 55, 59, 63-69.

27. A partially offsetting bias is that free women and children, who contributed in some measure to agricultural work, are not counted as members of the agricultural work force.

28. Clearly, this affects the analytical meaning of sectoral affiliation, a point taken up below. It also means that the results of estimating procedures of the type developed by David and utilized in this paper are subject to error, a point fully recognized by David. The margin of error on this account need not be wide, however, since shifts in the relationship between agricultural and non-agricultural work performed by agricultural workers are unlikely to be sudden and pronounced.

III

FARM PRODUCTION AND INCOME IN OLD AND NEW AREAS AT MID-CENTURY

Richard A. Easterlin[1]

University of Pennsylvania

This paper presents estimates for 1840 of agricultural output by state, along with previously published estimates of agricultural income and labor force (Table A-1). These data provide a summary picture of a number of geographic features of American agriculture at the time—the share of each state in output and income, the structure of interstate price differences, comparative levels of labor productivity and income per worker, and the degree of regional specialization in production. They throw further light on the contribution of the westward movement to the growth of labor productivity.

In addition, estimates of agricultural output and labor force based on consistent procedures are given for seven geographic divisions for 1840, 1850, and 1860 (Table B-1). These figures clarify regional trends in production and productivity in the two decades before the Civil War. Of special interest are comparative developments in Northern and Southern agricultural labor productivity during this period.

In the output estimates, products in every state or division are valued at the same prices—the United States average for each product. In the subsequent discussion these figures are sometimes termed "agricultural income at United States prices" (or constant prices) to distinguish them from previously published income estimates at state (or current) prices, in which products are valued at the prices actually received by farmers. In the current and constant price estimates by state for 1840 the prices used are averages for the period 1840-46; in the constant price estimates by division for 1840, 1850, and 1860, the prices used are the United States prices of 1879. States are classified by region as shown in Table A-1—the classification is the same as the present one of the Bureau of the Census, except that Delaware and Maryland are included in the Middle Atlantic division and the District of Columbia is omitted. Details regarding scope and concept of the output and income estimates along with methods of estimation are given in Appendixes A and B. The present discussion summarizes some of the principal results.

THE SITUATION IN 1840

Production shares and productivity.—In 1840, the output of United States agriculture, valued in terms of the average prices of 1840-46, amounted to $663 million or $173 per member of the agricultural labor force. Column 2 of Table A-2 shows which regions and states were principally responsible for producing this output. On a regional basis, output was nearly evenly divided between the eighteen Northern states and eleven Southern states, with the former producing slighly more than half. (If the regional groupings here were the Census Bureau's, with Delaware and Maryland included with the South, the division would be almost exactly fifty-fifty.) As one would expect, the older eastern regions typically had the largest shares. The Middle Atlantic and South Atlantic regions together accounted for somewhat under half of total output, and New England added almost another tenth. In contrast, the two westernmost divisions, the West North Central and West South Central, contributed in combination less than a twelfth.

New York was the leading agricultural state with over 12 per cent of national production. Next in importance came Pennsylvania and then a relatively new state, Ohio, both with somewhat over 8 per cent of the total. After these was a cluster of seven Southern states, led in order by Virginia, Tennessee, Kentucky, and Georgia, with shares ranging from 7 down to a little more than 4 percentage points. Only one other state, a northern one, Indiana, had a share exceeding 4 per cent. Altogether, these eleven leading states out of a total of twenty-nine, accounted for seven-tenths of the total agricultural production of the country.

A comparison of state shares in agricultural production with their shares in total population gives one an idea of the major markets for farm production entering into interstate trade (Table A-2, columns 2 and 5). The idea is only approximate, because such a comparison assumes, in effect, that per capita consumption levels are the same in each state, and disregards the effect on consumption of such things as interstate differences in population structure, tastes, per capita income, and relative prices. It also disregards the fact that there are state differences in the share of agricultural production flowing into foreign trade. Despite these drawbacks, the general picture is reasonably correct. The states with population shares greater than production shares—those which, implicitly, must rely partly on others for agricultural supplies—are almost wholly in the northern part of the country. The percentage point differences are greatest for those states with the major cities of the country—in order of size of production deficit: New York, Massachusetts, Pennsylvania, and Maryland.[2] In contrast, the Southern and Central states—with the notable exception of Ohio—typically have production shares in excess of population shares. This is especially marked in the case of states specializing in cotton, but since exports are unusually important for these states, their contribution to domestic markets is doubtless exaggerated by this statistic. Thus, the picture that emerges is basically one of production deficits in the Northeast, especially in the states with the main urban centers, which are supplied by surpluses produced elsewhere.

State differences in labor productivity—that is, agricultural output per worker—are implied by differences between state shares in production and those in agricultural labor force (Table A-2, columns 2 and 3). A share in output greater than that in labor force implies a level of output per worker above the national average. The magnitude of the deviation in labor productivity from the countrywide level can be made explicit by dividing the production share for each state by the labor force share. This yields average product per worker in the state expressed as a percentage of the national average.

The results of such a calculation show considerable differences among states in labor productivity (Table A-3, column 4). The range is from a low in the Carolinas, where output per worker is only three-fourths of the United States average, to a high in Louisiana, where it is about half again as great. There is a pronounced geographic pattern roughly consistent with that found by Parker and Klein [23] in their studies of individual crops.[3] In general, the older Eastern seaboard states are those with below average productivity, and the newer interior states, those with above average productivity. There are some important exceptions to this pattern, however. Among the older states in the northeastern part of the country, there are several with about average productivity levels (New York, Connecticut, and Massachusetts). But the striking exceptions in this area are New Jersey and Pennsylvania with productivity levels one-fourth or more above the average. Among the southern seaboard states, the only state with above average productivity is Florida, which at this time, in contrast to the other states in this group, was a new state experiencing in-migration. Finally, several of the states at the fringe of settlement (Iowa, Wisconsin, and Michigan) have below average productivity (though this is not true of all of the newest states—compare, for example, Arkansas). This observation regarding the frontier states suggests that it is perhaps more accurate to say that, typically, above average labor productivity characterizes the newer, though not necessarily, the newest states.

What of agricultural productivity in northern versus southern states—was the South in 1840 characterized by lower or higher labor productivity than the North? The answer is that there is no systematic difference. In both North and South there are both low and high productivity states—the geographic differential in productivity is an east-west one, not a north-south one.

This observation is based on a calculation which includes slaves along with free persons in the agricultural labor force denominator of the productivity calculation. A calculation of productivity based on free persons alone would markedly increase the relative position of the southern states, raising them as high as, and usually higher than, most Northern states. For example, for the South Atlantic division as a whole, whereas the 1840 level of agricultural output per worker as computed in Table A-3 was the lowest in the country, $140, a calculation in terms of the free population alone, would raise output per worker to $188, essentially the same level as that prevailing in the three highest northern divisions.[4] Since the South Atlantic division is the lowest productivity area in the South, this means a calculation based on free persons alone would, on balance, show a North-South productivity differential in favor of the South.

Price differences.—The price which a farmer could get for a given farm product in the mid-nineteenth century depended very much on his location. A bushel of wheat brought a farmer in New York, for example, more than twice as much as it did one in Missouri.[5] Interstate differences in prices varied, however, from one farm product to another. Map 1 gives a picture of the average of these price differences. It shows for each state the (appropriately weighted) ratio of the prices received by farmers in the state to national farm prices. In deriving this ratio, the farm products of the state are valued first at the prices actually received by farmers and then at United States prices, and the percentage of the former to the latter is computed.[6] Map 1 shows, for example, that farmers in Indiana got only 75 per cent of what they could have received for their output if they had been able to sell it at the average prices prevailing in the United States. On the other hand, farmers in Pennsylvania obtained 20 per cent more for their output than they would have received if they had sold it at United States prices.

What is quickly apparent from Map 1 is that farm prices in the bloc of interior states from Tennessee and Missouri northward tended to be substantially below the average, reflecting principally the greater distance of these states from the principal markets. Correspondingly, farmers in the regions with the principal urban population concentrations—the Middle Atlantic and New England divisions— benefited from prices considerably above the average. Needless to say, since the indexes used here are statewide averages, they give a misleading impression of the abruptness of geographic price variations. Thus in moving through Pennsylvania to Ohio, one would not find a sudden drop at the common border, but rather a gradual decline with prices in western Pennsylvania lower than those in the eastern part of the state and closer to those in Ohio [28, p. 366].

Subsequently, we shall look at differences among the states in the goods they produce—the "output mix". Because of these differences, it is not possible to compare directly the price indexes for each state—to say, for

Map 1

Average Ratio of Prices Received by Farmers in a State to United States Prices, 1840-46 (percent)

Source: Table A-1; column 3.

example, that prices in Pennsylvania bear a ratio to those in Indiana of 120/75. This applies most obviously to cotton versus non-cotton producing states. For many states, however, there is enough similarity in the output mix for the indexes to give a rough impression of the magnitude, as well as the direction, of interstate price differences. Thus, generalizing from Map 1, one might say that in 1840 farm prices in the northeastern part of the country were often as much as 50 per cent higher than in the interior central portion ($\frac{120\text{-}80}{80} \times 100$)—a difference of very substantial magnitude. It would be interesting to have a similar set of price indexes for 1860 to see whether the rapid expansion of the railroad network in the intervening two decades narrowed these differences substantially.

Income shares and income per worker.—The income received by a farmer depends on both his output and the prices received. The substantial geographic variation in prices just noted implies that state shares in farm income differed from those in output. The states in the interior of the country, where prices were relatively low, had lower shares in income than in output, and conversely for those states, principally in the Northeast, where prices were relatively high. Thus, the bloc of interior states from Tennessee and Missouri northward, while accounting for almost a third of total output, received only a little more than a quarter of farm income (Table A-2, columns 1 and 2). Most of the benefit of this reduced share went to the New England and Middle Atlantic states, whose total share is increased from more than a third of total output to over four-tenths of total income.

These differences imply that the pattern of state variations in per worker income was different from that in per worker output. Table A-3 provides a comparison of current price agricultural income per worker in each state with output per worker, each expressed as a percentage of the national average (columns 3 and 4). If one leaves aside the cotton producing states of the deep South, where, as Map 1 shows, interstate price variation was not substantial, some noteworthy shifts appear in state positions relative to the national average. Whereas in the newer Central states, productivity is typically above average, income per worker is below average. Correspondingly, in the New England and Middle Atlantic states, where productivity is often below average, income per worker is at or above average (except for Maine). Thus, aside from the deep South, the higher productivity levels in the newer states did not yield corresponding fruits in terms of income, because of the markedly less favorable price situation in these states.

While the relative position of most of the southern states is not substantially altered by the shift from product per worker to income per worker, it is seriously affected if the base of the comparison is shifted from the total to free labor force. This has already been pointed out above in comparing productivity in the South and North. The nature of the adjustment would be the same here, and the results similar—that is, per head of the free labor force, agricultural income in most of the Southern states would be as high as, or higher than, in most of the Northern states. In effect, from the viewpoint of Southern whites, agriculture was, on the average, as prosperous and productive as in the North, if not more so. However, the dispersion about the average was probably much greater in the South than in the North, since inequality in farm holdings was noticeably greater in the South [34, ch. III].

Structure of output.—The constant price estimates of farm output developed here can be used to compare, in broad terms, the structure of agricultural output in different states, and thus to identify regional patterns of agricultural specialization. Table A-4 gives the share in agricultural output in each state of several categories of farm products. For the United States as a whole, "small grains," comprising wheat, oats, barley, rye, and buckwheat, accounted for about 15 percent of total output. Cotton was responsible for a little under a tenth, dairy products for about 7 percent, and pork and beef, the two principal livestock products, for over a third. Altogether these four product classes accounted for two-thirds of United States agricultural production.

The importance of cotton in the states of the deep South comes as no surprise—in three states cotton accounted for around a third of total agricultural production and in two (Mississippi and Louisiana), about a half (see the Group IV states of Table A-4).

Outside the deep South, the pattern of specialization which emerges is as follows. The New England states show a disproportionate concentration in dairy products—milk, butter, cheese, etc. This category might be taken as a proxy more generally for a number of locally produced products destined for urban markets, for example, poultry, eggs, and vegetables, as well as the items just mentioned. A second group of states, comprising the Middle Atlantic states plus Virginia, Ohio, Michigan, and Wisconsin, is disproportionately specialized in small grains. (New York and New Jersey in the Middle Atlantic division also produce a sizeable share of dairy products, and can be viewed as intermediate in their specialization pattern between the first and second groups.) Finally, there are the North Central states plus Kentucky, Tennessee, and Arkansas, which are especially concentrated in livestock production.

The states in the Northeast have greater diversification of their production structures. This is implied by the lower proportions of total output accounted for by the four classes of specified products for the states of this area than for the states of the Central and Southern regions (Table A-4, column 5). In all regions of the country, there are states which deviate noticeably from the typical pattern of specialization—for example, sugar and rice are especially important in Louisiana, tobacco in Virginia, and potatoes in Maine. But, in general, the picture is one of more land-intensive, higher-transport-cost products being produced closer to the major northeastern markets, while land-extensive, lower-transport-cost products are produced at a distance. The argument, based on Guy Calender's classic article, that the cotton-growing South was the major market for the West's meat production has been questioned on a number of grounds,[7] but it is perhaps worth adding that the present figures indicate that the shares of livestock production in all cotton states other than Louisiana were about equal to or greater than the national average.

The westward shift and labor productivity.—The 1840 state estimates of labor productivity provide a new opportunity for examining the effect of the westward movement on the countrywide trend in agricultural output per worker. Did the opening up and settlement of western states, north and south, tend to raise or lower the national level of agricultural labor productivity?

A number of scholars have considered this question previously—Parker and Whartenby [24], Albert Fishlow (for the northern part of the country only) [10, pp. 220-222], Parker and Klein (for three crops—corn, wheat, and oats) [22, 23], and Paul David [6]. The findings have generally pointed to a positive productivity contribution from the regional shift, though of modest magnitude. The one exception is the first study noted, which inappropriately used state estimates of income per worker to estimate the contribution of the regional shift, rather than output per worker—in effect, the figures in Table A-3, column 1, rather than those in column 2. More recently, Edith Lang has attempted a more comprehensive analysis of the problem, based on an agricultural production function for

87

1860 estimated from state data, and taking account of possible links between shifts in the distribution of labor and other factors of production[17, 18].

The analysis here follows that of Paul David. David computed hypothetical values of the national weighted average of product per worker for each decennial year 1800 to 1840 by weighting the 1840 divisional values of agricultural product per worker by the divisional shares in agricultural labor force actually observed at each date. The change thus obtained in the national average is ascribed to the changing divisional shares in labor force—essentially the westward movement. For agricultural output per worker, David used my preliminary unpublished estimates by geographic division. The final estimates for the divisions published here are fairly close to those used by David, but there are some differences. I have replicated David's analysis by division using the final estimates and added a new calculation based on state data rather than those for geographic divisions. The issue, in using state rather than divisional data, is whether the results are noticeably affected by increasing the number of geographic units for which the analysis is done—from seven geographic divisions to twenty-nine states. In principal, the effect might be substantial—the critical issue is whether the seven geographic divisions are fairly homogenous internally with regard to both the change in labor force shares and level of product per worker. For the calculations by state there are, unfortunately, no agricultural labor force estimates for the dates before 1840, and I have used instead rural population data to compute the state shares to which the productivity weights are applied. At the divisional level, however, there are agricultural labor force estimates available for 1800-1830, developed by Paul David on a basis consistent with my 1840 estimates. To see what effect arises from the use of rural population rather than agricultural labor force data, I have done the divisional calculations using both sets of figures. All told, then, we have four calculations of the geographic shift effect—Paul David's earlier one, plus three new ones— all summarized in Table 1.

Table 1

Index of Average Agricultural Output per Worker due to Geographic Shift Effect Alone, 1790-1840, Derived by Four Methods

	(1)	(2)	(3)	(4)
Method	A (David)	B	C	D
Geographic Units	Divisions	Divisions	Divisions	States
Basis of Unit Shares	Agric. Labor Force	Agric. Labor Force	Rural Population	Rural Population
Productivity Weights	Prelim Est. by Division	Final Est. by Division	Final Est. by Division	Final Est. by State
1790	-	-	99.0	98.9
1800	100.0	100.0	100.0	100.0
1810	102.3	101.8	102.0	101.8
1820	104.5	103.4	103.2	103.0
1830	105.8	104.3	104.7	104.2
1840	108.3	106.0	106.2	105.6

Sources: Agricultural labor force shares, from David [6, p. 197] and Table A-2, col. 3; rural population shares, [31, pp. 1-29 through 1-37]; preliminary productivity weights, David [6, p. 179, n. 54]; final productivity weights, Table A-3, col. 2. For method of computing index, see text.

David estimated an 8.3 per cent rise from 1800 to 1840 in national average product per worker due to the regional shift effect. The principal result of the new estimates is to revise this somewhat downward—the best of the new estimates is the 5.6 per cent increase shown in column 4. This compares with an estimated labor productivity growth from all sources during this period of around 30 per cent [6, p. 177; 13, p. 206], indicating that at best only a modest productivity role can be attributed to the shift effect. As a comparison of the various columns indicates, the reduction in the contribution of the shift effect is due overwhelmingly to the revised estimates of productivity. The similarity of columns 2, 3, and 4 demonstrates that the use of states rather than divisions and of rural population rather than agricultural labor force has a negligible effect on the present results. The effect of the productivity revisions is due predominately to the somewhat lower productivity levels now estimated for the North Central states. The downward revisions for these states leaves them with divisional productivity averages about the same as that in the Middle Atlantic division, rather than higher, as in the figures used by David. As a result, the rise in share of the Central region, to the extent it merely compensates for a decline in that of the Middle Atlantic, has no positive effect on agricultural productivity.

The positive effects of the regional shift shown in Table 1 are due overwhelmingly to the steadily declining shares of the older, below average productivity, states along the Eastern seaboard—Maine, New Hampshire, Vermont, Rhode Island, and the tier of states from Delaware south to Georgia. According to the 1840 figures, productivity was almost always higher in the states west of these, so that the redistribution of agricultural activity away from the seaboard tended to raise the national level of agricultural productivity. Shifts in relative importance within the group of non-seaboard states, however, such as that from the Middle Atlantic to the North Central region, were more ambiguous in their effects on product per worker.

What is the likelihood that the 1840 pattern of differences in productivity by state prevailed throughout the first half-century before 1840?[8] The cogency of this question becomes clearer when one recalls that in several of the newest states (Iowa, Wisconsin, Michigan) productivity levels were below average and not much different from those in the older, lower productivity, states along the eastern seaboard. Might this have been true earlier of states undergoing settlement as population moved west across the Appalachians?

A reasonable answer to this question is, yes, that *initial* productivity levels in states undergoing settlement may have been low in relation to others at the time and also in relation to their own subsequent levels. Most evidence suggests that in the early stages of settlement inputs per worker, such as improved land and implements, were relatively low.[9] Moreover, new environments often required changes in methods of production, and in the early settlement phase not enough time had elapsed for such changes to take place. There is, in addition, the likelihood that initially a substantial share of labor time was required in farm capital formation—clearing timber, draining, fencing, and so forth [25-27]. Thus, productivity was often likely to be relatively low in new areas. This situation may well account for the low productivity levels shown by Iowa, Wisconsin, and Michigan in 1840.

Nevertheless, it is clear that once this early settlement stage was over—usually in only a decade or two—productivity levels were established in the new areas which were usually markedly superior to those in many of the older states. Thus, while the 1840 productivity differentials cannot be assumed to have persisted throughout the previous half-century, they provide for newer areas past the initial settlement phase a rough indication of their potential productivity advantage over the older areas. It is this potential productivity advantage that dominates the shift effect estimated here. This advantage and the shift effect derived from it have substantive meaning. The availability for expanding United States agricultural output of new lands with high productivity potential led to a positive impact on productivity that would not have occurred had such expansion been on newer lands of lower potential or required more intensive exploitation of the older coastal agricultural areas.

TRENDS IN PRODUCTION AND PRODUCTIVITY, 1840-60

Production shares and productivity.—To throw some tentative light on developments in the two decades before the Civil War, I have made rough census year estimates of agricultural production and labor force for the geographic divisions (Table B-1). The 1860 labor force estimate is based almost wholly on Edith Lang's work [18]. The estimating methods for the production estimates are essentially the same as those used to derive the state figures in United States prices in Appendix A. For reasons detailed in Appendix B, the 1840 figures in Table B-1 differ somewhat from those in Table A-1, though the regional patterns are quite similar.

The indicated trends in regional production and labor force shares in the two decades after 1840 are in the directions one would expect (Table B-2, columns 1-6). The three eastern seaboard divisions continue their declines, while the interior divisions, with one exception, show increases. The exception is the East South Central division, whose share peaks in 1850 and then enters a phase of decline, like that shown by the earlier settled regions.

The trends in labor productivity are shown in columns 7-9 of Table B-1. The United States average changes hardly at all between 1840 and 1850, and then shows a sizeable upsurge to 1860 of about 15 per cent. This, at least, is the pattern one obtains when Gallman's output estimates are combined with Lebergott's labor force figures, the United States totals to which the present regional estimates are keyed. The stability in United States agricultural productivity from 1840 to 1850 implied by these figures seems questionable.[10] This impression is reinforced when one looks at the implicit regional movements; for example, New England shows a sharp decline from 1840 to 1850, then an abrupt return to its 1840 level in 1860. If, as seems likely, the United States level of agricultural output per worker in 1850 is understated relative to the levels in 1840 and 1860, this bias would affect all of the regional figures. As a result the productivity changes shown by the divisions in the decade of the forties would be biased downward, while those for the fifties would be biased upward. Because of reservations about the validity of the decade changes, primary reliance here will be placed on the pattern of changes shown for the 1840 to 1860 period as a whole.

If the geographic divisions are ranked in order of magnitude of the 1840-60 productivity increase, one obtains the following:

Division	*Percent increase in agricultural production per worker, 1840-60*
East North Central	17.9
Middle Atlantic	13.1
E. So. Central	10.1
So. Atlantic	8.4
W. So. Central	2.5
New England	1.1
W. No. Central	-2.4

From this it appears that the national increase of 15 per cent obscures considerable regional variability in productivity growth. While four divisions showed substantial increases, two showed little change and one, a decline.

The productivity decline for the West North Central division deserves special comment for it reflects a phenomenon just touched on in the preceding section. The decline is attributable to a downward movement concentrated in the decade 1850-60, due to the weight exerted on the 1860 average by a sizeable new area characterized by low productivity (Minnesota, the Dakotas, Nebraska, and Kansas). The underlying relationships are illustrated by the 1840 figures for the two states in the division at that time, Missouri and Iowa. Whereas, the newer state in the division, Iowa, is about 20 per cent below the national productivity level, the older state, Missouri, is about 13 per cent above (Table A-3, column 4). It is likely that in 1860 the newer areas of Minnesota, Dakota, Nebraska, and Kansas are in a similar position relative to the two older states at that time, Missouri and Iowa. Moreover, in 1860 the effect of these newer areas is substantial enough to depress the divisional productivity figure below the national average.

It seems likely that if figures were available for the next decade or two, the West North Central division would show a productivity upsurge as the new areas of 1860 passed out of the early settlement phase. Such an upsurge probably took place in Iowa from 1840 to 1850 and played a part in the rise shown in the West North Central's level of product per worker in that decade, a rise which contrasts noticeably with the downward movements shown by most other divisions in this period. While the West North Central's productivity change is subject to the same possible downward bias in this period as those of the other divisions, the real productivity increase in this area was apparently substantial enough to offset it.

These remarks suggest more generally that a divisonal productivity average may show a downward fluctuation as very new areas are added, and then an upward shift as production conditions normalize in the area. It is possible that the V-shaped movement in the West South Central division from 1840 to 1860 may reflect something of this sort as Texas is added in 1850 (though the 1840 to 1850 decline is subject to the same qualifications about possible negative bias noted above). It is also likely that the striking rise in productivity in the West from 1850 to 1860 reflects the passing of California (the dominant state in this division's average) from the early settlement phase reflected in the 1850 figure to a more normal production situation in 1860.

To return to the 1840-60 productivity changes by division, perhaps the question of greatest interest is the comparative performance of the Southern divisions. Considerable controversy surrounds the question of the extent of economic progress in the South before the Civil War.[11] To judge from the productivity estimates here, the Southern divisions did not do badly. The East South Central and South Atlantic divisions showed medium productivity increases—better than those in the New England and West North Central divisions, and poorer than those in the Middle Atlantic and East North Central divisions. The West South Central division showed only a slight gain. However, this division had the highest productivity level in the country in 1840 and maintained its leadership during the 1840-60 period, even though its relative advantage declined. The absolute rates of increase shown above are possibly subject to bias because of difficulties mentioned earlier due to using Gallman's United States output estimates with Lebergott's labor force figures; however, the *relative* performance of the Southern divisions would be unaffected by the use of other United States totals for output or labor force.

The relatives of product per worker for the three Southern divisions all show a decline from 1840 to 1860, indicating slower growth than that in the United States average (Table B-2, columns 7 and 9). But so do the relatives for all of the northern divisions, except the East North Central, where a mild improvement is apparent. The trend in the United States average of product per worker reflects, as we have seen, not only the productivity changes within each division, but also the effect of shifts in the distribution of labor force among regions with different productivity levels. This latter effect provided a sizeable boost to the United States average in this period, as will be shown below. The positive effect on the United States average of the shift to high productivity regions was partly due to developments within the South, where resources were redistributed toward the high productivity West South Central region. If one computes the growth in product per worker for the three Southern divisions combined, the result reflects this regional shift as well as the changes within divisions.[12] Based on the data in Table B-2, one obtains for the South as a whole:

Output per Worker	*1840*	*1860*
Absolute amount, dollars	198	229
Per cent of U.S. average	98	98

This calculation shows that for the South as a whole productivity was just about equal to the United States average in 1840 and grew at the same rate as the United States average from 1840 to 1860. There is little in this indicator of agricultural performance to suggest noticeable economic retrogression in the South considered as a whole in the two decades before the Civil War.

The present figures throw light on the stability and magnitude of interregional productivity differences over time, a question which has already been touched on in regard to the pre-1840 period, though in speculative fashion only. The present estimates show substantial stability in the directions of the regional deviations from the national average. Over the 1840-60 period the West North Central division is the only one to change the direction of its deviation—from above to below the United States average—and, if the previous discussion is correct, this was probably a temporary phenomenon. As for the average magnitude of the productivity differentials, this shows some increase over the period as a whole. The arithmetic mean deviation from the United States average is 16.8 per cent in 1840. It drops to 11.9 per cent in 1850, but then rises to 27.0 per cent in 1860. The very high productivity level shown by the West in 1860 is especially important in accounting for this sharp rise. Since the share of the West in United States agriculture is small, however, a dispersion measure which weights the divisional deviations in terms of their labor force shares may be more meaningful. Such a measure shows little change in the mean deviation between the first two dates (11.7 per cent in 1840 and 11.0 per cent in 1850), and then a mild rise to 1860 (14.5 per cent). All in all, the impression that emerges is one of considerable stability during this period in both the direction and magnitude of regional productivity differences.

Effect of the westward shift on agricultural productivity. The estimates for 1840-60 make possible an extension and expansion of the earlier analysis of regional shift effects on agricultural productivity growth, subject, of course, to the usual reservations attaching to such index number analyses of components of change. At issue is how much the observed growth of 15 per cent in the United States average of agricultural output per worker was due to (a) intra-regional changes in productivity versus (b) labor force shifts toward higher productivity regions. The answer is that component (a) contributed about two-thirds and (b) one-third of the productivity increase in the 1840-60 period. The contribution of (a) was obtained by computing the hypothetical 1860 product per worker that would have prevailed if the actual 1860 productivity levels of each division had existed, but the labor force distribution by division were that of 1840. This works out to be $223, about a 10 per cent increase over the $203 level that actually existed in 1840. The contribution of component (b) is then the balance between the hypothetical 1860 figure of $223 and the actual figure of $234, amounting to $11, or about a 5 per cent increase. (This is identical with the change in agricultural product per worker that one obtains if the 1860 divisional productivity figures are weighted first by the 1840 labor force distribution by division and then by the 1860 distribution.) Compared with the pre-1840 trend (Table 1, column 4) this result suggests a substantial acceleration in the regional shift effect. In the two decades after 1840, the effect was almost as great as in the four decades before.

Mention has been made of the likelihood of sizeable fluctuations in the divisional productivity levels as regions undergo settlement. In principle, this could alter the results of calculations such as the above. Thus, as we have seen, the 1860 level of product per worker in the West North Central division is below the United States average, whereas the 1850 level is above. Since this region is gaining importance as a result of the westward shift, the direction of its contribution to United States productivity growth will differ depending on which date's productivity figures are used. If one considers this region's influence alone, a calculation of the interregional shift effect based on 1850 figures would show a larger (algebraic) contribution than one based on 1860 figures. When one considers all regions taken together, however, the reverse proves to be the case—the shift effect, 1840-60, based on 1850 productivity differentials is less than that based on 1860 differentials (3.3 per cent versus 5.0 per cent). The reason is that the adverse productivity change in the West North Central division from 1850 to 1860 is more than compensated for by favorable movements of productivity levels in the West South Central and Western divisions, where, as suggested earlier, production conditions were probably tending to normalize. It seems likely that this tendency for the results of the shift effect to be dominated by newer regions where production conditions are normalizing, rather than by those in a very early settlement phase, is a typical one, because of the larger proportion of the population likely to be involved in the more advanced phase of settlement. Hence as long as the productivity potential of the newer regions is above the average of the older, the contribution of the regional shift effect is likely to be positive.

SUMMARY

The principal aim of this paper has been to make available 1840 estimates of agricultural production by state to supplement my previously published estimates of agricultural income. New estimates have also been presented of agricultural production by geographic division for 1840, 1850, and 1860.

Among other things, these data indicate that in the mid-nineteenth century agricultural labor productivity (output per worker) was typically higher in the newer states beyond the Appalachians. In some of the newest states, however, productivity was not especially high, suggesting that during the early phase of settlement a state may undergo a transition from relatively low to higher productivity. In the bloc of interior states from Tennessee and Missouri northward, the prices received by farmers were markedly lower than elsewhere, so much so that despite their relatively high productivity, these states had relatively low income per worker. A pattern of regional specialization existed with land-intensive, higher-transport-cost products being produced closer to the major northeastern markets, while land-extensive, lower-transport-cost-products were produced at a distance.

Comparisons between northern and southern states, either of agricultural output per worker or income per worker, do not reveal any marked systematic differences. The South is not a comparatively backward agricultural area at this time. Indeed, if comparisons are based on the free rather than the total labor force, the southern states would typically be relatively high in both productivity and income per worker. Similarly, the productivity trends from 1840 to 1860 do not reflect adversely on the South's performance. For the South as a whole, productivity grew at about the national average. When divisions are ranked by rate of productivity increase from 1840 to 1860, the three southern divisions fall in the middle of the distribution.

The effect of the westward movement on the average level of agricultural productivity was positive, though of quite modest magnitude. There was, however, some acceleration in the magnitude of the effect in the two decades just before the Civil War.

These observations are but a start on the analytical potentials of the estimates presented here. Indeed, when one considers the possibilities that would be opened up by a set of decennial agricultural income and product estimates by state from 1840 down to the present, done in more systematic fashion than the present estimates, one can only wonder why the new economic history has been so slow in filling the gap. The basic data for such a contribution are there in the federal censuses and similar sources; let us hope that the opportunity will soon be realized.

APPENDIX A

ESTIMATES FOR 1840 OF AGRICULTURAL INCOME IN EACH STATE AT UNITED STATES PRICES OF 1840-46

Columns 1 and 2 of Table A-1 give estimates of agricultural income in each state in 1840 under two different schemes of valuation. In the estimates "at state prices" products are valued "at the places of production, or where they are sold by the producer," [28, p. 452], that is, at the prices current in each state. In the estimates "at U.S. prices", the outputs in every state of a given product are valued at the same price, the national average. In both cases, the prices used are an average for the period 1840-46. The income and output estimates include deductions for the portion of output consumed as seed and feed, but none for depreciation of farm capital. In this sense, they are estimates of gross, not net, income originating in each state. They include the value of agricultural improvements done by the farmer (clearing, fencing, draining, and so forth), but exclude income from the services of dwellings and the value of home manufactures. Income from the production of fuelwood is included in the estimates.

The methods used to obtain and test the previously published current price estimates in column 1 are described in detail in an earlier study [7, Appendix B]. The figures are basically those of Ezra Seaman with one major exception, the estimate of income from the production of animal products, which was made by me following Robert E. Gallman's procedures.

To obtain the constant price figure for each state shown in column 2, the specific procedure was as follows. The outputs for each of sixteen product classes were valued both at state and United States prices. The differences between the current and constant price estimates for all sixteen products were summed, and then the published current price agricultural income estimate for the state was adjusted by this amount to obtain the constant price estimate. The procedure is illustrated below for two states (all figures in millions of dollars):

		Penna.	*Indiana*
1.	Sixteen product classes		
	a. Valued at state prices	52.5	12.5
	b. Valued at U.S. prices	41.0	19.3
	c. Difference (1a-1b)	11.5	–6.8
2.	All product classes		
	a. Agricultural income at state prices	68.1	20.4
	b. Agricultural income at U.S. prices (2a-1c)	56.6	27.2

The sixteen product classes were chosen on the basis of their quantitative importance and the ready availability of state as well as United States price data. They comprise wheat, oats, barley, rye, buckwheat, Indian corn, potatoes, wool, hemp, tobacco, rice, cotton, cane sugar, hay, pork, and beef. While they include a little over half of the number of census categories of agricultural products, they account at the national level for almost three-quarters of the value of agricultural income. Since the other census product classes are included at current dollar values in both

101

estimates,[13] the present adjustment to obtain the constant dollar estimate is a minimum adjustment. For all farm products in a given state, deviations from the United States price tend to be in the same direction. I could have assumed, therefore, that the relative magnitude of the deviation was the same for all products combined as the average for the sixteen for which I had data, and derived a constant dollar estimate that included an allowance for all products for the difference between state and United States values. The direction of bias in the resulting estimate, however, would have been uncertain. I preferred, therefore, to use the present procedure which leaves one certain about the direction of bias in the constant dollar estimate. Specifically, for states where the present constant price estimate exceeds the current price estimate (as in the case of Indiana), the constant price figure is understated. For states where the constant price estimate is less than the current price estimate (as for Pennsylvania), the constant price figure is overstated.

The important products, judged in terms of value of output, which are included at state prices in both current and constant price estimates are dairy products, poultry and eggs, products of domestic gardens, orchard products, and fuelwood. Except for the last, only the value of output of these products was returned in the agricultural census.

Agricultural Income Valued at State and United States Prices of 1840-46, Implicit State Price Index, and Agricultural Labor Force, by Geographic Division and State, 1840

Geographic Division and State	(1) Agricultural Income At State Prices (millions)	(2) Agricultural Income At U.S. Prices (millions)	(3) Implicit Price Index(percent) [100×(1)/(2)]	(4) Agricultural Labor Force (thousands)
U.S.	663.4	663.4	100	3827.7
New Eng.	71.5	62.6	114	393.7
Maine	14.8	13.5	110	101.6
N.H.	10.8	9.4	115	59.5
Vt.	14.1	11.8	120	73.2
Mass.	17.4	15.6	112	87.8
R.I.	2.5	2.2	114	14.6
Conn.	11.9	10.2	116	57.0
Mid Atlan.	198.2	167.5	118	879.3
N.Y.	93.9	81.1	116	456.0
N.J.	16.2	14.0	116	58.7
Pa.	68.1	56.6	120	266.8
Del.	3.0	2.3	127	16.0
Md.	16.9	13.5	125	81.8
E. No. Cent.	88.6	112.3	79	601.3
Ohio	44.5	54.0	82	283.6
Ind.	20.4	27.2	75	148.8
Ill.	16.2	22.2	73	105.3
Mich.	6.5	7.7	85	56.5
Wis.	0.9	1.2	80	7.0
W. No. Cent.	15.0	20.4	73	107.3
Iowa	1.1	1.5	72	11.0
Mo.	13.8	18.9	73	96.2
So. Atlan.	144.2	136.6	106	972.9
Va. & W. Va.	49.2	45.6	108	318.8
N.C.	31.4	28.1	112	226.1
S.C.	27.6	25.7	108	198.4
Ga.	33.5	34.6	97	215.7
Fla.	2.4	2.7	90	14.0
E. So. Cent.	117.2	134.2	87	752.1
Ky.	30.3	38.3	79	197.7
Tenn.	32.3	41.0	79	227.7
Ala.	26.6	27.6	96	186.9
Miss.	28.1	27.3	103	139.7
W. So. Cent.	28.8	29.8	97	121.2
Ark.	5.5	5.8	94	28.3
La.	23.3	24.0	97	92.9

Calculations were carried through on unrounded figures. Detail does not necessarily add to totals because of rounding. Wisconsin includes eastern Minnesota, and Iowa includes western Minnesota and the eastern part of North and South Dakota. The District of Columbia has been omitted.

In Colume 1, products are valued at average prices received by farmers in each state; in column 2, at average United States prices.

Source: Columns 1 and 4 from [7, pp. 97-98]. See Appendix A for method of estimating column 2.

Table A-2

Percent Distribution by Geographic Division and State of Agricultural Income Valued at State and United States Prices of 1840-46, Agricultural Labor Force, Rural Population, and Total Population, 1840

Geographic Division and State	(1) Agricultural Income — At State Prices	(2) Agricultural Income — At U.S. Prices	(3) Agricultural Labor Force	(4) Rural Population	(5) Total Population
U.S.	100.0	100.0	100.0	100.0	100.0
New Eng.	10.8	9.4	10.3	11.8	13.1
Maine	2.2	2.0	2.7	3.0	2.9
N.H.	1.6	1.4	1.6	1.7	1.7
Vt.	2.1	1.8	1.9	1.9	1.7
Mass.	2.6	2.4	2.3	3.0	4.3
R.I.	0.4	0.3	0.4	0.4	0.6
Conn.	1.8	1.5	1.5	1.8	1.8
Mid Atlan.	29.9	25.2	23.0	27.2	29.8
N.Y.	14.2	12.2	11.9	12.9	14.3
N.J.	2.4	2.1	1.5	2.2	2.2
Pa.	10.3	8.5	7.0	9.3	10.1
Del.	0.4	0.4	0.4	0.5	0.5
Md.	2.5	2.0	2.1	2.3	2.8
E. No Cent.	13.4	16.9	15.7	18.5	17.2
Ohio	6.7	8.1	7.4	9.4	8.9
Ind.	3.1	4.1	3.9	4.4	4.0
Ill.	2.4	3.3	2.8	3.1	2.8
Mich.	1.0	1.2	1.5	1.3	1.2
Wis.	0.1	0.2	0.2	0.2	0.2
W. No. Cent.	2.3	3.1	2.8	2.7	2.5
Iowa	0.2	0.2	0.3	0.3	0.3
Mo.	2.1	2.8	2.5	2.4	2.3
So. Atlan.	21.7	20.6	25.4	21.0	19.6
Va. & W. Va.	7.4	6.9	8.3	7.7	7.3
N.C.	4.7	4.2	5.9	4.9	4.4
S.C.	4.2	3.9	5.2	3.7	3.5
Ga.	5.0	5.2	5.6	4.4	4.1
Fla.	0.4	0.4	0.4	0.4	0.3
E. So. Cent.	17.7	20.2	19.6	16.6	15.1
Ky.	4.6	5.8	5.2	4.9	4.6
Tenn.	4.9	6.2	6.0	5.4	4.9
Ala.	4.0	4.2	4.9	3.8	3.5
Miss.	4.2	4.1	3.6	2.4	2.2
W. So. Cent.	4.3	4.5	3.2	2.3	2.6
Ark.	0.8	0.9	0.7	0.6	0.6
La.	3.5	3.6	2.4	1.6	2.1

See notes to Table A-1.
Source: Columns 1, 2, and 3 from Table A-1. Columns 4 and 5 from [31, pp. 1-16, 1-17, and 1-29 through 1-37].

Agricultural Income Per Worker Valued at State and United States
Prices of 1840-46: Absolute Value and as Percentage of United
States Average, by Geographic Division and State, 1840

Geographic Division and State	(1) Absolute Value At State Prices	(2) At U.S. Prices	(3) Percentage of U.S. Value At State Prices	(4) At U.S. Prices
U.S.	173	173	100	100
New Eng.	182	159	105	92
Maine	146	132	84	76
N.H.	182	158	105	91
Vt.	193	161	112	93
Mass.	199	178	115	103
R.I.	170	149	98	86
Conn.	208	179	120	103
Mid Atlan.	225	190	130	110
N.Y.	206	178	119	103
N.J.	276	238	160	138
Pa.	255	212	147	123
Del.	185	146	107	84
Md.	207	165	120	95
E. No. Cent.	147	187	85	108
Ohio	157	190	91	110
Ind.	137	183	79	106
Ill.	154	211	89	122
Mich.	116	136	67	79
Wis.	132	165	76	95
W. No. Cent.	140	190	81	110
Iowa	101	139	58	80
Mo.	144	196	83	113
So. Atlan.	148	140	86	81
Va. & W. Va.	154	143	89	83
N.C.	139	124	80	72
S.C.	139	129	80	75
Ga.	155	160	90	93
Fla.	171	190	99	110
E. So. Cent.	156	178	90	103
Ky.	153	193	88	112
Tenn.	142	180	82	104
Ala.	142	148	82	86
Miss.	201	196	116	113
W. So. Cent.	238	246	138	142
Ark.	194	206	112	119
La.	251	258	145	149

See notes to Table A-1.
Source: Calculated from Table A-1, columns 1, 2, and 4.

TABLE A-4

Value of Specified Products as Percentage of Agricultural Income, by State, 1840

State	(1) Dairy Products	(2) Small Grains	(3) Pork and Beef	(4) Cotton	(5) Total Cols. 1-4
U.S.	7	15	36	9	66
Group I					
Maine	15	8	13	0	35
N.H.	23	9	18	0	50
Vt.	23	10	23	0	55
Mass.	20	5	11	0	36
R.I.	14	4	12	0	30
Conn.	18	9	15	0	42
Group II					
N.Y.	17	21	23	0	61
N.J.	13	17	17	0	47
Pa.	8	32	25	0	65
Del.	7	20	29	. . .	56
Md.	5	26	26	. . .	57
Va. & W. Va.	4	24	40	1	69
Ohio	5	29	35	0	69
Mich.	5	28	34	0	66
Wisc.	4	22	38	0	64
Group III					
Ind.	4	16	49	. . .	69
Ill.	3	16	57	. . .	76
Iowa	2	11	56	0	68
Mo.	1	7	55	. . .	62
Ky.	3	15	49	. . .	68
Tenn.	2	11	56	5	74
Ark.	1	2	59	8	70
Group IV					
N.C.	3	8	50	13	74
S.C.	3	4	35	17	60
Ga.	2	5	40	34	82
Fla.	1	. . .	47	33	81
Ala.	1	3	45	31	81
Miss.	2	1	35	51	89
La.	1	. . .	18	46	65

See notes to Table A-1. States are grouped according to pattern of specialization. Small grains includes wheat, oats, barley, rye, and buckwheat. Products in each class and agricultural income are valued at United States prices of 1840-46.

. . . indicates less than 0.5 per cent.

Source: From worksheets for constant price income estimates.

106

APPENDIX B-1

ESTIMATES FOR 1840, 1850, AND 1860 OF AGRICULTURAL
INCOME IN EACH GEOGRAPHIC DIVISION AT UNITED STATES
PRICES OF 1879

The basis for these estimates is Robert E. Gallman's national figures for gross agricultural income (in 1879 prices) by type of product for the census years 1839, 1849, and 1859 [14]. Gallman's estimate is built up from estimates for about thirty-four product classes. My procedure was to allocate his total for each product class among the geographic divisions according to their respective shares in the volume of production as reported in the census. Thus, if New England accounted for 10 per cent of wheat production, it was allocated one-tenth of Gallman's estimate of the amount of gross agricultural income attributable to wheat. This procedure is equivalent to valuing output in each state at the average United States price prevailing in 1879.

The scope of the estimates is the same as for those in Appendix A, except that fuelwood was omitted because data for the regional allocation were not available in 1849 and 1859. In the actual estimation process no allocations were done for seven product classes—flaxseed, veal, peas and beans, molasses and maple syrup, flax, honey and wax, and wine. These minor products accounted at each date for 2 per cent or less of United States agricultural output. My figure for United States gross agricultural income differs from Gallman's because of the omission of these products, forest products, and home manufactures. For poultry and eggs, farm and market garden products, and orchard products, the allocations by division were based on value of output rather than physical production.

The 1840 estimates for geographic divisions obtained here can be compared with those of Appendix A. Since we are

107

especially interested in productivity, the following compares the estimates of agricultural product per worker as a percentage of the United States average:

	Appendix A	Appendix B
West South Central	142	158
Mid-Atlantic	110	106
West North Central	110	102
East North Central	108	107
East South Central	103	108
New England	92	86
South Atlantic	81	82

The results are quite consistent. The West South Central division is noticeably above the United States average, and New England and the South Atlantic division are at the bottom of the productivity array. The other four regions are clustered together though with some differences in their ordering.

The differences in the estimates are due entirely to the estimates of agricultural output, because the relative magnitudes of the regional estimates of labor force are the same in Appendixes A and B. The output differences arise from several sources, as follows. The Appendix A estimates take Seaman's current price estimates (revised) as a benchmark; the constant price figures are then derived by applying an estimated adjustment to the current price figures (see Appendix A). In contrast, in Appendix B the constant price value is estimated directly, not derived by adjusting the current price value. Also, the methods used by Seaman in deriving his estimates differ in various details from those used by Gallman (for example, in the percentage allowances for seed and feed). Furthermore, the Appendix A estimates are at United States prices of 1840-46, while those in Appendix B are at 1879 prices; hence, differences between the two dates in relative product prices alter the regional estimates. Finally, as previously noted, the Appendix B estimates omit fuelwood and seven minor product classes.

Without a much more systematic effort than is attempted here to derive current and constant price estimates by state for 1840, 1850, and 1860, one cannot judge with certainty the relative merits of the divisional constant price estimates for 1840 in Appendixes A and B. Those in Appendix B are not carried out as comprehensively as they might be. On the other hand, the estimates in Appendix A are keyed to the Seaman current dollar estimates. In my previous study, I tested Seaman's estimates and they seemed reasonably sound, but it is possible that some biases in Seaman's current dollar figures may have been carried over to the constant dollar figures. Without a definitive basis for judging the relative merits of the Appendix A and B estimates, the recommended procedure is that followed in the text here. Where the concern is with current versus constant price comparisons the Appendix A estimates are to be preferred. When the analytical purpose is the study of output trends over time, the Appendix B estimates are recommended.

TABLE B-1

Agricultural Income Valued at United States Prices of 1879, Agricultural Labor Force, and Agricultural Income per Worker, by Geographic Division, 1840, 1850, and 1860

Geographic Division	(1) 1840	(2) 1850	(3) 1860	(4) 1840	(5) 1850	(6) 1860	(7) 1840	(8) 1850	(9) 1860
	Income ($ millions)			Labor Force (thousands)			Income per Worker ($)		
United States	723.6	900.7	1378.8	3569.9	4520.0	5880.2	203	199	234
New Eng.	64.4	53.9	64.7	367.2	369.4	364.4	175	146	177
Mid Atlan.	175.8	185.6	233.6	820.1	903.0	965.8	214	206	242
E. No. Cent.	122.0	178.3	306.6	560.8	811.0	1193.4	218	220	257
W. No. Cent.	20.7	40.3	90.5	100.0	189.6	447.5	207	212	202
So. Atlan.	151.7	183.1	225.0	907.4	1064.5	1240.3	167	172	181
E. So. Cent.	152.9	194.5	269.1	701.5	909.8	1122.5	218	214	240
W. So. Cent.	36.1	59.4	153.5	113.0	245.9	470.2	319	241	327
West		5.6	35.9		26.7	76.1		212	472

Calculations were carried through on unrounded figures. Detail does not necessarily add to totals because of rounding.
The figures in column 1 here differ from those in Table A-1, column 2, for reasons noted in Appendix B, but are consistent in method of derivation with those in columns 2 and 3 here. Figures in column 4 differ from those in Table A-1, column 4, only in that a proportional adjustment was uniformly applied to obtain here the United States total published by Stanley Lebergott [19, p. 510].

Source: See Appendixes B-1 and B-2 for methods of estimating columns 1 through 6.

APPENDIX B-2

ESTIMATES FOR 1840, 1850, AND 1860 OF
AGRICULTURAL LABOR FORCE BY GEOGRAPHIC
DIVISION

The United States totals are the agricultural labor force estimates of Stanley Lebergott [19, p. 510, T.A-1]. At each date these were distributed by division, as follows: for 1840, my state labor force estimates, a revision of the original census figures, were used for the divisional allocation; for 1860, I used the estimates made by Edith Lang in her dissertation.[14] For the present purpose, the Lang estimates are less than ideal since they are in adult male equivalents, that is, women and children in the labor force were converted to adult male equivalents on the basis of relative wage rates. However, a test based on the trend in rural population shares presented below suggests that the 1860 Lang estimate together with my 1840 estimate implies an 1840-60 labor force trend that is in the right direction and of a reasonable order of magnitude.

The 1850 figures for distributing the United States total were obtained by interpolation between 1840 and 1860 on the basis of rural population estimates for each date. Ratios for each state of agricultural labor force to rural population were computed for 1840 and 1860. These ratios were almost always quite close in magnitude. An average of the figures for 1840 and 1860 was then applied to the 1850 figure for the rural population of the state to obtain the estimated agricultural labor force. The sum of the state figures thus obtained fell short of the 1850 Lebergott total by only two-tenths of one per cent. The state figures were then adjusted upward by this proportion to yield the United States total estimated by Lebergott.

The estimates of agricultural labor force for 1840, 1850, and 1860 thus obtained were compared with the census data on rural population. Since agriculture accounts for the preponderant share of rural population, one would

111

expect that a division which is experiencing a falling share in rural population would show a similar trend for agricultural labor force. In the tabulations below, at each date the first figure for a division is the change in labor force share; the second figure, that in rural population:

Division

| | 1840-60 | | 1840-50 | | 1850-60 | |
	Ag.L.F.	Rural Pop.	Ag.L.F.	Rural Pop.	Ag.L.F.	Rural Pop.
New Eng.	−4.1	−3.9	−2.1	−1.9	−2.0	−2.0
Middle Atlan.	−6.6	−5.9	−3.0	−2.4	−3.6	−3.5
E. No. Cent.	+4.6	+5.2	+2.2	+2.5	+2.4	+2.7
W. No. Cent.	+4.8	+4.8	+1.4	+1.3	+3.4	+3.5
So. Atlan.	−4.3	−4.3	−1.8	−1.9	−2.5	−2.4
E. So. Cent.	−0.5	−1.6	+0.5	−0.2	−1.0	−1.4
W. So. Cent.	+4.8	+3.7	+2.2	+1.7	+2.6	+2.0
West	+1.3	+1.9	+0.6	+0.8	+0.7	+1.1

Not only the directions of change but the magnitudes are quite similar for each period. This result was not built in by the estimating procedure, since the 1840 estimate of labor force by division was made independently of the rural population data and this was very largely the case too with regard to the 1860 estimate.[15] This comparison thus suggests that the labor force estimates are reasonable.

1. The research on which this paper is based was supported by NICHD grant 1 RO1 HD-05427-02. I am grateful for assistance to Janet S. Berens, Gretchen A. Condran, Dana E. Lightman, and Cynthia Schneider, and for comments to Robert Douglas, Stanley L. Engerman, Robert E. Gallman, and Joseph D. Reid, Jr.

2. Ohio and Maine show production deficits in relation to population of about the same order of magnitude as Maryland. The four states mentioned in the text plus these two account for over eight-tenths of the aggregrate shortfall of production compared with population shares.

3. For a convenient summary, see David, [6, p. 181].

4. In this calculation, slaves are treated by analogy with working animals. The agricultural output consumed by them is estimated at $26.6 million, obtained by multiplying the total slave population in the division, 1.33 million, by $20. The latter, a commonly used figure for the average maintenance cost per slave [12, p. 334, n. 35] may be high for this purpose, since it includes nonagricultural as well as agricultural consumption needs of slaves. On the other hand, Seaman estimated the total maintenance cost of slaves in 1840 at $30 per head [28, p. 462]. Deducting $26.6 million from the original estimate of agricultural output of $136.6 million (Table A-1, column 2) yields a new estimate of agricultural output net of slave consumption of $110 million. The free agricultural labor force is estimated

TABLE B-2

Per Cent Distribution of Agricultural Income Valued at United States Prices of 1879 and of Agricultural Labor Force, and Agricultural Income per Worker as Percentage of United States Average, by Geographic Division, 1840, 1850, and 1860

Geographic Division	(1) Income 1840	(2) Income 1850	(3) Income 1860	(4) Labor Force 1840	(5) Labor Force 1850	(6) Labor Force 1860	(7) Income Per Worker 1840	(8) Income Per Worker 1850	(9) Income Per Worker 1860
United States	100.0	100.0	100.0	100.0	100.0	100.0	100	100	100
New Eng.	8.9	6.0	4.7	10.3	8.2	6.2	86	73	76
Mid Atlan.	24.3	20.6	16.9	23.0	20.0	16.4	106	103	103
E. No. Cent.	16.9	19.8	22.2	15.7	17.9	20.3	107	110	110
W. No. Cent.	2.9	4.5	6.6	2.8	4.2	7.6	102	107	86
So. Atlan.	21.0	20.3	16.3	25.4	23.6	21.1	82	86	77
E. So. Cent.	21.1	21.6	19.5	19.6	20.1	19.1	108	107	102
W. So. Cent.	5.0	6.6	11.1	3.2	5.4	8.0	158	121	139
West		0.6	2.6		0.6	1.3		106	201

See notes to Table B-1.
Source: Table B-1.

at 583.7 thousand, obtained by multiplying the total agricultural labor force, 972.9 thousand, by 0.6, the ratio of the free to the total population. (This is probably a maximum estimate of the free agricultural labor force since the share of free persons in the total population is probably greater than that in the total agricultural labor force.) The quotient obtained by dividing total output, $110 million, by the free labor force, 583.7 thousand, is agricultural output per head of the free labor force, $188.

5. Cf. [28, p. 366]. References to price data for other products are given in [7, Appendix B].

6. Technically, the price index of a state equals $\Sigma p_s q_s / \Sigma p_{us} q_s$, where the United States price of a product is an average of the state prices, with each state's price weighted according to the state's share in the output of each crop.

7. Cf. [3] and North [21]. Recent contributions to the subject include those by Battalio and Kagel[1], Engerman [9], Fishlow [11], Gallman [15], and Lindstrom [20].

8. David provides a valuable discussion of this question regarding the products specifically covered in the Parker and Klein studies[6, p. 182].

9. This is implied, for example, by the time trends shown in the studies by Bogue [2, pp. 242, 286] and Curti [4, T.12 and ch. VIII].

10. In his estimate of total factor productivity, based in part on the same data as the present estimate of labor productivity, Gallman shows a decline between 1840 and 1850, and gives reasons for doubting its validity. He later notes the possibility of bias in the pre-1840 and post-1840 rates of change shown by the Lebergott labor force estimates. His discussion raises the possibility that the rate of change computed here for 1840 through 1860, as well as that for 1840-50, may be biased [13, p. 208, n.31 and p. 210].

11. Fogel and Engerman [12] provide a valuable review and analysis of the relevant literature.

12. Fogel and Engerman point this out in their analysis of per capita income trends in the region [ibid., p. 335]. The per capita income figures, which are based largely on earlier estimates of mine [8], are influenced in substantial measure by the agricultural productivity movements shown here. The per capita income estimates are somewhat less reliable than those of agricultural productivity, because the data base is less complete (for example, income originating in the service sector is omitted) and because the estimating technique involves a larger number of assumptions. Jonathan Hughes in a review of the Fogel and Engerman article makes the valid point that for certain purposes one is interested in comparisons not between the South as a whole and the North as a whole, but between specific areas within each section [cf. *Explorations in Entrepreneurial History*, Vol. 10, No. 1 (Fall, 1972), pp. 122-23].

13. An exception is the estimate for agricultural improvements, which by virtue of Seaman's particular estimating procedure is, in effect, included at constant prices in both estimates [28, pp. 452-53].

14. [18, p. 169, T.C.9]. No 1860 estimates were given by Lang for five small states or territories—Dakota, Nebraska, Kansas, Nevada, and Washington. I added rough estimates for these areas, taking the reported census total of farmers and farm laborers as equal to the agricultural labor force.

15. Only for the slave labor force in 1860 were rural-urban population data used to estimate the agricultural-nonagricultural labor force distribution [18, p. 167].

REFERENCES AND SHORT BIBLIOGRAPHY

1. Battalio, Raymond C. and Kagel, John, "The Structure of Antebellum Southern Agriculture: South Carolina, A Case Study" in William N. Parker, ed., *The Structure of the Cotton Economy of the Antebellum South.* Washington: The Agricultural History Society, 1970, pp. 25-37.
2. Bogue, Allan G., *From Prairie to Cornbelt.* Chicago: Quadrangle Books, 1968.
3. Callender, Guy S., "The Early Transportation and Banking Enterprises of the States in Relation to the Growth of Corporations," *Quarterly Journal of Economics,* XVII (1903), pp. 111-62.
4. Curti, Merle, *The Making of an American Community.* Stanford: Stanford University Press, 1959.
5. Danhof, Clarence H., *Change in Agriculture: The Northern United States 1820-1870.* Cambridge: Harvard University Press, 1969.
6. David, Paul, "The Growth of Real Product in the United States Before 1840: New Evidence, Controlled Conjectures," *Journal of Economic History,* Vol. 27, No. 2 (June 1967), pp. 151-97.
7. Easterlin, Richard A., "Interregional Differences in Per Capita Income, Population, and Total Income, 1840-1950," in *Trends in the American Economy in the Nineteenth Century, Studies in Income and Wealth,* Vol. 24. Princeton: Princeton University Press, 1960, pp. 73-140.
8. ———, "Regional Income Trends, 1840-1850," in Seymour E. Harris, ed., *American Economic History.* New York: McGraw-Hill Book Co., Inc., 1961, pp. 525-47.
9. Engerman, Stanley L., "The Antebellum South: What Probably Was and Should Have Been," in William N. Parker, ed., *The Structure of the Cotton Economy of the Antebellum South.* Washington: The Agricultural History Society, 1970, pp. 127-42.
10. Fishlow, Albert, *American Railroads and the Transformation of the Ante-Bellum Economy.* Cambridge, Mass.: Harvard University Press, 1965.
11. ———, "Antebellum Interregional Trade Reconsidered," in Ralph Andreano, ed., *New Views on American Economic Development.* Cambridge, Mass.: Schenkman Co., 1965.

12. Fogel, Robert William and Engerman, Stanley L., "The Economics of Slavery," in Robert W. Fogel and Stanley L. Engerman, eds., *The Reinterpretation of American Economic History*. New York: Harper & Row, 1971.

13. Gallman, Robert E., "Changes in Total U.S. Agricultural Factor Productivity in the Nineteenth Century," *Agricultural History*, Vol. 46, No. 1 (January 1972), pp. 191-210.

14. ———, "Commodity Output, 1839-1899," in *Trends in the American Economy in the Nineteenth Century, Studies in Income and Wealth*, Vol. 24. Princeton: Princeton University Press, 1960, pp. 13-72.

15. ———, "Self-Sufficiency in the Cotton Economy of the Antebellum South," in William N. Parker, ed., *The Structure of the Cotton Economy of the Antebellum South*. Washington: The Agricultural History Society, 1970, pp. 5-23.

16. Gates, Paul Wallace, *The Farmer's Age: Agriculture, 1815-1860*. New York: Holt, Rinehart & Winston, 1960.

17. Lang, Edith, "The Effects of Net Interregional Migration on Agricultural Income Growth: The United States, 1850-1860," *Journal of Economic History*, Vol 32, No. 1 (March 1972), pp. 393-95.

18. ———, "The Effects of Net Interregional Migration on Agricultural Income Growth: The United States, 1850-1860," unpublished doctoral dissertation, University of Rochester, 1972.

19. Lebergott, Stanley, *Manpower in Economic Growth: The American Record since 1800*. New York: McGraw Hill, 1964.

20. Lindstrom, Diane L., "Southern Dependence upon Interregional Grain Supplies: A Review of the Trade Flows, 1840-1860," in William N. Parker, ed., *The Structure of the Cotton Economy of the Antebellum South*. Washington: The Agricultural History Society, 1970, pp. 101-13.

21. North, Douglass C., *The Economic Growth of the United States, 1790-1860*. Englewood Cliffs, New Jersey: Prentice-Hall, 1961.

22. Parker, William N., "Productivity Growth in American Grain Farming: An Analysis of its 19th Century Sources," in Robert W. Fogel and Stanley L. Engerman, eds., *The Reinterpretation of American Economic History*. New York: Harper & Row, 1971.

23. ———, and Klein, Judith L. V., "Productivity Growth in Grain Production in the United States," in *Output, Em-*

ployment, and Productivity in the United States after 1800, Studies in Income and Wealth, Vol. 30. New York: National Bureau of Economic Research, 1966, pp. 523-79.

24. ——— and Whartenby, Franklee, "The Growth of Output Before 1840," in *Trends in the American Economy in the Nineteenth Century, Studies in Income and Wealth*, Vol. 24. Princeton: Princeton University Press, 1960, pp. 191-212.

25. Primack, Martin L., "Farm Construction and Labor," *Journal of Economic History*, Vol. 25, No. 1 (March 1965), pp. 114-25.

26. ———, "Farm Fencing in the Nineteenth Century," *Journal of Economic History*, Vol. 29, No. 2 (June 1969), pp. 287-89.

27. ———, "Farm Formed Capital in American Agriculture, 1850-1910," unpublished doctoral dissertation, University of North Carolina at Chapel Hill, 1963.

28. Seaman, Ezra, *Essays on the Progress of Nations*. New York: Charles Scribner, 1853.

29. Towne, Marvin W. and Rasmussen, Wayne D., "Farm Gross Product and Gross Investment in the Nineteenth Century," in *Trends in the American Economy in the Nineteenth Century, Studies in Income and Wealth*, Vol. 24. Princeton: Princeton University Press, 1960, pp. 255-312.

30. Tucker, George, *Progress of the United States in Population and Wealth in Fifty Years*. New York: Press of Hunt's Merchant's Magazine, 1855, and Reprints of Economic Classics, New York: Augustus M. Kelley, Bookseller, 1964.

31. U.S. Bureau of the Census, *Census of Population: 1960, United States Summary*. Washington: Government Printing Office, 1963.

32. U.S. Census Office, *Preliminary Report on the Eighth Census, 1860*. Washington: Government Printing Office, 1862.

33. ———, *Statistical View of the United States. Compendium of the Seventh Census*. Washington: Beverly Tucker, Senate Printer, 1854.

34. Wright, Gavin, "The Economics of Cotton in the Antebellum South," unpublished doctoral dissertation, Yale University, 1969.

IV

NINETEENTH CENTURY PUBLIC LAND POLICY: THE CASE FOR THE SPECULATOR

Edward H. Rastatter

Office of Management and Budget

INTRODUCTION

One of the most maligned figures in American history has been the land speculator. In buying large plots of public land, he "prevented the small farmer from buying,"[1] and "forced widespread dispersion of population."[2] He is supposed to have forced settlers to pay higher prices for the public lands, thereby forcing them onto poorer land, and "held land out of the market for at least a time and so compelled settlement to pass around or across it."[3] He bought so great a proportion of the land sold and held it out of the market for so long that "there is no evidence even to suggest that additions to the farming area of the West kept pace with land sales; no such amount of land could be assimilated in so short a time."[4] This used to be the historical concensus of the part played by the speculator. After a century and a half, a more dispassionate view of the speculator has evolved.[5]

A speculator in any commodity reacts to expected changes in supply-demand conditions. To the extent his expectations are correct, he helps smooth out price fluctuations by buying in "glut" time and selling in "shortage" times. Seldom if ever can speculators "corner the market"; and even if they could do so, they would not sit on their holdings indefinitely, since invested funds have opportunity costs. The speculator pays out his holdings at a rate which he hopes will maximize his profits or minimize his losses.[6] Land speculation is no exception.

Stated more rigorously, some historians contended that speculators raised the price of good land and skimmed off quasi-rents, thereby forcing settlers to buy and develop poorer land, and in general delayed land settlement. On theoretical grounds alone these assertions are suspect. The vast quantities of land offered for sale by the government virtually assured a "glut" condition somewhere during the entire period when speculators are alleged to have done their worst damage. Finding it impossible to act as monopolists, most speculators would have found it necessary to accept resale prices far below those which skimmed off all or even most of the quasi-rents. One would expect to find that settlement and production were highly correlated with the actual value of land, and that settlement—at least on land with value in agricultural production—followed hot on the heels of its purchase at auction. The rest of this paper presents some evidence that this was true. Assuming eventual agricultural use of the land, an agricultural model is constructed for the State of Ohio for the period 1820-40, the period of greatest speculative activity, and an attempt is made to estimate the returns to land.

EXPLANATION OF THE MODEL

The return on an investment can be computed by using the capital-value formula,

$$(1) \quad V = \sum_{j=1}^{n} \frac{R_j}{(1+r)^j} ,$$

119

where V is the cost of the investment, the summed R_j's are the future net annual returns from the investment, r is the marginal efficiency of capital, and n is a reasonable period of time, say 10 years. If (1) is solved for r, and r is found to be greater than or equal to the currently attainable rate of interest, then the investment is said to be profitable.

The cost of the investment is, then

$$(2) \quad V = C_1 + C_k,$$

where C_1 represents the sale price of one acre of land; C_k is the cost of capital improvements—clearing, fencing, and equipping the settler with basic implements.

The annual returns may be expressed as

$$(3) \quad R_j = (p_x . q_x) - (C_o + C_t),$$

where x is the crop produced on the particular plot of land, p is its wholesale price and q_x is the yield per acre in a given year; C_o comprises all current operating costs of producing one acre of the crop chosen, and C_t is the cost of transporting the crop to the market.

Current operating cost, C_o, is here represented solely by labor costs. Other costs such as seed and recurring capital costs were probably not significant enough to dwell on. Although the frontier labor market was far from being organized, there are patterns evident in independent observations to render a relatively reliable wage rate. While the settler and his family generally performed all of the labor necessary for the production of a crop, there was an opportunity cost involved because the laborer, whether paid explicitly or not, is undergoing the cost of not earning farm wages elsewhere.

C_t is set by the location of the land relative to the market for agricultural goods. Transportation costs will be greater the farther the location from the market. Thus, the location of land closer to market may compensate for a lower crop yield per acre. Costs of transporting the crop to market may decrease over time in either or both of two ways. First, the distance to market may decrease as new markets arise; and second, ton-mile rates of transporting goods may be lowered by such things as canals and railroads. It is assumed, however, that markets were more or less competitive so that prices in all markets in the frontier vicinity were equal to those of the "secondary markets", such as Cincinnati, except for transportation costs. Thus, if new markets arise nearer the point of production, transportation costs would fall, but the decrease would be negated by a lower price for the goods. The only real decrease in the costs of transportation came through a reduction of rates per ton-mile.

Costs of transportation and initial costs of clearing and fencing the land were the most significant costs of farming on the frontier. It is assumed here that land improvement costs were about the same throughout a given region; hence the rate of settlement was influenced mainly by the costs of transportation. That is, the potential net returns to land determined the time and rate of settlement of the region. If a particular plot of land was located nearer the market and transportation rates were held constant, it was settled before land located farther from the market. The decrease in transportation costs brought about by the canals brought unsettled land into production. On the frontier, as in modern times, the rate of return determined the feasibility of investment.

THE COST OF THE INVESTMENT

The capital investment in the land included the original sale price of the unimproved land, the costs of improving the land to suit it for production—clearing and fencing—and an outlay for the basic capital implements with which the typical small-scale settler worked. The land price assumed here is the Government's minimum, $1.25 per acre. (Later there is a substitution of hypothetical higher prices, to see how the price charged by the speculator might have affected the rate of return.) Data show that this was about the usual price paid the land offices.

For land clearing costs, Primack[7] uses a median figure of thirty-three man days per acre. This is supported by independent data stating that the commonly accepted cost of clearing the land of trees ran between $10.00-12.00 per acre or about one man's labor for one month; and a figure for pulling stumps of about thirteen man days per acre. Based on twenty-six working days per month, the cost of stumping would be roughly $5.00-6.00. The cost of completely clearing an acre of land was thus approximately $15-18. Gallman,[8] however, suggests that the cost was probably closer to $11.00 per acre for clearing *and* fencing land. A conservative figure of $15.00 per acre is used here.

Fencing cost is a function of acreage and the shape of the area to be fenced.[9] Two independent figures put the size of the average farm in Ohio during this period at 114 acres[10] and 125 acres.[11] For simplicity say the average was at 121 acres, then the average acre (assuming a square area) would require only 25 yards to be fenced, or less than 10 per cent of the cost of fencing a single acre. Computations made on Danhof's data[12] yield a fencing cost of $2.75-$3.25 per acre (median and mean, respectively) on an average size farm of 129 acres, close to the Ohio average size. A compromise figure of $3.00 per acre is used.

For farm implements, estimates[13] are that it cost approximately $25.00 to equip a slave to work 30-35 acres of cotton land in the ante-bellum South. Assuming that the cost of northern agricultural implements did not differ significantly from those of the South and that a northern laborer could take care of about 36 acres, it cost about $86.50 to farm the entire 121 acres, the cost of implements thus being about $.72 per acre. The total cost of the investment, then, was about $19.97, or $20.00 per acre.[14]

PRICES OF AGRICULTURAL PRODUCTS

Relatively good price data for agricultural goods are available for the Ohio Valley, notably Cincinnati. It can reasonably be assumed that the market for home consumption was not extensive enough on the frontier to support large-scale market-oriented production. Thus, the large cities such as Cincinnati and (later, with the Erie Canal in operation) Cleveland functioned largely as "secondary markets", where goods were bought and gathered for export to the "primary markets" of New Orleans and the large cities on the East Coast. Prior to the Erie Canal, opened in 1825, the standard trade routes from the West (including Ohio) to the Northeast were overland for high-value manufactured goods and by the Ohio River to New Orleans and coastwise trade to the Northeast for bulky, low-value goods. During the 1830's this pattern began changing, and with the completion of the Ohio canals "a gradual redirection of western produce to the eastern seaboard" took place.[15]

It is clear, then, that prices in these secondary markets were a function of (a) supply and demand conditions in the primary markets and (b) the cost of transporting the goods to these markets. That is, prices in Cincinnati can be generally taken as roughly equal to eastern prices minus the costs of transporting the goods to the eastern markets. Prices on the frontier, in the smaller "tertiary markets" which supplied the secondary markets, were probably roughly equal to prices in the secondary markets less the cost of transporting the goods to those markets. The routes to market are assumed to have been chosen to minimize the costs of transportation. With these assumptions laid down, it is possible to concentrate attention on Cincinnati prices as approximations of Ohio prices in general.[16]

There is overwhelming evidence that "after 1815 . . . the West became a surplus grain- and livestock-producing kingdom, supplying the growing deficits of the South and the East."[17] In addition it is rather clear that, of the grain that was grown in Ohio, the great bulk consisted of wheat and corn. Attention on prices and productivity is centered on the data for these two cash crops and their derivatives.

Probably the best price series available have been compiled by Cole[18] and Berry.[19] However, for the purposes of this study, their monthly prices should be adjusted by the monthly volume of goods shipped to market, to find an annual index of prices.

Demand for agricultural products is more or less stable; thus, short-run price instability is associated primarily with irregularities in supply conditions. Specifically, high prices would characterize the months of low supply, and low prices the months of abundant supply. Berry has computed a seasonal index for selected goods at Cincinnati for the years 1824-36, 1836-48, and 1848-60. These are shown in Table 1. In addition, monthly volume figures are available for the Ohio canals for various points in the years 1833 and 1834. There is reason to believe that there was some lag between the arrival of goods and the adjustment of prevailing prices. In Table 1, it is shown that there exists a high degree of inverse correlation between the Monthly Index of Volume and the Price Index for wheat[20] if prices are permitted to lag one month behind volume. The Monthly Index of Volume thus provides appropriate weights for the annual price series.

Hog prices are given by Berry on a monthly basis. It is clear that there was a definite "season" for marketing hogs during the period, mainly from November to February, but occasionally from October to March. Since hog prices remained relatively stable within a "season", little accuracy is lost if a simple numerical average is used to represent an annual price of hogs. As the season includes the end of one year and the beginning of the next, the average season price of hogs is arbitrarily given to

124

Table 1
Monthly Index of Wheat Prices 1824-36, 1836-48, and 1848-60, and Average Monthly Percentages of Annual Crop Shipped on Ohio Canals, 1833-34

	Jan.	Feb.	Mar.	Apr.	May	June	July	Aug.	Sept.	Oct.	Nov.	Dec.
(1) 1824-36	100.3	100.2	100.2	100.1	100.0	99.9	99.8	99.7	99.7	99.6	100.5	100.4
(2) 1836-48	104.8	101.8	101.2	98.7	99.4	95.4	87.8	95.5	95.5	103.0	105.4	107.6
(3) 1848-60	104.7	105.2	104.5	103.0	108.0	101.2	92.3	91.9	91.9	95.8	98.0	102.2
(4) Index of Volume	.017	.026	.019	.051	.142	.144	.100	.097	.127	.140	.127	.131

Rows 1-3 from Berry, *Western Prices Before 1861*, pp. 566-57 (Jan.-Dec. = 1200).
Row 4 computed from Canal Receipts on Ohio Canals, 1833-34, (Jan.-Dec. = 1000).

the year in which the season begins. The Berry hog prices apply to live hogs, per hundred pounds; as the average hog weighed about two hundred pounds at market, the Berry price was doubled to give the average annual price per live hog.

CROP YIELD PER ACRE

There seems to be little data available for crop yields in Ohio for the period under study. In a study by Parker, the wheat productivity of Ohio soil is estimated by extrapolating U.S. Department of Agriculture estimates for 1866-75 backward to 1843-55. This method gives the productivity range for wheat as 10 to 35 bushels to the acre, with a median value of 15.[21] Other figures are available for productivity in wheat and corn for the years 1850-55.[22] These studies were probably undertaken to assess the value of the land for taxes.[23] Therefore, the figures probably understate the true productivity of the land. The mean productivity in wheat is 13.4 bushels per acre. This includes an extremely poor year (1854) during which many counties average less than five bushels to the acre, and several showed averages of less than one bushel,[24] indicating that a mean somewhat higher and closer to Parker's median might be correct. In the case of corn, the average over the years 1850-55 was 35.5 bushels. On the average, the percentage of tilled land that was devoted to corn and wheat over the years 1850-55 was 55 per cent and 45 per cent respectively.[25] Assuming these percentages held in the years 1820-40, an acre of Ohio land could produce approximately 35.5 bushels of corn or 15 bushels of wheat or a mixture of 19.5 bushels of corn and 6.75 bushels of wheat.

Very little corn was marketed as corn during this period since it was high-bulk and low-value. However, it was easily converted into hogs and whiskey on the frontier and then marketed in the derived form. In the West hogs required approximately 15 bushels of corn to be fattened for market.[26] It is assumed here that all corn was marketed as hogs.

LABOR COST

In order to compute the labor cost involved in the production of one acre of wheat and corn, it is necessary to know the wage rate for farm labor and the average labor time required to perform the various tasks of securing the crop.

The traditional reference work on wage rates is the study by Adams concerning Vermont farm laborers. It is usually cited with a cautionary note indicating that the corresponding western wage rate was probably somewhat lower than the Vermont wage.[27] Later studies indicate that the note of caution is well-founded. The data of Lebergott[28] and Holmes[29] are consistently below those of Adams for farm wages. However, since the Adams data are supposedly sound,[30] they are used here.

Farm wages in the nineteenth century are usually given in the form of a daily and a monthly wage, and often also with a separate monthly rate if hiring is by the year. The expected annual income from farm labor would tend to be the same, regardless of the length of the contract, given the uncertainty of constant employment on a daily basis. The monthly wage is used here with its bias in the direction of overestimation since the farm family, "hired" on an annual basis, probably performed most of the labor. The traditional Adams data is here multiplied by a factor of one and one-third to allow for board.[31]

Figures on the productivity of farm labor are sparse. Rogin[32] presents a small set of data concerning the labor time required to produce one acre of wheat for the years 1820-21, 1829-30, 1831-32, 1835-36, 1837, and 1847. Although these data concern different regions (Michigan, Maryland-Virginia, and New York) and years, the figures are re-

127

markably close together, indicating that, after land clearing, labor time was probably comparable over a wide area of the United States. This fact suggests that there should be no reason for labor-time requirements to differ significantly among the regions of Ohio. Rogin breaks down his figures into "putting crop in" and "harvest" labor, the labor time in hours averaging 15 hours and 40 minutes, and 53 hours and 30 minutes per acre, respectively, or a total of 69 hours and 10 minutes.[33] While there are no data available concerning labor requirements in the production of corn, they would probably be lower for corn than for wheat, given that most corn was used for feeding hogs. Using a ten-hour working day and a twenty-six working-day month, it required .269 month to produce one acre of crops at $10.34 monthly wages, or $2.78. Including an allowance of one-third wages for board, labor costs were about $3.71 per acre.

TRANSPORTATION COSTS

Cost of transporting the goods to market comprise at once the most intricate problem in the analysis and the most critical determinant of profitability in the region under study. Assuming that labor costs were comparable and that the cost of the investment was approximately equal over the entire region, then the residual return after transportation costs varied inversely with the distance to market.

The problem here is intricate because of the unknowns that must be found or inferred: (a) the route to market from each point of production; (b) the distance by land routes; (c) the distance by water routes; (d) wagon rates per ton-mile; (e) water rates per ton-mile; (f) the weight of one acre of produce. The problem is further complicated by the coming of the canals. In other words, the costs of transportation to market must be computed in the presence *and* the absence of the canals, since the costs and routes taken to market may have differed in the two cases.

To find the route to market, it will first be assumed that the route was chosen to minimize the costs of transportation. As was pointed out earlier, it has been assumed that prices in the interior of the region of Ohio—the tertiary markets—were roughly equal to prices in the secondary markets less transport costs. Thus, the relevant transportation costs are those from production point to the secondary markets.

The period 1820-40 is divided into two sub-periods, a tactic necessitated by the coming of the canals. In the "pre-canal" period, 1820-30, northern routes to the East were fairly unimportant. Prior to the opening of the Erie Canal in 1825, the direct route to the East was simply not economically feasible, considering the high costs of wagon transport and the mountainous terrain. Even after 1825, it took several years to change the traditional route to the East in order to take advantage of the relative cheapness of the new canal route; hence, in the pre-canal period, it is assumed that trade traffic moved toward Cincinnati.

The second period, 1830-40, is the "canal" period. Ohio canals began opening for traffic as early as 1827, but complete routes were not available until approximately 1830 or 1833. At that time, the combination of the Erie Canal, Lake Erie, and the Ohio canal system made the northern route to the East economically feasible. With the beginning of this period, traffic began to move on a northeasterly path in Ohio, as well as on the established southwest path. In the second period, then, both the Cincinnati and Cleveland markets are considered collection points for exports, or secondary markets. At some point in Ohio on a northeast-southwest line, it became a matter of indifference in choosing the market toward which to ship.

To estimate the average distance from the point of production to a water-shipping point, the center of the county is found and its distance from a water point is measured in straight "airline" distance, then multiplied by a factor of 1.4, which is the ratio Fogel found between highway and straight-line distances in a random sample of modern high-ways.[34] It is assumed that only the Ohio, Scioto, Muskingum, and Little Miami rivers were navigable and carried shipments to market. In the latter period the canals are added as water routes. Since water rates were much lower than wagon rates, it is assumed that farmers used wagons to haul their produce to the nearest of these water routes, then shipped the rest of the way to market by water, as both Cleveland and Cincinnati were water ports. Most water distances can be closely gauged, as the canals usually paralleled a river, and the distances on the canals were published.

There is some dispute concerning the costs of shipping by wagon. A commonly used figure is $.25 per ton-mile, but this probably involves quite a large overstatement. Taylor estimates that "by the fifties, 15 cents was considered the usual rate on 'ordinary highways.' "[35] Whereas Fogel mentions $.25 as a possible rate, he explains why it was not actually that high, and poses another figure of $.2032 per ton-mile. Since most of the discussion of wagon rates falls within the $.15 to $.25 range, perhaps a compromise figure on the order of Fogel's $.2032 per ton-mile would not be far amiss.[36]

Water rates per ton-mile are also disputed. Fogel's estimate that "the average water rate per ton-mile (was) 3.18 cents"[37] appears high, as rates by downstream steamer were only 1.3 cents,[38] and 0.186 cents per ton-mile for the lake and canal route.[39] Allowing for what Fogel calls the "neglected costs" of "insurance, cargo losses in transit," and "transshipment costs," it is assumed that the total cost of shipping by water prior to the canal period was 3.18 cents per ton-mile, except for the Ohio River, for which the rate was known to be 1.3 cents per ton-mile downstream.

Computation of the cost of shipping one acre's worth of produce is a relatively simple matter. A bushel of corn weighed 56 pounds, a bushel of wheat, 60 pounds,[40] and a hog averaged 200 pounds.[41] From the average productivity figures outlined above, an average acre of Ohio land produced 1.3 hogs (19.5 bushels of corn) and 6.75 bushels of wheat. Thus, an acre-weight is 665 pounds or .3325 ton. With wagon rates set at $.2032 per ton-mile, it cost 6.76 cents per mile to ship one acre-weight by wagon. Given the average cost of shipping by water as 3.18 cents per ton-mile, it cost 1.06 cents per mile to ship an acre weight by water.

Unfortunately, there are no good data on prices in the Cleveland market. There are two alternatives available in lieu of direct data: it can be assumed that Cleveland prices were at least as high as Cincinnati prices in the canal period, which is known to be true; or Cleveland prices can be simulated with Cincinnati prices and the relative costs of shipping to the East from Cincinnati and from Cleveland. The latter alternative is taken here.

It can be safely assumed that the route taken from Cleveland to New York was Lake Erie to Buffalo, Erie Canal to Albany, and Hudson River to New York. The average cost of shipping one ton from Buffalo to New York City over the period 1830 to 1850 was $8.81.[42] Assuming that the cost of lake shipping over this route was in established traffic and was no more than the cost of shipping downstream on the Ohio River, 1.3 cents per ton-mile (Taylor states a cost of .10 cents for 1853[43]) is used. Thus, the cost of shipping one ton from Cleveland to New York City was about $10.01. The rate for shipping flour from Cincinnati to New York via New Orleans averaged $1.21 per barrel over the period 1837-50.[44] This rate is equivalent to $12.35 per ton, or $2.34 per ton higher than the rate from Cleveland. In other words, a ton of produce at Cleveland should have been worth $2.34 more than a ton at Cincinnati. Cleveland prices are computed as Cincinnati prices plus $2.34 divided by the produce weights.

THE RETURNS TO INVESTMENT IN LAND

Under the assumptions outlined above, it is possible to impute the returns to average Ohio land for the years 1820-

131

40. The average is weighted across counties by their agricultural population.[45] Table 2 shows the average annual returns under the assumption that Ohio land was devoted to production of wheat and corn in the proportions that held in the year 1850-55. Table 2 also shows the present value of those returns at six and eight per cent,[46] and the land price the settler should have been willing to pay to yield such returns. It is evident that the potential returns to land were rising rapidly over time. Although at the beginning of

Table 2

Annual Returns and Break-Even Price for Average Ohio Land, 1820-40[a]

Opportunity Cost Rate of Return

Year	Annual Return	6% Present Value[b]	Price[c]	8% Present Value[b]	Price[c]
1820	$ 2.65	22.59	3.84	20.40	1.65
1821	0.49	25.62	6.87	22.88	4.13
1822	1.44	31.37	12.62	28.10	9.35
1823	3.53	36.48	17.73	32.74	13.99
1824	3.09	39.13	20.38	35.04	16.29
1825	1.92	46.02	27.27	40.99	22.24
1826	1.78	57.06	38.31	50.75	32.00
1827	1.78	64.63	45.88	57.89	39.14
1828	3.89	75.58	56.83	68.03	49.28
1829	4.75	81.58	62.83	73.91	55.16
1830	6.56	85.64	66.89	78.18	59.43
1831	8.03	86.33	67.58	79.42	60.67
1832	8.46	85.36	66.61	79.07	60.32
1833	8.52	84.14	65.39	78.43	59.68
1834	7.53	82.63	63.88	77.56	58.81
1835	14.00	82.18	63.43	77.76	59.01
1836	18.46	74.41	55.66	70.64	51.89
1837	10.82	63.81	45.06	60.09	41.34
1838	16.03	59.15	40.40	55.68	36.93
1839	10.01	48.65	29.90	45.26	26.51
1840	7.53	44.90	26.15	41.34	22.59

[a]Annual returns were projected to 1850, but 1841-50 are not shown here. All numbers are on a per-acre basis.
[b]Present value at n=10 years. This provides another understatement of the true returns, since some of the years beyond 10 add significantly.
[c]Present value minus $18.75, the estimated investment cost per acre for clearing, fencing, and implements.

132

the period the break-even price of land even at 6 per cent may have been quite close to the government minimum price of $1.25, it is clear that as the period wore on the break-even price rose far above the minimum.

Data concerning the actual sale price of land between private parties are not rich enough to base comfortable assertions on them, but it is the contention of this paper that the price the speculator exacted from the settler seldom was above the reservation prices shown in Table 2.[47] The glut of land on the market throughout the period is consoling evidence.

RETURNS TO LAND AND POPULATION PATTERNS

If the speculator significantly distorted the pattern of land settlement, most agricultural production should have been taking place on land with the lowest potential rates of return, while the speculator held the most valuable land out of the market. However, theory suggests that the relationship between the potential returns to a given area of land and the volume of production on that land should be strongly positive, not negative. The value of land (present value at 6 per cent) in each of the eighty-eight counties of Ohio for the decades of the 1820's and 1830's was regressed against their respective agricultural population for the years 1820 and 1840, respectively, to show the relationship before and after the period of greatest speculation. The results, in Table 3 below, show quite emphatically that population varied positively and significantly with land values. High-value land drew a significantly higher population than low-value land.

THE DELAY IN LAND SETTLEMENT

In the absence of direct data on annual population or agricultural production, changes in receipts on Ohio canals were used as a proxy and correlated with land sales. First differences in canal receipts resulted primarily from

133

Table 3

Regression Results, Population per Square Mile versus Land Value, 1820 and 1840

Year	Constant Term	Regression Coefficient	R^2 Adjusted
1820	3.8342** (11.87)[a]	+ .0588** (5.21)	.2311**
1840	5.7624** (11.24)	+ .0924** (2.96)	.0817**

[a]t-values in parentheses
**significant at .01.

increases of acreage in production since yields per acre, fraction of yields marketed, canal tolls, and canal shipping patterns remained relatively constant over the period in question.

Table 4 shows the results of correlating land sales and changes in canal receipts, using various lags. The best fit is obtained with a lag of two years. A lag of one year yields somewhat poorer results, but lags longer than two years show no relationship whatever between the variables. These results strongly suggest that, by and large, land was settled and in production within two years of its sale at public auction.[48]

Table 4

Land Sales versus Canal Receipts, 1827-40

Lag (Years)	r	R Adjusted	t
0	-.0321	-.0898	- 0.11
1	.5389*	.2259	2.12*
2	.7859**	.5829	4.22**
3	.2521	-.0216	0.86
4	.1566	-.0642	0.53

*Significant at .10.
**Significant at .01.

NINETEENTH CENTURY PUBLIC LAND POLICY

CONCLUSION

While the consensus among historians might be that speculation made an already poor public land policy even worse, the evidence presented here casts further doubt on this contention. First, given the value of land as an income-producing asset and the huge quantities of land for sale at any one time, it is doubtful whether speculators were able to charge so high a price as to confiscate all or even most of the returns to the land. Second, it was shown that the most valuable land was put into production first, while the land that had low or negative potential returns did not attract population and production until lowered transportation costs and higher prices combined to make possible a profitable return. Third, evidence was offered to suggest that land was settled and producing within two years of its sale at public auction. Therefore, it appears highly unlikely that the land speculator could have significantly retarded or distorted the settlement of the public lands.

1. Benjamin H. Hibbard, *A History of the Public Land Policies* (New York: Macmillan Co., 1924), p. 211.

2. Paul W. Gates, "The Role of the Land Speculator in Western Development," *The Public Lands*, ed. Vernon Carstensen (Madison, Wisc.: The University of Wisconsin Press, 1963), p. 361. Cited hereafter as Carstensen.

3. Hibbard, p. 219.

4. *Ibid.*, p. 215.

5. Since the research for this piece was completed, several fine works have been published. See especially Robert P. Swierenga, *Pioneers and Profits* (Ames: The Iowa State Press, 1968); and Robert W. Fogel and Jack L. Rutner, "The Efficiency Effects of Federal Land Policy, 1850-1900: A Report of Some Provisional Findings," *The Dimensions of Quantitative Research in History*, ed. William Aydelotte, Allan Bogue and Robert Fogel (Princeton: Princeton University Press, 1972), pp. 390-418.

6. See Fogel and Rutner, pp. 412-416, for an excellent theoretical treatment of this point.

7. Martin L. Primack, "Land Clearing Under Nineteenth-Century Techniques," *The Journal of Economic History*, XXII (December 1962), pp. 485-91.

8. Robert E. Gallman, "Discussion," *The Journal of Economic History*, XXII (December 1962), p. 516.

9. For a given acreage, the more nearly square the plot of land, the lower the fencing cost per acre. And, as acreage increases, average and marginal cost decline.

10. Paul W. Gates, *The Farmer's Age*, Vol. III: *The Economic History of the United States* (New York: Holt, Rinehart, Winston, 1962), p. 58.

11. Francis P. Weisenburger, *The Passing of the Frontier, 1825-50*, Vol. III: *The History of the State of Ohio*, ed. Carl Wittke (Columbus: Ohio State Archaeological and Historical Society, 1941), p. 58.

12. Clarence H. Danhof, "Farm-making Costs and the 'Safety Valve': 1850-60", *Journal of Political Economy*, LXIX (June, 1941), pp. 285-59. Observations (g) and (x) were excluded as extreme values.

13. Alfred H. Conrad and John R. Meyer, "The Economics of Slavery in the Ante Bellum South," *Journal of Political Economy*, LXVI, No. 2 (April, 1958), pp. 100-101.

14. Coincidentally the value of the average farm of 125 acres in Ohio in 1850 was estimated at $2,495, or about $20.00 per acre. See Weisenberger, p. 58.

15. Douglass C. North, *The Economic Growth of the United States, 1790-1860* (Englewood Cliffs, N.J.: Prentice-Hall, Inc. 1961), pp. 102-103.

16. Later, Cleveland prices are estimated, but the estimates are based on Cincinnati prices.

17. Louis B. Schmidt, "Internal Commerce and the Development of a National Economy Before 1860," *Journal of Political Economy*, XLVII (December, 1939), p. 799.

18. Arthur H. Cole, *Wholesale Commodity Prices in the United States 1700-1861, Statistical Supplement* (Cambridge: Harvard University Press, 1938).

19. Thomas S. Berry, *Western Prices Before 1861: A Study of the Cincinnati Market* (Cambridge: Harvard University Press, 1943).

20. Correlation between mean average of rows 1-3 and row 4, or between Price Index and Monthly Index of Volume, with prices lagged one month, r = -.854, significant above .001 when it is assumed Price Index is independent of Index of Volume.

21. William N. Parker, *Productivity Change in the Small Grains*, A Preliminary Report to the Conference on Research in Income and Wealth, September 4-5, 1963, Prepared by the National Bureau of Economic Research (New York: The Conference, 1963), p. 8. Cited hereafter as Parker, *Grains*.

22. *Annual Report of the Board of Agriculture of the State of Ohio*, 1857, pp. 21-23, 29-31. Cited hereafter as *Annual Report*.

23. William T. Utter, *The Frontier State*, Vol. II: *The History of the State of Ohio*, ed. Carl Wittke (Columbus: Ohio State Archaeological and Historical Society, 1942), pp. 131, 133.

24. *Annual Report*.

25. *Ibid*.

26. A. L. Kohlmeier, *The Old Northwest As the Keystone of the Arch of American Federal Union* (Bloomington, Indiana: The Principia Press, 1938), p. 32, n. 33.

27. See, e.g., W. N. Parker and F. Whartenby, "The Growth of Output Before 1840," *Trends in the American Economy in the Nineteenth Century*, Vol. XXIV

of Studies in Income and Wealth, Conference on Research in Income and Wealth, National Bureau of Economic Research (Princeton: Princeton University Press, 1960), pp. 208-209.

28. Stanley Lebergott, *Manpower in Economic Growth: The United States Record Since 1800* (New York: McGraw-Hill Book Co., 1964), pp. 257-63.

29. G. K. Holmes, *Wages of Farm Labor* (USDA Statistical Bulletin No. 99, 1912), pp. 14-21.

30. Parker and Whartenby, p. 208.

31. Lebergott, pp. 141, 262.

32. Leo Rogin, *The Introduction of Farm Machinery in Relation to the Productivity of Labor in the Agriculture of the United States During the Nineteenth Century* (Berkeley: The University of California Press, 1931), pp. 206-207, 234-35.

33. Parker, *Grains*, Appendix 12, Table B-2 gives figures which total very close to Rogin's, for the period 1835-60.

34. Robert W. Fogel, *Railroads and American Economic Growth: Essays in Econometric History* (Baltimore: The John Hopkins Press, 1964), p. 68. Hereafter cited as Fogel, *Railroads.*

35. George R. Taylor, *The Transportation Revolution, 1815-1860,* Vol. IV: *The Economic History of the United States* (New York: Holt, Rinehart, Winston, 1951), p. 134.

36. Roger L. Ranson, *Government Investment in Canals: A Study of the Ohio Canal, 1825-1860* (unpublished Ph.D. dissertation, University of Washington, 1963), p. 63, uses a wagon rate of 20 cents.

37. Robert W. Fogel, "The Intra-Regional Distribution of Agricultural Products," Preliminary Draft of Chapter 3 of Fogel, *Railroads,* p. 41.

38. Taylor, p. 442.

39. Fogel, *Railroads,* p. 39.

40. Berry, p. 152.

41. *Ibid.,* p. 230.

42. Taylor, p. 137.

43. *Ibid.,* p. 442.

44. Berry, Table 9, p. 561, weighted by Table 14, p. 563.

45. Agricultural population figures are available for 1820 and 1840. Since farm population as a per cent of total population for those years was 19 per cent and 18 per cent, respectively, 1830 farm population is estimated to be 18.5 per cent of total 1830 population. Inter-census year farm population is interpolated linearly.

46. Conrad and Meyer, pp. 101-103, judge a fair rate of return before 1860 at 6-8 per cent, from the rates charged on prime commercial paper in the principal money markets.

47. The estimates by Swierenga for a later period (1845-1889) and a different region (Iowa) are that the average resale price of land was only about $3.10. Swierenga, pp. 195-196. See also Allan Bogue and Margaret Bogue, " 'Profits' and the Fronter Land Speculator," *Journal of Economic History,* XVII (March, 1957), pp. 1-24.

48. Swierenga estimates the delay in Iowa for a later period averaged only slightly more than two-and-a-half years. Swierenga, *Ibid.*

V

HUMAN FERTILITY AND AGRICULTURAL OPPORTUNITIES IN OHIO COUNTIES: FROM FRONTIER TO MATURITY, 1810-60

Don R. Leet

California State University, Fresno

The movement from high to moderate levels of fertility has traditionally been associated with the rise of industrialization and urbanization. According to the classical view of the fertility transition, lower birth rates are the outcome of the diffusion of new values which, in turn, are a product of the new urban environment. In this urban-industrial milieu, traditional agrarian attitudes about children and family size are reshaped by the economic and social realities of urban life.[1]

The foregoing view of the American fertility experience was, until recently, a comparatively unchallenged one. However, in light of population studies which established the downward trend of birthrates for the nation as a whole from the beginning of the nineteenth century, doubt has been cast on the traditional interpretation. It would now appear that the decline in birth rates antedates any significant urbanization or industrialization. As the Taeubers wrote:

> Ratios of numbers of children under 5 years of age to women aged 20 to 44 for the whole white population show declines in fertility throughout the nineteenth and early twentieth centuries. . . . The most striking aspect of these ratios is that the major absolute declines occurred in the first three quarters of the nineteenth century, a period when the country was mainly rural and agricultural.[2]

The purpose of this study is to investigate the fertility experience of the white population in Ohio for the five decades preceeding the American Civil War. During this time Ohio remained largely a state of farmers, although the forces of industrialization and urbanization were continually growing in importance. The data in Table I reveal the overwhelming rural orientation of Ohio throughout the period. In 1820 only Cincinnati with less than 2 per cent of the state's population can qualify as an urban place, and even by mid-century only one-eighth of state's population lived in towns of more than 2500. While both the number and the proportion residing in towns increased, the growth was substantially confined to a few well defined counties, so that on the eve of the Civil War almost two-thirds of the urban population was still to be found in the five largest cities.

The unit of study in this paper will be the county and the analysis will often be restricted to the 83 counties of 1860 which did not contain a major urban center.[3] Thus Cuyahoga, Franklin, Hamilton, Lucas, and Montgomery counties containing Cleveland, Columbus, Cincinnati, Toledo, and Dayton respectively will frequently be separated from the other counties in order to clarify the more purely agrarian influences within the state.

Measuring birth rates in ante-bellum Ohio is a rather difficult task. Early in the period birth registration was non-existent, and although it later became possible to register births, the system was little used. As a result the historian is forced to rely on the less precise but still reliable child-woman ratio:[4]

$$\frac{\text{number of white children } 0\text{-}9}{\text{number of white women } 16\text{-}44} \times 1000$$

The child-woman ratio (or fertility ratio) tends to exceed the general fertility rate, i.e., the number of births per thousand women in the childbearing ages, by a factor of eight to ten. This is a result of the differences in the size of the numerators of the two ratios. The numerator of the child-woman ratio would be ten times as large as that for the general fertility rate if the number of births were the same in all years and assuming that there were no infant or child mortality. Of course not all children survived to age ten and thus a survival ratio on the order of .80 to .95 should be applied to exclude those dying before the end of the period. This adjustment would tend to reduce the size of the fertility ratio in relation to the general fertility rate. With a secular decline in births, however, the child-woman ratio would be even larger relative to the general fertility rate since the number of children in the youngest age class, zero to one year, would be smaller than those in each successive age class. The strength of these conflicting forces determines whether the child-woman ratio is nearer the lower or upper bound in a comparison with the general fertility rate.

Two questions seem relevant at this point. First, could inter-county differences in these underlying factors, especially infant and child mortality, distort cross sectional comparisons of fertility? And second, in interpreting the secular trend of birth rates from the fertility ratio, what bias does infant and child mortality introduce? The answer to the first question is that of course differential mortality experience among counties could disrupt any analysis of fertility based on the child-woman ratio. However, it seems unlikely that mortality conditions varied

Table I

The Rural-Urban Population of Ohio 1810 to 1860

	1810	1820	1830	1840	1850	1860
Total Population	228,220	581,295	937,093	1,519,467	1,980,329	2,339,511
Total Urban Urban as a proportion of total	2,540	9,642	36,673	83,491	243,331	406,510
	1.11	1.65	3.91	5.49	12.28	17.37
Population of Cincinnati	2,540	9,642	24,831	46,338	115,435	161,132
As a proportion of total	1.11	1.65	2.64	3.04	5.82	6.88
As a proportion of urban	100.00	100.00	67.70	55.50	47.43	39.63
*Population of five major cities	2,540	9,642	27,496	64,524	165,157	257,476
As a proportion of total	1.11	1.65	2.93	4.24	8.33	11.00
As a proportion of urban	100.00	100.00	74.97	77.28	67.87	63.33

*The five major cities are: Cincinnati, Cleveland, Columbus, Dayton, and Toledo.

Sources: Charles Cist, *Cincinnati in 1841: Its Early Annals and Future Prospects* (Cincinnati: 1841), p. 35. *Statistical Report of the Secretary of State for 1868* (Columbus: 1869), pp. 143-144.

significantly between agricultural counties for any time before 1860.[5] If this is correct, then a fertility ratio should not produce results far different from actual birth rate data. As to the second question, there is some dispute as to the trend of infant and child mortality in early nineteenth century America. Nevertheless the general directions of the biases can be outlined. If infant and child mortality can be assumed to be falling (rising) throughout the period, then the child-woman ratio would tend to understate (overstate) the fall in the birth rate, since at every time a higher (lower) proportion of children ever born would have survived. The general problem is still that the fertility ratio reflects births over the past ten years whereas the fertility rate pertains only to births in a given year.

A general overview of fertility in Ohio from 1810 to 1860 should serve to clarify the secular trend. Table II displays the essential features of white fertility over the fifty years under study. Line 1 shows the mean fertility ratio for the state as a whole. In each decade fertility was lower than the previous one, so that by 1860 mean

Table II

Measures of Central Tendency and Dispersion in Fertility Ratios[1]
for Ohio Counties 1810-60

	1810	1820	1830	1840	1850	1860
Mean	2312	2154	1946	1769	1554	1416
Standard Deviation	118	173	179	193	192	178
Coefficient of						
Variation (per cent)	5.1	8.0	9.8	10.9	12.4	12.6
Quartiles						
First	2222	2033	1820	1620	1434	1314
Second (median)	2314	2168	1917	1765	1553	1392
Third	2423	2270	2062	1892	1712	1573
Number of Counties	36	59	73	79	87	88
Total White						
Population (000)	229	577	928	1502	1955	2303

Notes: [1] Ratios of children under 10 to women 16-44

fertility ratios had fallen by almost 40 per cent from the 1810 level. Dispersion about the mean can be seen to be increasing throughout the period so that even by 1860, more than sixty years after initial settlement, there were considerable differentials among counties. The last two lines of the table concern the number of counties and the white population. Although both continue to rise during the entire period, the rate of change had greatly slowed by 1860. Whereas from 1810 to 1820 the white population more than doubled, it rose by less than 18 per cent during the 1850 to 1860 decade. All of these trends point toward the filling-up or maturation process taking place in Ohio. From 1810 to 1860 Ohio moves from a frontier state ranking thirteenth in terms of overall population to a well settled area with a population density greater than any other state in the Old Northwest and with a white population larger than any other state in the Union except for New York and Pennsylvania.[6]

Figure I disaggregates the Ohio data by regions. The downward trend of fertility and the pervasive nature of this trend in every region is even more apparent when viewed at the regional level. At the beginning of this period Central Ohio was just being opened up, and the Backbone Counties of East Central Ohio showed the highest fertility of any region at that time. By 1860 only in the Northwest and parts of the Central West regions could areas of virgin land still be found. These regions also generally exhibited higher fertility relative to other Ohio regions.

Settlement in Ohio can be roughly seen as progressing from south to north and east to west. Thus the counties along the Ohio river are the oldest in the state, while the counties in in the Northwest are the youngest. Figure I generally reflects this pattern throughout the period if newer settled areas are thought to have higher fertility than older ones. Indeed, a simple bivariate regression between the fertility ratio in 1860 and the age of the county

Figure I

Trends in Fertility Ratios for Regions of Ohio, 1810 to 1860.

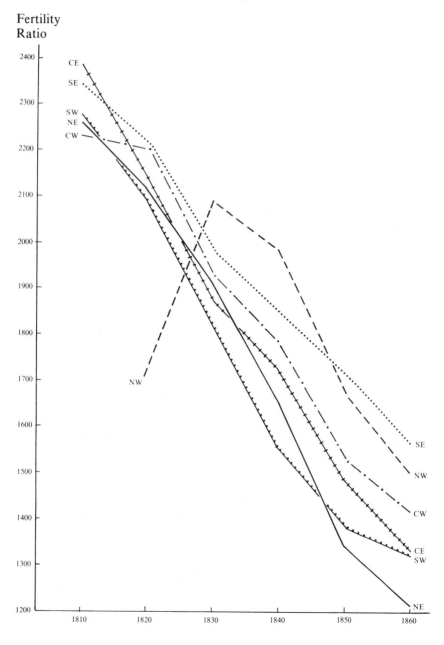

at that date indicates a statistically significant negative relationship at the .01 level.[7]

This observation suggests the desirability of a fuller investigation of the relationship between fertility and the agricultural settlement process. The general hypothesis is that in a virgin area land will be plentiful relative to the number of potential young farmers in the county and thus early marriage and high marital fertility will be the rule.[8] With great supplies of land, a large family conceived as rapidly as possible would be an economic asset. On the other hand, as the land becomes settled the amount of unused virgin land necessarily decreases. The farmers, and especially the prospective new farmers, of any given county will necessarily find it more difficult to enlarge their present farmstead or to obtain a virgin farmsite. This increasing scarcity of land with respect to demanders will, theoretically, produce a delay in the age at marriage and possibly promote intramarital fertility restriction. Both a rise in the age at marriage and the increased use of abortion or contraception would reduce the fertility rate.[9]

The foregoing hypothesis is similar to that of Yasukichi Yasuba, who associated population density with fertility in the United States over the period 1800 to 1860. He interpreted density as a measure of land availability, such that a higher population density meant relatively scarce land, and thus the value of children would be lower while the cost of setting up new farmsteads would higher than in the low density case.[10] More recently Colin Forster and G.S.L. Tucker have used a similar density measure to refine and buttress Yasuba's findings on the negative relationship between population density and birth rates.[11]

All of the above research roughly associates fertility behavior with the settlement process. People are seen to be adjusting their fertility to their environment.[12] However, identifying the various phases of the settlement process and uncovering the environmental experience have proved to be difficult. A given geographical area, e.g., a county, passes from an area of agricultural opportunity to one in which opportunities are much more limited and stress is consequently experienced by all farmers, but especially by the young potential farmers. The difficulty arises in the attempt to quantify this agricultural "stress" factor. Frequently a population density measure such as the one Yasuba calculated has been used to estimate this stress experience. A typical stress measure, such as the ratio of the total population of a county to the cultivable area of that county, can roughly approximate the agrarian situation. However this measure ignores a number of important factors: first, the relevant demanders are mostly young men between the ages of 15 and 25 rather than the entire population; secondly, the average farm size may vary between counties and with it the amount of land considered necessary for a new farmsite; finally, it is difficult to compare density measures between counties, since the measure has no upper bound and no critical value to differentiate between a situation of opportunity and one of stress.

Clearly, another measure is called for. Preferably the new index would illuminate the interplay of both supply and demand in addition to avoiding the other drawbacks of a simple density measure. Table III is an example of such an index, but it should be noted here that this index of economic stress is only one of a number of alternative stress measures which could be employed. Sections A through C of Table III concern the supply of farmsites which will be made available at some time during the decade of the 1850's. Section A applies a mortality rate to all white males aged 25 and over in each county. Every person in this category is assumed to hold a farm, and thus his death releases a farmstead and so contributes to the total farmsites available over the 1850 to 1860 period (line C). The other major component of the supply of farms is undeveloped land (line B3). This can be estimated by differencing the amount of land which is potentially cultivable (line B1) and the amount of land already improved (line B2). If the amount of potentially cultivable land not in use is then divided by the average farm size in the county (line B4), the number of potential

Table III

An example calculation of an Index of Economic Stress for two Ohio Counties, 1850-60.

	Columbiana	Allen
A. Farm sites becoming available over the period through death of farmers		
1. White males in the county in 1850 (000)	6.536	2.152
2. Mortality rate of white males aged 25+ in Ohio	.1549	.1549
3. Deaths, 1850-60, of those in line A1 (000) [line A1 × line A2]	1.012	.333
B. Farm sites not yet developed		
1. Cultivable land (000) acres	223.0	232.3
2. Improved land, 1850 (000) acres	173.2	50.8
3. Cultivable land not in use, 1850 (000) acres [line B1 - line B2]	49.8	181.5
4. Average improved land per farm in county, 1850	72.7	44.5
5. Farm sites undeveloped (000) [line B3 ÷ line B4]	.685	4.079
C. Total farm sites available, 1850-60 (000) [line A3 + line B5]	1.697	4.412
D. White males, aged 15-24 in county in 1850 (000)	3.389	1.177
E. Economic stress		
1. Excess demand for farm sites, 1850-60 (000) [line D line C] negative sign indicates excess supply	1.692	-3.235
2. Percentage of demanders unsatisfied, 1850-60 [(line E1 ÷ line D) × 100]	+.499	
3. Percentage of available farm sites not required for local demand, 1850-60 [(line E1 ÷ line C) × 100]		-.733

Sources and notes:

Line A2 is the mortality rate of Ohio native white males aged 25+ for 1870-80, calculated from the 1870 and 1880 age distribution in Simon Kuznets, *et al.*, *Population Redistribution and Economic Growth, United States, 1870-1950*.

Line B1 is land defined as cropland (classes I-IV) in an inventory of Ohio soil capabilities published as *Ohio Soil and Water Conservation Needs Inventory*, Columbus 1961.

All other data from the U.S. Censuses of Population and Agriculture.

147

undeveloped farmsites can be estimated (line B5). Thus an estimate of the supply of farmsites can be derived for the 1850 to 1860 decade. For example in Columbiana county there were 1,692 farmsites coming available whereas in Allen county there were 4,412. It is also interesting to note the composition of the supply for these two counties. Columbiana was a much older county, having been organized in 1803, and, as might be expected, almost two-thirds of the newly available farmsites were a product of the mortality factor, whereas in Allen county less than one-tenth of the available farmsites were due to the deaths of older farmers (line A3/line C).

The demand for these farmsites will depend upon the number of young men in the county seeking farms. In the example calculation all white males aged 15 to 24 were assumed to be potential farmsite demanders. Thus in Columbiana county 3,389 demanders were vying for 1,697 farmsites, while in Allen county 1,177 young men in the county faced a situation of excess supply since there were potentially 4,412 farmsites available. The resolution of these two situations can be seen in section E of the table. In Columbiana county almost 50 per cent of those young men reaching household forming age will find no farms available, whereas in Allen county all young men could obtain a farm and still almost 75 per cent of the potential farmsites would go unclaimed by local demanders.

Unlike the simple density measure, this new stress measure provides data which are readily comparable with other areas since every area's stress experience can be recorded on a scale from +100 to -100. The upper bound indicates that 100 per cent of the demanders will be unable to find a farmsite, while the lower bound means that none of the supply of farmsites will be taken by local men aged 15 to 24. In addition a region's passing from an area of economic opportunity to economic stress is signified by the movement from a negative to a positive observation on the stress scale.

It should also be noted that this new stress index relates to a period of time, not a single point in time. Men 15 to 24 years old in 1850 will be seeking farms between 1850 and 1860. The possibility of their getting farms is directly related to both the mortality conditions of older farmers during this period and the amount of potentially cultivable land not already taken up by 1850 in improved land. This measure, then, relates to prospective demand and supply conditions over the 1850 to 1860 decade. Unfortunately, this index can only be estimated for the decade of the 1850's, because the United States Census did not collect data on improved land until 1850.

Table IV shows the distribution of the 82 agricultural counties of Ohio[13] arranged by region with respect to the index of economic stress. It is readily apparent from this table that very few counties exhibit high levels of negative stress, i.e., opportunity. Those counties with the highest

Table IV

Frequency Distribution of Ohio Counties Classified by Economic Stress According to Regions for 1850-60

Economic Stress (per cent)	Ohio	South East	Central East	North East	South West	Central West	North West
61 to 80	3	0	2	1	0	0	0
41 to 60	9	1	3	3	1	0	1
21 to 40	8	2	0	2	3	1	0
1 to 20	15	3	5	3	2	2	0
0 to -19	13	0	1	4	7	1	0
-20 to -39	11	3	1	3	1	2	1
-40 to -59	6	3	0	0	0	1	2
-60 to -79	5	0	0	0	0	3	2
-80 to -99	12	0	0	0	0	3	9
Subtotal (positive stress)	35	6	10	9	6	3	1
Subtotal (negative stress)	47	6	2	7	8	10	14
Total	82	12	12	16	14	13	15

levels of opportunity are located for the most part in the West, and especially in the Northwest. This reflects the historical reality of the movement of the frontier in Ohio, for it was not until the late 1840's and early 1850's that Northwestern Ohio was settled on a large scale. The older regions of Ohio, particularly the East and the Southeast show high and positive degrees of economic stress. Again this coincides with historical experience, as these areas were settled early in the nineteenth century.

In Table V the 82 non-urban counties are distributed in a cross classification between fertility levels and an index of economic stress for the 1850's. In this cross tabulation counties with highly negative stresses are generally associated with high fertility ratios, while those counties with high positive stress usually fall into the lower fertility categories. A simple bivariate regression of the index of

Table V

Frequency Distribution of Ohio Counties Cross Classified by Economic Stress and Fertility Levels for 1850-60

Economic Stress (per cent)		Fertility Ratio			
	Ohio	1000 to 1199	1200 to 1399	1400 to 1599	1600 to 1799
61 to 80	3	1	2	0	0
41 to 60	9	1	6	1	1
21 to 40	8	0	5	2	1
1 to 20	15	0	9	6	0
0 to −19	13	3	5	4	1
−20 to −39	11	2	5	3	1
−40 to −59	6	0	1	2	3
−60 to −79	5	0	0	4	1
−80 to −99	12	0	0	3	9
Subtotal (positive stress)	35	2	22	9	2
Subtotal (negative stress)	47	5	11	16	15
Total	82	7	33	25	17

economic stress versus the dependent variable, the fertility ratio, shows a negative relationship significant at the .01 level.

That there is a strong association between the availability of land and the birth rate is clearly suggested by the foregoing, but three questions arise. The first question pertains to a comparison of the density measure and the index of economic stress, namely, which offers a better explanation of human fertility behavior? The second question deals with the "exceptions" to the land availability hypothesis. Why do some counties experience higher stress than others and yet maintain higher fertility? And third, if the five urban counties were reintroduced, would urbanization significantly aid in the explanation of the variance in the fertility ratios?

As to the first question, the density measure which was used in the comparison was composed of two parts: the denominator, containing the amount of potentially cultivable land as given in the soil census; and the numerator, with the total white population of the county in 1850. This density measure is similar to Yasuba's, except that in his measure he used the amount of land actually cropped in 1949 for the denominator. There are two major reasons for not duplicating the Yasuba density measure. First, a soil census would seem to be a better indicator of the amount of potentially cultivable land; and second, the comparison between the two measures would be made clearer if the data basis for each were similar. A comparison of the density and the stress measures can be made from the first two lines of Table VI. For the non-urban counties over the decade of the 1850's the stress measure can be seen to have the greater explanatory power in that it explains a greater proportion of the variance. In fact, for this decade in Ohio the density measure fails the test of statistical significance even at the .10 level.

Southeastern Ohio contains several "exceptions" to the land availability hypothesis. As can be most easily seen in Figure I, the fertility of this region ranks consistently high when compared with other areas, and yet land is less available there than in the Northwest region. The possibility exists that some other factor may be consistently inflating the fertility ratio of the Southeast. In the case of Ohio, the geographic regions of the migrants may have influenced the families' taste for children.[14] For example, southern Ohio was largely settled by migrants from Virginia and Kentucky, while the Northeast was originally settled by New Englanders.[15] These first settlers brought with them different traditions of age at marriage and desired family size. In the early nineteenth century the American South was a region with higher fertility than the United States as a whole, while New England had significantly lower

Table VI

Bivariate Regression Analysis of Fertility and Various Independent Variables for Agricultural Counties of Ohio, 1850-60

Independent Variables	Regression Coefficient	Stnd. Error	T-value	Correl. Coeff.	Proportion of Total Variance Explained
1. Density	-0.150	0.150	-0.997	0.111	0.012
2. Economic Stress	-216.259	36.188	-5.975	-0.555	0.308
3. Southerners	17.649	6.340	(**) 2.783	0.297	0.088
4. New Englanders	-58.467	11.549	-5.062 (**)	-0.492	0.242
5. Urbanization	-3.511	1.677	-2.093 (*)	-0.227	0.051

Notes:
(**) T-values are significant at the 0.01 level.
(*) T-values are significant at the 0.05 level.
Sources and Definitions
Density is the total white population of a county per thousand acres of potentially cultivable land in that county.
Economic Stress calculated as in Table III for the 1850-60 period.
Southerners as a per cent of total county population in 1870 were defined as Ohio residents born in Virginia, West Virginia, or Kentucky.
New Englander as a per cent of total county population in 1870 were defined as residents of Ohio born in the New England states. These data were not directly obtainable from the 1870 U.S. Census and had to be estimated.
Urbanization is defined as all population living in towns of 2,500 or more as shown in the 1860 U.S. Census of Population. It is shown as a per cent of total county population.

fertility.[16] Thus it appears likely that migrants from these regions carried these and other values with them to the Ohio frontier. As a result, even in the earliest period, comparable frontier areas had different fertility levels.

Quantifying the impact of New England or Southern influence is difficult because the data on the state of origin of Ohio residents is not tabulated on a county basis until 1870, and even then the number of New England migrants must be estimated. However, differences among counties in 1870 in the proportions of Southerners or New Englanders may be viewed as a heritage from early nineteenth century Ohio. It can be seen from Table VI that both measures are significantly related to the 1860 fertility ratios and in the direction expected, namely, New England migrants are negatively correlated with fertility and Southerners are shown to be positively related.

Urbanization also appears to be significantly related to fertility, although the relationship is not so strong as that for economic stress. (See Table VI). The question next becomes which variables or combination of variables best explains fertility in Ohio over this period. In order to answer this question multiple regression analysis is needed. This technique allows for the standardization of other influences and thus permits the relationship between the dependent variable, fertility, and any independent variable to be analyzed holding the influence of other variables constant. It also permits the ranking of variables in terms of the proportion of the variance in the dependent variable that they explain. From Table VII (using only the 82 non-urban counties) and Table VIII (using all 87 counties) it is apparent that economic stress is the most important independent variable. Urbanization, even when using all 87 counties, is a relatively weak variable. In the multivariate regressions, urbanization fails the test for statistical significance even at the .05 level. When the urbanization variable is omitted from the analysis, the adjusted coefficient of determination falls only slightly from .6148 to

Table VII

Multivariate Regression Analysis of Fertility and Various Independent Variables for the 82 non-urban counties of Ohio, 1850-1860.

Economic Stress	Proportion Southerners	Proportion New Englanders	Urban Proportion	Constant	Multiple Correlation Coefficient	Adjusted Coefficient of Determination
-226.650 (-7.755)**	+12.482 (+2.514)*	-54.124 (-5.763)**	-1.876 (-1.541)	1478.00	.7989	.6148
-243.653 (-8.924)**	+10.193 (+2.132)*	-55.032 (-5.820)**		1467.32	.7919	.6080
-215.809 (-5.415)**			-0.043 (-0.027)	1393.79	.555	.2824

Table VIII

Multivariate Regression Analysis of Fertility and Various Independent Variables using all 87 counties of Ohio, 1850 to 1860.

	Economic Stress	Proportion Southerners	Proportion New Englanders	Urban Proportion	Constant	Multiple Correlation Coefficient	Adjusted Coefficient of Determination
1.	− 227.647 (−7.989)**	+ 10.573 (+2.256)*	− 54.160 (−5.873)**	− 0.801 (−1.052)	1476.29	.8000	.6181
2.	− 240.567 (−9.351)**	+ 9.995 (+2.146)*	− 54.766 (−5.946)**		1468.03	.7970	.6176
3.	− 208.981 (−5.454)**			− 0.623 (−0.610)	1398.97	.5731	.3045

.6080 as seen in Table VII. The introduction of the major urban counties does not alter the conclusion that, in the Ohio case, urbanization does not appear to have played the major role in the transition from high to moderate levels of fertility during the first half of the nineteenth century.

Thus land availability does appear to be most significantly related to the fertility pattern in Ohio counties for the decade of the 1850's. When a measure of stress reflecting land availability was combined with various sociological factors, namely the proportion of Southerners or New Englanders, almost two-thirds of the variance in fertility among counties was explained. It may be hazardous to generalize from a cross-sectional analysis of one decade to the fertility experience of Ohio counties over four decades. However, it does seem that a causal mechanism based on land availability has been outlined for the 1850's, and that this thesis is applicable to the earlier period as well. Certainly it has been demonstrated that urbanization could not have been responsible for the major portion of the fertility decline. And while the proportion of migrants from different sections was important in the cross-sectional analysis, they did not vary significantly over time and thus were not involved in the secular decline. There remains only one factor which varied both among counties and over time, namely land availability.

As with so many concepts, this one was anticipated by a number of scholars. One of the most notable and prescient was Alfred Marshall. In the eighth edition of the *Principles*, published in 1920, he wrote:

> [T]he longer marriages are postponed beyond the age that is natural to the country, the smaller is the birth rate . . . [T]he average age at marriage depends chiefly on the ease with which young people can establish themselves, and support a family according to the standard of comfort that prevails among their friends and acquaintances.

156

[T]he gradual rise in the value of land and its growing scarcity is tending to check the increase of population
in some districts . . . On the other hand there seem to be
no conditions more favorable to the rapid growth of numbers than those of the agricultural districts of new countries.
Land is to be had in abundance . . . The "farmer", as the
peasant proprietor is called in America, finds therefore
that a large family is not a burden but an assistance to
him.[17]

I wish to thank R. A. Easterlin, G. Masnick, E. Rotella, and E. R. Weiss-Altaner for their comments on an earlier draft.

1. The classic explanation of the fertility transition and its connection with urbanization and industrialization was given by Frank W. Notestein in the *Proceedings of the Eighth International Conference of Agricultural Economists.*

2. Conrad Taeuber and Irene B. Taeuber, *The Changing Population of the United States* (New York: 1958).

3. A major urban center will be defined as any city containing a population of more than 10,000 in 1860.

4. This ratio was also used by Yasukichi Yasuba in his work, *Birth Rates of the White Population in the United States, 1800-1860* (Baltimore: 1962). His method of computing the fertility ratio is followed throughout this text.

5. It seems highly unlikely that mortality conditions varied significantly be-tween agricultural counties in Ohio for any time before 1860. Urban counties, on the other hand, were probably more unhealthful places and thus counties with large urban populations may have had lower fertility ratios than their birth rates would indicate.

6. *Preliminary Report on the Eighth Census, 1860* (Washington: 1862), pp. 120-21.

7. In the simple regression between the fertility ratio and the age of the county, the regression coefficient was 7.150; the standard error of the regression coefficient was 1.307; and the computed T-value equalled 5.467 with a correlation coefficient (r) of 0.510. The age of the county was determined by its date of political formation unless the population density of the new county was greater than the density of the state as a whole. If this was the case, the county was then assigned the mean age of those counties which were contiguous. This was done in order to avoid classifying a county as a frontier area when, in point of fact, it had been created as a mere sub-divison of a well-settled county.

8. This concept was originally used in: Richard A. Easterlin, "Effects of Agrarian Population Pressure: Some Prospective Lines of Analysis" (mimeo, University of Pennsylvania: 1971).

9. There is some evidence that abortion was practiced on a wide scale in Ohio as early as 1830. In 1834 the state legislature passed a law prohibiting physicians from performing abortions under penalty of one year in jail or a fine of $500. See Jona-

157

than Forman, "Organized Medicine in Ohio, 1811 to 1926", *Ohio State Medical Journal*, 1947, p. 170.

10. Yasuba, p. 159.

11. Colin Forster and G. S. L. Tucker, *Economic Opportunity and American Fertility Ratios, 1800-1860* (New Haven: 1972).

12. Richard A. Easterlin, "Does Human Fertility Adjust to the Environment?" *American Economic Review*, May, 1971, pp. 399-407.

13. The five counties containing major urban centers have been deleted and, in addition, Noble county has been subdivided into its neighboring counties, since it did not appear until 1852.

14. For a model of fertility behavior, see: Richard A. Easterlin, "Towards a Socio-economic Theory of Fertility: A Survey of Recent Research on Economic Factors in American Fertility", in S. Behrman, ed., *Fertility and Family Planning: A World View* (Ann Arbor: 1969), pp. 127-56.

15. Robert E. Chaddock, *Ohio Before 1850* (New York: 1908).

16. Yasuba, pp. 50-54.

17. Alfred Marshall, *Principles of Economics*, 8th edition, 1920 (London: 1962), pp. 150-53.

VI

MIGRATION AND THE OLD NORTHWEST

Richard K. Vedder
and Lowell E. Gallaway

Ohio University

Migration created the Old Northwest. More precisely, nearly all of the substantial population growth in the East North Central states from the time of the founding of the Republic to the Civil War resulted from the direct and secondary effects of that great human migration, the Westward Movement. At the time of the ratification of the American Constitution, there was not one permanent settlement in the Old Northwest. By 1860, 6,926,884 persons (22 per cent of the total population of the United States) were living in the five East North Central states (Ohio, Indiana, Illinois, Michigan, and Wisconsin). Largely because of this tremendous influx into the Old Northwest, the population center of the United States moved so far west that by 1860 it was near Chillicothe, Ohio—about fifty miles *west* of the first permanent settlement in the Northwest Territory at Marietta, Ohio, which had been founded only seventy-two years earlier. This great migration, then, was largely responsible for the Old Northwest states becoming the heartland of America. Interestingly, the population center of the United States has remained in the three lower

East North Central states ever since.[1] In this chapter, we intend to examine the magnitude and cause of this massive movement of persons and labor resources.

I. THE MAGNITUDE OF MIGRATION

Population change in a given area results from variation in four factors: the number of births, the number of deaths, in-migration into the area, and out-migration from the area. The first two factors comprise the "natural" population increase, while the last two determine net migration. Any population change different from that explained by natural factors (births and deaths) is, by definition, attributable to net migration.

Since reasonably accurate decennial total population estimates are available since 1790 in the various censuses of population, it is possible to estimate net migration if some determination can be made of the magnitude of natural population increase. Using this "residual" approach, we have calculated decennial net migration estimates for the Old Northwest for the first six decades of the nineteenth century (Table I). Basically, the procedure used was this: birth rates were assumed to vary from the national average directly and proportionately with the "refined child ratio", which is the ratio of children zero to nine years of age to women between the ages of sixteen through forty-four, adjusted for the proportion of women in this age group in the total population.[2] Given the scanty nature of the data on mortality, plus given the fact that the demographic structure of the population of the Old Northwest does not seem to suggest radically different mortality rates, we assumed death rates were the same as an estimated national average (the relatively small proportion of population in high mortality older age groups was offset, we judged, by a larger proportion of infants, for whom mortality rates were also high, as well as by possibly less adequate professional medical care in the region). From our estimated birth and death rates, we can estimate the rate of natural population increase, which, subtracted from total population increase, yields net migration (for a more detailed explanation of the estimation technique, see the Appendix).

Table I

The Components of Population Change, The Old Northwest, 1800-1860

Decade	Beginning Population	Natural Increase	Net Migration	End Population	Migration Rate [*]
1800-1810	51,006	26,119	195,199	272,324	382.70%
1810-1820	272,324	117,142	403,252	792,719	148.08
1820-1830	792,719	345,371	341,928	1,470,018	43.13
1830-1840	1,470,018	601,720	852,990	2,924,728	58.03
1840-1850	2,924,728	1,107,373	491,159	4,523,260	16.79
1850-1860	4,523,260	1,556,208	847,416	6,926,884	18.73

[*] Net migration divided by beginning population.

Table I reveals that migration into the Old Northwest was indeed extensive. Before 1840, migration accounted for the majority of population increase in the region. Although migration's importance in a relative sense declined after that date, the absolute volume of net migration remained very high, reaching a peak in the 1850's. Actually, in-migration into the region climbed more rapidly in the 1850's than Table I might suggest, because out-migration from the region, which was relatively unimportant before 1850, grew dramatically during that decade, as the Old Northwest was losing its status as being a truly "western" area. For example, in 1850, 96,708 persons born in the Old Northwest were living in the states or territories of Minnesota, Iowa, Missouri, and Kansas. By 1860, that number had grown to 350,524.[3] Thus, well over 250,000 persons migrated West out of the Old Northwest in the 1850's. Before 1850, when the Old Northwest was closer to (or on) the Western frontier, there was very little out-migration from the East North Central states. Certainly,

161

few persons moved back East. For example, in 1850 only 18,759 persons living in New England and the Mid-Atlantic states were born in the Old Northwest; by contrast, some 858,658 persons born in New England and the Mid-Atlantic states were living in the Old Northwest. "Net-migration" was almost the same amount as "in-migration".

The general trend towards increasing absolute amounts of net migration was interrupted (if Table I is reasonably accurate) in both the 1820's and 1840's. While we cannot be certain, we suspect this drop reflected the effects of the Panics of 1819 and 1837 on westward migration. Certainly, descriptive historical accounts of the region at this time are vivid with stories of severe depression and unemployment.[4] Both panics, indeed, were closely related to western land speculation.

Interstate Variations in Net Migration

While the amount of net migration was increasing (and the migration rate decreasing) throughout the period (with some cyclical variation), there were some very important differences in the net migration patterns of the five Old Northwest states, as indicated in Tables II through VI.

Table II

The Components of Population Change,
Ohio, 1800-1860*

Decade	Beginning Population	Natural Increase	Net Migration	End Population	Migration Rate*
1800-1810	45,365	23,698	161,697	230,760	356.44%
1810-1820	230,760	99,214	251,459	581,434	108.97
1820-1830	581,434	246,144	110,325	937,903	18.97
1830-1840	937,903	362,480	219,084	1,519,467	23.36
1840-1850	1,519,467	537,624	− 76,762	1,980,329	− 5.05
1850-1860	1,980,329	633,358	−274,176	2,339,511	− 13.84

* Net migration divided by beginning population.
* Decennial results are not strictly comparable owing to boundary changes.

162

Table III

The Components of Population Change, Indiana, 1800-1860*

Decade	Beginning Population	Natural Increase	Net Migration	End Population	Migration Rate[+]
1800-1810	5,641	2,421	16,458	24,520	291.76%
1810-1820	24,520	10,977	111,681	147,178	455.47
1820-1830	147,178	71,723	124,130	343,031	84.34
1830-1840	343,031	155,691	187,144	685,866	54.56
1840-1850	685,866	293,470	9,080	988,416	1.32
1850-1860	988,416	402,161	− 40,149	1,350,428	− 4.06

[+] Net migration divided by beginning population.
* Decennial results are not strictly comparable owing to boundary changes.

Table IV

The Components of Population Changes, Illinois, 1810-1860*

Decade	Beginning Population	Natural Increase	Net Migration	End Population	Migration Rate[+]
1810-1820	12,282	5,284	37,645	55,211	306.51%
1820-1830	55,211	27,277	74,957	157,445	135.76
1830-1840	157,445	72,870	245,868	476,183	156.16
1840-1850	476,183	203,750	171,537	851,470	36.02
1850-1860	851,470	306,950	553,531	1,711,951	65.01

[+] Net migration divided by beginning population.
* Decennial results are not strictly comparable owing to boundary changes.

Table V

The Components of Population Change, Michigan, 1810-1860*

Decade	Beginning Population	Natural Increase	Net Migration	End Population	Migration Rate[+]
1810-1820	4,762	1,667	2,467	8,896	51.81%
1820-1830	8,896	3,087	19,656	31,639	220.95
1830-1840	31,639	10,679	169,949	212,267	537.15
1840-1850	212,267	63,344	122,043	397,654	57.49
1850-1860	397,654	111,222	240,237	749,113	60.41

[+] Net migration divided by beginning population.
* Decennial results are not strictly comparable owing to boundary changes.

Table VI

The Components of Population Change,
Wisconsin, 1840-1860*

Decade	Beginning Population	Natural Increase	Net Migration	End Population	Migration Rate˙
1840-1850	30,945	9,185	265,261	305,391	857.20%
1850-1860	305,391	102,517	367,973	775,881	120.49

˙ Net migration divided by beginning population.
* Decennial results are not strictly comparable owing to boundary changes.

The interstate comparisons dramatically illustrate the westward nature of American population movement. Ohio, the oldest Old Northwest state, had its greatest amount of positive net migration in the 1810-1820 decade; its neighbor to the west, Indiana, experienced peak net migration in the 1830's, while Illinois' net migration was greatest in the 1850's. Interestingly, the peak in net migration in both Indiana and Illinois came twenty years later than the state directly to the east. The pattern in the upper Northwest states, Michigan and Wisconsin, was different, reflecting the relative lateness of the settlement of those states. Both states reached the maximum amount of net migration in the 1850's. By the Fifties, the *rate* of net migration of Wisconsin was the greatest for the entire Old Northwest, while in terms of absolute numbers the migration was second only to Illinois.

The growing maturity of the region is reflected in the fact that Ohio became a net exporter of human resources after 1840, followed in the 1850's by Indiana. By the Fifties, negative net migration resulted in Ohio's population growth being reduced more than 40 per cent from that caused by natural increase. In one half of a century, Ohio had moved from being a raw frontier state to being a mature "older" area which was losing population to newer areas to the west.

Immigration

Up to this point, nothing has been said about immigration. As estimated, net migration includes both domestic and international in and out-migration. What proportion of the tremendous amount of net migration was the result of international immigration?

Unfortunately, that question is an extremely difficult one to answer for the early part of the period, owing to a paucity of data. Before 1850, the only relevant data available are for the total number of immigrant arrivals; even this information is not available before 1820. Except for New York Port after 1847, the intended destination of arriving immigrants was not recorded. In 1850 and 1860, however, nativity information from the Censuses gives us some idea of the importance of immigration in the 1850's. We estimated net migration of the foreign born, noting that net migration equaled the increase in the foreign born population in the Old Northwest in the 1850's, plus that proportion of 1850 foreign born population that died (we assumed 20 per cent died, or an annual mortality rate of about twenty-two per thousand population). The results are presented in Table VII.

Table VII

Native and Foreign Net Migration,
Old Northwest, 1850-60

State	Total Population Increase	Natural Increase	Native Net Migration	Net Migration of Foreign Born
Ohio	359,102	633,358	-427,971	153,695
Indiana	362,012	402,161	-113,975	73,826
Illinois	860,481	306,950	318,402	235,129
Michigan	351,459	111,222	134,906	105,331
Wisconsin	470,490	102,517	189,428	178,545
Old Northwest	2,403,624	1,556,208	100,890	746,526

165

The massive amount of net migration from other countries is estimated to have accounted for 88 per cent of the total net migration in the Old Northwest in the 1850's. However, in no state experiencing positive net migration did this immigration account for as much as 50 per cent of the total (it amounted to 40 to 50 per cent in the three states with positive net migration). This seeming contradiction is explained by the fact that there was fairly substantial positive net migration of foreign born in Ohio and Indiana, both of which had substantial net outflows of native born. All in all, though, the unprecedented absolute amount of net migration recorded in the 1850's was very largely due to immigration. Native net migration, in fact, was probably at the lowest level for any period after 1800 (more about that later).

Estimating the amount of foreign net migration before 1850 is a trickier proposition, and one subject to considerable error. Nonetheless, we have estimated the foreign born population of the Old Northwest in 1840 at 203,172, compared with 550,837 in 1850 and 1,197,198 in 1860. Our estimate is based on two major assumptions: the ratio of the increase in the foreign born population of the United States to the number of immigrant arrivals was the same in the 1840's as the 1850's, and that the ratio of the per cent increase in the foreign born population in the Old Northwest to that increase for the United States was the same in the 1840's as in the 1850's. Using the same procedure as before, we estimate that net foreign migration in the 1840's was 388,299 in the Old Northwest. Since we previously estimated total net migration to have been 491,159, this implies that native net migration was only 102,860, only slightly greater than for the 1850's. Again it appears that immigration accounted for the bulk (79 per cent) of total net migration in the Old Northwest.

Any estimate of the importance of immigration in the Old Northwest before 1840 would be little more than a guess. Fortunately, the national statistics of immigrant arrivals suggests that immigration was comparatively unimportant before that date. We would guess that there were perhaps 75,000 foreign born in the Old Northwest in 1830, suggesting that perhaps 140,000 of the total net migration of 853,000 in the 1830's was attributed to immigration, or about 16 to 17 per cent.

In summary, there seems to have been a tendency for native net migration to decline over time as the Old Northwest became more settled. Not only did in-migration probably decline somewhat, but out-migration from the region increased substantially. This absolute decline in native net migration was completely offset, however, by a substantial influx of foreign born. Francis A. Walker may have been thinking in part of this region when he hypothesized that increases in the foreign born population lead to a decline in the increase in the native born. There is nothing in this analysis, of course, that proves that natives were "pushed" west by the immigrant influx.

II. CAUSES OF MIGRATION

What were the causes of migration into the Old Northwest? In earlier studies, we have argued that both American interstate migration and immigration to the United States have been largely shaped by economic opportunity.[5] Specifically, with respect to interstate internal migration, we have demonstrated, using a log-linear multiple regression model, that migrants, *ceteris paribus*, tended to move to areas with higher levels of per capita income and more jobs, and that they preferred, *ceteris paribus*, to move short distances (in order to avoid movement costs). Also, migrants preferred to move, *ceteris paribus*, to areas with similar physical and cultural climates and to less congested areas, presumably because land is more readily available (cheaper) in these areas. Using 1850 Census data, we generally observed statistically significant relationships between each of these factors and migration, although the relationship between migration and income was somewhat weak, probably in part because of the data used (we did not have the benefit of Richard Easterlin's price differential adjustments included in this volume). Even so, the mean elasticity of migration with respect to per capita income was estimated to be nearly unity (0.89). The evidence is rather strong, then, that migrants were responding to economic opportunities in making their moves.

An interesting aspect of this earlier study was the differential behaviorial responses of migrants born in different regions. In particular, migrants born in the Old Northwest appeared much more sensitive to economic opportunities, in particular to per capita income differentials, in making their location decisions than persons from any other region. Moreover, within the Old Northwest, migrants from the "newer" states seemed more responsive to income differentials (though not to wealth differentials) than those from the old states of Ohio and Indiana (Table VIII). This may suggest that the "frontier man" was the ultimate maximizer.

Table VIII

Elasticity of Migration with Respect to
Per Capita Income and Wealth, 1850

State of Birth	Income Elasticity'	Wealth Elasticity'
Ohio	0.31	4.80**
Indiana	0.45	1.55**
Illinois	1.58*	4.24**
Michigan	3.24**	3.18**
Wisconsin	2.44**	3.50**
Old Northwest (weighted state means)	1.58	3.19
United States (weighted state means)	0.89	2.19

' Per capita income estimates of Richard Easterlin for 1840 were used, as well as per capita wealth estimates for 1860 calculated by us from census real and personal property data.

Not only were those migrants born in the Old Northwest more sensitive to income differentials, they were also more affected by the costs associated with migration, as measured by distance. We estimated the mean elasticity of migration with respect to distance for persons born in the Old Northwest to have been –2.79, compared with –1.84 for the nation as a whole. This might partly reflect the poorer transportation network in the Old Northwest and that region's position on the western frontier.

All in all, the citizens of the Old Northwest resembled the economist's conceptualization of "economic man" even more than do Americans in general. It is important to note here that the bulk of the out-migration recorded in this study for persons born in the Old Northwest actually took place within the region. For example, of the 1,514,885 persons born in Ohio and living in the United States in 1850, 295,453 (19 per cent) had left that state, but 210,491 (71 per cent of the migrants) had moved to other states in the Old Northwest. Only in Illinois, which had comparatively few out-migrants, did a substantial majority of these migrants leave the Old Northwest. Thus, much of this searching for economic opportunity was taking place within the confines of the region.

A Closer Perspective

To gain somewhat greater insight into migration in the Old Northwest, we looked at the relationship between the migrant status of an unbiased sample of 2,437 persons living in the lower Old Northwest and certain characteristics of those individuals or the area (county) in which they were residing in 1860.[6] The sample was based on the manuscript census returns for 1860 for the states of Ohio, Indiana, and Illinois. Only heads of households were included in the sample. Since the only migration information given was the state or nation of birth, we were investigating the "lifetime" or "permanent" migration patterns of an essentially adult population. Persons who had made an interstate migration only to return to the state of birth are recorded as "non-migrants". In the case of some migrants, the interstate migration occurred well before 1860 (the region's most famous person, Abraham Lincoln, made his interstate move to Illinois in two steps, the last of which was in 1830).

Some basic characteristics of the sample population and the areas in which they lived are indicated in Table IX. The importance of migration in the development of the lower Old Northwest is strikingly illustrated. Even in the oldest, most "mature" state, Ohio, fewer than 30 per cent of the heads of household were born in that state. In Illinois, only *eight* per cent of household heads were born in that state. In both Ohio and Illinois, there were more heads of households born in other *countries* than in the state of residence in 1860. This certainly tends to refute the impression given by some modern commentators, such as Alvin Toffler, that the nomadic traits of the American population are a fairly recent development.[7]

Table IX

Characteristics of Sample of
2,437 Household Heads, 1860

Characteristic	Three States	Ohio	Indiana	Illinois
Sample Size	2,437	1,053	612	772
Per cent Migrants	78.99	70.37	77.29	92.10
Per cent Native Born Migrants	52.19	40.55	59.48	62.31
Per cent Foreign Born Migrants	26.80	29.82	17.81	29.79
Per cent Non-Migrants	21.01	29.63	22.71	7.90
Mean Age	40.58	41.66	39.63	39.62
Per cent Male	93.60	92.78	93.63	94.69
Per cent in Farming	52.98	45.49	61.93	56.09
Mean Real Property	$2211	$2171	$2231	$2251
Mean Personal Property	$ 741	$ 731	$ 652	$ 824
Total Mean Property	$2952	$2902	$2883	$3075
Percent Living in Poor Soil Area (terminal morraine)	17.03	22.13	22.55	5.70
Percent of 1910 Improved Land Developed	63.01	73.28	54.90	55.41

Some other characteristics of the sample are worth noting. The average head of household was rather young (around forty) with that average falling a bit as one progresses westward. Also, the proportion of the sample engaged in agriculture becomes greater as one progresses westward, although Illinois' proportion is slightly less than Indiana's, presumably reflecting the comparative advantage the newer states had in land intensive pursuits. The average wealth figure of nearly $3,000 is similar for all three states. Interestingly, the average wealth figure was actually highest in the newest state, with the youngest population, Illinois. Using 1910 as a base year when the cultivation of land (as measured by "improved acres") was about at its maximum in the region, we can estimate the proportion of arable agricultural land that was improved (or, conversely, that was still unimproved) in 1860. The evidence is that a much smaller proportion of potentially improved arable land was unimproved in Ohio in 1860 (25 per cent) than in either Indiana or Illinois (45 per cent).

Finally, the geological impact of the Ice Age on soil quality is considered by noting the proportion of the population living below or outside the terminal moraine, a region that includes much of southern Ohio, Indiana, and a few counties in southern and extreme northwestern Illinois. As can be seen, a much smaller proportion of the Illinois sample resided in this geologically disadvantaged area.

The Determination of Migrant Status

What impact did any of these factors have on the migrant status of the population of these states? Using multiple regression analysis, we tried to "explain" the migrant status of the population in terms of seven factors: age, sex, occupation (whether the sampled person was a farmer or not), the longitude of the county of residence in 1860 (a measure of "Westwardness"), whether the residence was located outside the terminal moraine, the proportion of "free" land available in the county of residence (measured by the difference between 1860 and 1910 improved acres), and total wealth (real and personal property). "Migrant status" was simply measured by a dummy variable that took the value of zero for persons living in the state of birth and a value of one for all others (migrants). Dummy variables were similarly constructed to measure sex and occupational status. The results are presented in Table X.

Table X

Relationship Between Migrant Status and Other Factors,
Old Northwest, 1860

Variable	Coefficient	Statistical Significance
Age	.00996	Significant at 1% level.
Sex (0=female; 1=male)	.00806	Not significant.
Occupation (0=non-farmer; 1=farmer)	−.10402	Significant at 1% level.
Longitude	.02990	Significant at 1% level.
Soil quality (terminal morraine)	−.13899	Significant at 1% level.
Land availability	−.03044	Not significant.
Wealth	−.00000	Not significant.

R=.41   F-ratio:68.530
DF = 2429

The results suggest that older heads of households were more likely to have migrated, *ceteris paribus*, than younger ones, which is not surprising since older persons had a longer time span to make an interstate move. The positive sign on the sex variable suggests that male heads of household were more likely to migrate, but the results are not statistically significant. The negative coefficient on the occupation variable suggests that *migrants were less likely*, other factors equal, *to be farmers than non-migrants*. The result is highly significant in a statistical sense. The coefficients suggests that, controlling for other factors, for a group of one hundred migrants there would typically be about ten fewer farmers than in a comparable group of non-migrants. The newer settlers, then, were not all agriculturists who turned to the older, established population for their non-agricultural needs (indeed, the reverse appears to be closer to the truth).

The westward nature of American migration is indicated by the longitude variable. Each degree further west one went, the proportion of migrant heads of household increased by almost 3 per cent. *Ceteris paribus*, within any group of one hundred household heads living on the 88th meridian (Illinois), one would typically find fifteen more migrants than in a group of the same size living on the 83rd meridian (Ohio).

The terminal moraine variable works extremely well, and suggests that migrants tended to avoid those "geologically disadvantaged" counties with poor soil quality —counties in the Southern portion of the three states. Specifically, for every one hundred heads of household in these poor soil counties, there were typically fourteen fewer migrants than among one hundred heads of household outside these counties. Thus the rather sharp regional disparity observed today between the southern and the northern and central parts of these states appears to have been developing before 1860, and may well at least in part be a result of a geological phenomenon that had an impact on earning capacity in agriculture. The relative poverty of southern Ohio, Indiana, and Illinois may well have predated the demise of coal mining in those regions.

The results suggest, somewhat surprisngly, no statistically significant relationship between land availability and migration, although the importance of the land factor has already been recorded in the terminal moraine variable described above. Likewise, migrants tended to be neither more wealthy or less wealthy than non-migrants. One might interpret this as supporting the contention that the tremendous socioeconomic mobility and opportunities of a quasi-frontier society permitted newcomers to achieve economic equality with established residents. The evidence is much too sketchy in our judgment, however, to draw that conclusion.

The basic sample was disaggregated by state and the same analysis applied, with generally similar results. The "terminal moraine" factor was not significant in Illinois, perhaps reflecting the relatively small land area in that state that was "geologically disadvantaged". Just as interesting, the tendency of migrants to be relatively less involved in agriculture declines as one moves west (the coefficient is –.15 for Ohio, –.10 for Indiana, and –.04 for Illinois, and in the latter case is significant at only the 10 per cent level). Migrants to Illinois, then, were relatively more agriculturally oriented than those living to the immediate east.

III. Conclusions

The massive migration of human resources into the Old Northwest after 1800 may well be both the cause and the effect of that region's economic vitality. The migrants seemed to be acutely aware of economic opportunities and strove to maximize their economic advantage. Within the lower Old Northwest, they avoided the southern counties with poorer soils and also tended to enter nonagricultural pursuits, which even then seemed to offer higher rewards. The picture that emerges is that resources were allocated efficiently in the Old Northwest—probably more so than in the rest of the nation during this period. This probably contributed significantly to the observed relatively high rate of economic growth of the East Central states discussed in the introduction to this book. In any case, there is little question that migration resulted in the region moving from being the extreme western frontier to being the Heartland of America—a position it still holds.

APPENDIX

The procedure used for estimating natural population increase in the various states was as follows: the national

174

decennial rate of natural increase was obtained by calculating the per cent population change by decades. From 1850 to 1860, an adjustment for immigration was made by noting the change in the foreign born population. The foreign born population for 1820, 1830, and 1840 was estimated by assuming that the foreign born population increased by 72 per cent of the immigrant arrivals during the relevant decade. The statistic (.72) was the ratio of the change in foreign born population, 1850 to 1860, to immigrant arrivals in that period. We assumed the increase in the foreign born before 1820 to be 40,000 in the 1790's, 60,000 in the decade from 1800 to 1810, and 80,000 in the 1810-20 period.

To calculate a state's (or the Old Northwest's) deviation from the national rate of natural increase, we estimated the relevant birth rate by multiplying: $\dfrac{\text{state's refined child ratio}}{\text{U.S. refined child ratio}}$ × national crude birth rate (estimated). The national (also the state's) death rate was then subtracted to obtain population increase. The estimates of national demographic rates used were: birth rates of 50 per 1000 for the period 1800 to 1820, 45 per 1000 for the period 1820 to 1850, and 40 per 1000 during the 1850's; the death rate was assumed to be 24 per 1000 in the period 1800 to 1820, 20 per 1000 in the period 1820 to 1850, and 18 per 1000 in the 1850's.

Let us illustrate by estimating national increase in Indiana in the 1840's. The national rate of natural increase was calculated as described above. The refined child ratio for Indiana was 1846, compared with a national figure of 1452. The refined child ratio of Indiana was 1.272 that of the U. S. Multiplying that times an estimated U. S. birth rate of 45 gives us an estimated birth rate in Indiana of 57.246. Subtracting the death rate of 20 yields us an increase of 37.246, compared with an estimated national figure of 25. Dividing 37.246 by 25 yields a 49 per cent higher rate of increase in Indiana. Had Indiana grown at the national rate, natural increase would have been 196,981. Since we estimated natural increase to be 49 per cent greater in Indiana, we multiplied 196,981 × 1.49 to yield our estimate of 293,470.

Using quite different techniques, Stanley Lebergott obtained some estimates for four of the states for some of the decades in question. His estimates, expressed as migration *rates* based on mid-decade population, may be found in his "Migration Within the United States, 1800-1960: Some New Estimates," *Journal of Economic History*, December, 1970, 30:839-847.

* The authors express their deep appreciation to David C. Stockdale who performed the data processing chores with his usual high level of competence. All computations were performed at the Ohio University Academic Computer Center.

1. This statement may not be true for long. The 1970 geographic center was in St. Clair County, Illinois, in the St. Louis (Missouri) metropolitan area.

2. The "refined child ratio" statistics used were compiled by Yasukichi Yasuba, *Birth Rates of the White Population in the United States, 1800-1860* (Baltimore: Johns Hopkins Press, 1962).

3. As indicated in the 1850 and 1860 censuses of population. All subsequently cited migration statistics are derived from the decennial censuses.

4. For example, see Richard C. Wade, *The Urban Frontier* (Cambridge: Harvard University Press, 1959), for a good account of the panic of 1819 on the emerging western cities.

5. See for example, our "Mobility of Native Americans," *Journal of Economic History*, September, 1971, 31:613-649, and our "Emigration from the United Kingdom to the United States, 1860-1913," *Journal of Economic History*, December, 1971, 31:885-97.

6. We used microfilms of the manuscript census material. Observations were chosen by making five cranks of the microfilm reader and choosing a name. For the first observation, the first head of household on the page was taken. For subsequent observations, we took the second, third, fourth, etc., head of household on each manuscript page. Since a sample geographically distributed according to the actual distribution was desired, a purely random sampling technique was not used.

7. See for example, Toffler's *Future Shock* (New York: Random House, 1970).

VII

INDIVIDUAL WEALTH IN OHIO IN 1860

David Klingaman

Ohio University

The Ordinance of 1787 provided for the organization of the Northwest Territory on the land lying east of the Mississippi River and north of the Ohio River. Eventually this region became the states of Ohio, Indiana, Illinois, Michigan, and Wisconsin. In making the cession of her western lands to the federal government, Connecticut had reserved a strip of land lying between the forty-first parallel and Lake Erie. It extended 120 miles westward from the Pennsylvania line and was known as the Western Reserve. By 1795 the western portion had been given away, and the rest had been sold to thirty-five buyers at a price of $1,200,000. The Connecticut Land Company was formed to assist in the survey and resale venture, and the region rapidly increased in population from fifteen families in 1798 to over thirteen hundred persons two years later. Following Cleveland in 1796, Youngstown was founded in 1798 and Warren in 1799. Statehood came in 1803, and northeastern Ohio gradually became more populous as settlers poured in from New England and the Middle Atlantic States. The work on the Ohio Canal to connect Cleveland and Portsmouth on the Ohio River was begun in 1825, and about this time the town of Akron was founded along the proposed route. Youngstown, Warren, and Akron, then, were well settled population areas before the Civil War era.

Information on wealth held by individuals as long ago as 1860 is especially valuable to the economic historian, since income data are generally not available. In lieu of both income and wealth information, data on wealth alone provide a reasonably good basis for appraising the material well-being of the individuals owning that wealth. It is true that people with large holdings of wealth occasionally have low incomes, as when wealth is inherited, and the reverse is also true in some cases. Generally speaking, however, a high stock of wealth is associated with a high flow of income; thus the wealth of individuals is a rough guide to their incomes as well. The *Eighth Census of the United States*, taken in 1860, offers an unusual opportunity to examine how individuals fared in the economy more than one hundred years ago. This is possible because the census-takers asked each person not only his age, occupation, and nativity but also the value of his holdings of real estate and personal estate. Personal estate meant the value of any of his possessions not included in the category of real estate. Such assets as money, bonds, livestock, jewelry, and furniture were included as personal wealth—probably only clothing was excluded from consideration. At least in part, the real and personal wealth data were probably a total before the subtraction of debt. The census records were not to be made public, and the marshals of the census were forbidden to divulge their findings. Separate checks indicate that the wealth declarations were fairly reliable. In 1940 the federal government made the census returns through 1880 available for purposes of historical research, and the source for this study is the microfilms of the original census sheets for 1860.

This paper measures the amounts and distribution of wealth held by individuals in northeastern Ohio in 1860. The computations in Tables 1 through 6 were made from the census returns of the three counties of Mahoning, Summit, and Trumbull. In each of these counties, the largest town and a representative rural township were studied: Youngstown village and Canfield township; Akron village and Tallmadge township; and Warren village and Brookfield township. The three towns are at most fifty miles apart, and the township selected in each county is within a few miles of the village selected for that county. Warren, Youngstown, and Akron were selected for a study of wealth distribution because they were located in populous and industrial northeastern Ohio, were settled relatively early in the Old Northwest, and were, therefore, established population centers before 1860. In addition, the towns had a representative industrial base in 1860. Akron was primarily a flour and meal manufacturing center along the Ohio Canal. Warren was much more balanced: pig, bar, and sheet iron; flour and meal; and lumber. Youngstown, an incipient steel center, was heavily engaged in producing pig iron, followed in importance by coal products, flour and meal, and nail production.[1]

Because nearly all of the wealth in 1860 was owned by adult males, the focus of this study is on males twenty years of age and older. Table 1 gives the population of the six areas, the number of adult males, and the percentage of those males born in Ohio and in foreign countries. Note that the percentage of foreign-born was highest in the towns, especially in Akron and Youngstown. Each of the townships had a population of slightly more than one thousand persons. Akron was the largest town with nearly thirty-five hundred inhabitants, and Warren was the smallest with approximately twenty-four hundred inhabitants.

Table 2 shows the average value of real estate and personal estate owned by adult males in six areas of north-

179

eastern Ohio in 1860. The relatively high average wealth of the Warren resident is noticeable. The average adult male in Warren, who had wealth of approximately $3000, was nearly three times as well off as his counterpart in Akron and Youngstown. It is not clear why this great disparity existed. Warren is only about fifteen miles from Youngstown, and both towns were settled at approximately the same time. However, Warren was the county

Table 1

Population, Number of Males Twenty and Over, and
Composition According to Ohio Born and Foreign
Born in the Representative Areas in 1860

Township or Village	Township or Village Population	Males Twenty and Over		
		Number Present	Percentage Ohio-Born	Percentage Foreign-Born
Akron	3485	864	23.9	44.9
Tallmadge	1086	295	44.4	27.1
Warren	2399	670	43.3	25.2
Brookfield	1204	321	42.4	17.8
Youngstown	2755	792	21.5	36.4
Canfield	1091	296	43.9	17.9

Source: U. S. Bureau of the Census, Population, Schedule 1, *Eighth Census of the United States: 1860.*

Table 2

Average Wealth of All Males Twenty and Over
in the Representative Areas in 1860

Township or Village	Average Real Wealth	Average Personal Wealth	Average Total Wealth
Akron	$ 883	$ 344	$1,177
Tallmadge	1,808	365	2,173
Warren	1,762	1,249	3,011
Brookfield	1,209	466	1,675
Youngstown	654	366	1,019
Canfield	1,520	379	1,899

Source: Schedule 1, *Eighth Census of the United States.*
Note: Akron and Youngstown were sampled 50%; the rest were complete enumerations.

seat of Trumbull county, which was the first county organized in the Western Reserve and the seventh in the state. Originally Trumbull contained twenty-five townships, and it was not until 1846 that Mahoning county was formed from part of Trumbull county.[2] Thus Warren was for nearly fifty years the seat of the county which included Youngstown, and for this reason it may well have attracted wealthier and more established families. For example, Warren had a higher percentage of its population engaged in professional occupations and a lower percentage engaged in laboring occupations than either Akron or Youngstown.[3] Another reason for the high wealth among Warren residents is that Warren had a lower percentage of foreign-born than did Akron and Youngstown. As will be seen, foreign-born males had much less wealth than did native-born males. Whatever the causes, Warren had much richer families than did Youngstown or Akron, and the contrast of Warren with the other two towns must have been noticeable to the traveler of the day.

The average wealth of the rural adult male was nearly $2,000 and considerably exceeded that of the average adult male in Youngstown or Akron. It was not personal wealth but real estate wealth that made for this disparity. Most of the farmers owned some land and buildings; the average rural male had about $1,500 worth of such property. Only the inhabitants of Warren owned that much real property on the average; in Akron and Youngstown $600 to $800 was the average amount of real estate owned. Among the rural townships, Tallmadge residents were relatively wealthier. The explanation appears to lie in the land values in Tallmadge and in the quantity of agricultural implements owned by the farmers. In Trumbull and Mahoning counties the average cash value of farms per acre was $29 and $38 respectively. In contrast, Summit county had land values which averaged $41 per acre. In addition, the value of agricultural implements per farm in Summit county was approximately $150, more than twice that in Mahoning and

Trumbull counties.[4] It is not clear why the Tallmadge farmers were wealthier than the farmers in the other two townships although the better transport network (rail and canal) in Summit county may have been partly responsible.[5] Farms within easy hauling distance of a railroad or a canal would be in a position to receive higher profits on their crops since transport costs would be less. The consequence of this would be higher land values on farms located nearer to rails or canals. Such factors are especially relevant for comparisons between Tallmadge and Brookfield townships.

The average wealth of individuals in the six geographic areas implies nothing about the inequality of wealth holdings within each village or township. The concept of average wealth in itself does not mean much if most of the people were either rich or poor. Table 3 provides some information on the question of inequality by showing what per cent of the total wealth in each area was held by the richest one-tenth of the adult males. In Youngstown, where wealth was distributed more unequally than in any other area, the top 10 per cent owned 72.4 per cent of the wealth; the remaining 90 per cent of the adult males owned the other 27.6 per cent of the total wealth. In order to be included in the top 10 per cent of the wealth in Youngstown, it was necessary for a person to hold at least $2,500, not a very high figure compared to that of Warren or the three rural townships. The inequality among wealth-holders in Youngstown was only slightly greater than that prevailing in Akron. The big difference is found between Warren and the other two towns. The richest 10 per cent owned a smaller fraction of the total wealth in Warren than in the other two towns, and the lower bound, or wealth limit, of the richest 10 per cent class was much higher in Warren than in Akron and Youngstown. This meant, in effect, that while the rich were richer in Warren than they were in Akron or Youngstown, the lowest 90 per cent of the wealthholders in Warren were considerably better off than their counterparts in Akron and Youngstown. In the rural townships,

182

the richest 10 per cent held roughly 45 to 50 per cent of all the wealth, indicating that there was much less inequality in the rural areas than in the towns. In addition, the lower bound of the top 10 per cent of the wealthholders was much higher in the rural townships than in either Akron or Youngstown.

Table 3

Total Real and Personal Wealth Held by the Richest 10
Per Cent of All Males Twenty and Over

Township or Village	Total Wealth of Top 10 Per cent	As Per Cent of Total Wealth Held by All Individuals	Lower Bound of the Top 10 Per Cent Class
Akron	$ 836,900	67.9	$3,000
Tallmadge	353,000	52.0	7,000
Warren	1,435,462	62.5	8,000
Brookfield	266,093	46.9	5,300
Youngstown	762,400	72.4	2,500
Canfield	274,200	45.7	5,850

Source: Schedule 1, *Eighth Census of the United States.*
Note: Women were also included in the richest 10 per cent if they held wealth at least equal to the lower bound. The number of women included is a negligible percentage of the total number.

Professor Lee Soltow has estimated that in the northern United States the richest one-tenth of the adult males owned about two-thirds of all the wealth.[6] Inequality was much higher in ten large northern cities. Approximately 90 per cent of total wealth was owned by the upper 10 per cent.[7] A simple unweighted average of the six areas studied in Ohio in the present study indicates that the richest one-tenth had approximately six-tenths of the total wealth. The inequality of wealth has probably not decreased much since 1860. Presently, the richest one-tenth of individuals owns nearly two-thirds of the total wealth.

An important factor responsible for both the generally lower wealth and the higher inequality of wealth between the towns and the rural areas was the higher proportion of foreign-born in the towns. These were persons who had not yet had time to accumulate wealth. Not having the money necessary to purchase a farm, they moved to the towns and sold their services. In Youngstown the average wealth of the foreign-born adult male was slightly under $600, compared to about $1,250 for the native-born adult male. The same pattern seemed to hold for the rural areas. In Brookfield the foreign-born person had wealth of about $950 compared to approximately $1,830 for the native-born person.[8] This information is provided in Table 4. It is interesting that although the foreign-born male was about one-half as rich as the native male, both were about equally likely to own *some* wealth. In the towns, the foreign-born male actually was more likely to hold some wealth than the native male. This was probably true because the young foreign-born immigrant required minimal liquid wealth for initial expenses associated with the new life. The general inequality of wealth which prevailed in all the areas studied is underlined by the fact that only about one-half of the adult males owned wealth of any kind.

Table 4

Average Wealth of Males Twenty and Over
and the Percentage Holding Wealth for
Foreign-Born and Native Americans in 1860

Township or Village	Average Wealth of Foreign-born	Percentage of Foreign-born Having Wealth	Average Wealth of Native-born	Percentage of Native-born Having Wealth
Akron	$811	59	$1,475	48
Youngstown	598	68	1,259	51
Brookfield	954	40	1,831	52

Source: Schedule 1, *Eighth Census of the United States.*

An interesting and unusual breakdown of individual wealth is possible, based on classification according to occupation. Table 5 reveals that the professional person was fairly well off in all three towns, having average wealth of about $6,000 per adult male. In stark contrast, laborers in the three towns had only about $275 per adult male. Except for Warren, farmers had less wealth than professionals but generally more than any other occupation group. Quite a number of wealthy farmers resided in Warren village, but whether they were active farmers or retired landowners is not clear. The average wealth of merchants in the three towns displays a wide disparity, ranging from approximately $5,500 in Warren to only $1,500 in Akron. Skilled workers had wealth of approximately $800 although there was considerable variation among the six locations.

Table 5

Average Wealth of Males Twenty and Over
by Occupational Categories in 1860

Occupation[a]	Akron	Tallmadge	Warren	Brookfield	Youngstown	Canfield
Professional	$5,302	$ -	$6,802	$ -	$5,989	$ -
Skilled	906	438	1,364	788	452	877
Merchants	1,516	-	5,559	-	3,612	-
Farmers	-	4,092	14,706	2,913	-	3,992
Laborers	278	-	206	-	341	433

[a]Professional includes: doctors, lawyers, accountants, editors, publishers, printers, and teachers. Skilled includes: craftsmen, machinists, coopers, masons, builders, moulders, carpenters, blacksmiths, tanners, painters, plasterers, tailors, and milliners. Merchants include: merchants and millers. Farmers include: farm proprietors. Laborers include: laborers, servants, domestics, teamsters, timers, miners, coal diggers, boatmen, and draymen.

Source: Schedule 1, *Eighth Census of the United States: 1860.*

Note: Hyphens indicate that the number of observations was too few to provide meaningful averages.

After 1860 the only other census to record total wealth held by individuals was that of 1870. Because of the taxes instituted during the Civil War, respondents to the 1870 census may have been circumspect in their declarations of wealth. The extent to which the 1870 census on individual wealth may be biased to the low side is not known. It seems likely that any understatement of wealth is apt to have been comparatively small although one can simply not be sure about this. Individual wealth in Warren village and

185

Brookfield township in 1870 was computed, and the results shown in Table 6 disclose a pronounced increase in nominal wealth in Warren but a much smaller increase in Brookfield. In fact there was a decline in wealth in Brookfield when

Table 6

Comparison of Individual Wealth in 1860 and 1870 in Warren Village and Brookfield Township in Current Dollars

Category of Wealth	Warren	Brookfield
Real Wealth in 1860	$1,762	$1,209
Real Wealth in 1870	3,061	1,682
Personal Wealth in 1860	1,249	466
Personal Wealth in 1870	1,829	328
Total Wealth in 1860	3,011	1,675
Total Wealth in 1870	4,890	2,010

Source: Schedule 1, *Eighth Census of the United States* and *Ninth Census of the United States*.
Note: The 1870 data is based on a 50 per cent sample.

account is taken of the approximately 40 per cent rise in the consumer price index between 1860 and 1870.[9] With the value of the dollar shrinking by two-fifths, the real percentage increase in adult male wealth in Warren would be 16 per cent between 1860 and 1870 and a negative 14 per cent in Brookfield.

In the case of Brookfield, average real estate holdings of males twenty and over remained unchanged in dollars of constant purchasing power while there was a substantial decline in personal wealth. Much of this can be explained by the influx of immigrants. Brookfield's population more than doubled over this decade and the percentage of foreign-born rose from about 18 per cent to nearly 38 per cent. These new immigrants, many of whom were from Wales, found employment principally in the newly developed coal mines of the township. Wages were low, and the opportunity to acquire wealth in such a short span of time was virtually nil. What happened in Brookfield was that the farmers, mechanics, and merchants continued to accumulate wealth slowly while the nearly eight hundred new foreign-born arrivals pulled the average wealth down. This must have been a typical experience for rural areas where coal was available and where there were nearby industrial users, e.g., in this case Warren and Youngstown. The population of Warren grew substantially during the Civil War decade, rising from 2,400 to 3,500 persons. There were no structural changes in either population or occupations comparable to that in nearby Brookfield township. Taken together, Warren village and Brookfield township exhibited a growth of total individual wealth in real terms of less than 10 per cent for the decade.

A rough approximation is that the consumer price level sextupled between 1860 and today (1975), so that one dollar in 1860 would have the purchasing power of six dollars today.[10] A simple unweighted average of the six areas in Table 2 yields an average wealth of about $1,825 per adult male. Although intertemporal comparisons of this magnitude can be very deceptive, this amount of wealth in 1860 might be equivalent to $10,950 today.

An interesting sample from the whole Ohio population was taken by Professors Richard Vedder and Lowell Gallaway. A sample of size 1,053 was taken from Schedule 1 of the 1860 Population Census. Their results are particularly interesting because the sample consisted exclusively of heads of households. Of those sampled, approximately 45 per cent were farmers, 30 per cent were foreign-born, and 93 per cent were males. Average head of household wealth was approximately $2,900. This consisted of $2,171 of real wealth and $731 of personal wealth. One would expect household heads to be richer than adult males because the former would tend to be older and more established. Roughly speaking, household heads were probably about $1,100 richer than the average adult male.

187

Using the $2,900 wealth figure for heads of households, it is feasible to make a crude comparison between wealth in 1860 in Ohio and wealth in recent times in the United States. A Federal Reserve survey conducted in 1963 sampled consumer units as defined by the Census Bureau. Each group of two or more persons related by blood, marriage, or adoption, and living together, as well as each individual not living with relatives, is defined as a consumer unit. This classification seems fairly close to the head of household classification in the sample for 1860. It was estimated that the average wealth of consumer units in December, 1962, was approximately $37,000 in 1975 dollars.[11] If one inflates the 1860 head of household wealth figure six times in order to approximate the value of 1860 wealth in 1975 dollars, the result is $17,400. One can speculate that average head of household wealth in 1860 in Ohio was approximately 47 per cent of that for consumer units in the United States in 1962. Obviously such a comparison should be treated with caution.

Measuring wealth increases across a great time span is a hazardous process, even when it is done much more carefully than is attempted here. It has become common to express wealth accumulation growth rates in very precise terms, and frequently the figures are used as a convenient proxy (often implied) for a growth in material welfare. Quite apart from the adequacy of the data on which the measures rest, wealth estimates may be unreliable as a measure of the real increase in command over goods and services. This can occur because price indices over so long a period are crude estimates of the actual cost-of-living changes. The result is that the "real" value of a dollar of wealth today versus the "real" value of a dollar of wealth long ago can only be very roughly approximated. Besides the dollar's changing value, changes in consumer tastes are also a factor of great importance to real wealth comparisons made between distant points in time. Hence, this study is useful mainly to provide a picture of individual wealth differences at a point in time between rural versus city people in the same county, among occupation categories in a single town, and among towns in proximity to each other.

A final note may help to set this study in perspective. In *Men and Wealth in the United States, 1850-1870*, Lee Soltow found average wealth for northern adult males to be $2,040.[12] Northeastern Ohio wealth was not quite that high. It may, however, have been slightly more equally distributed. This would be despite the fact that nearly half of the adult males had no wealth. Most of these were young men who had not yet had the time to accumulate. At least up to a point, the older the man the more likely he was to have wealth. Although the average young man or immigrant was apt to have little wealth, he could observe that wealth was an increasing function of time. Of course, the static wealth distribution of this study provides no insight into the question of opportunities. One needs generation transition matrices to determine whether opportunities existed. The paper by Soltow in this volume relates to this very question. The manifest accumulation of wealth with age may have tended to offset discontent arising from the considerable inequality that prevailed.

* I am indebted to the Earhart Foundation for financial assistance during the summer of 1972. For help in data gathering, I am indebted to Mr. Willis Sommers.

1. U. S. Bureau of the Census, *Eighth Census of the United States: 1860, Manufactures*, pp. 464-65, 476-78.

2. Harriet Taylor Upton, *History of the Western Reserve*, I (Chicago: The Lewis Publishing Co.,1910), pp. 54, 59, 150.

3. About 10 per cent of the adult males in Warren listed occupations which fit the Professional category, compared to 7 and 3 per cent for Akron and Youngstown, respectively. Warren had nearly 15 per cent of its adult males engaged in laboring occupations compared to 21 per cent and 22.5 per cent for Akron and Youngstown. For Akron, Warren, and Youngstown the relevant percentages of the work force engaged in Skilled jobs was 35, 32, and 40 per cent. The relevant figure for Mer-

chants was 14, 15, and 8.7 per cent. Computed from Schedule 1, *Eighth Census of the United States.*

4. U. S. Bureau of the Census, *Eighth Census of the United States: 1860. Agriculture,* p. 116.

5. Albert Fishlow, *American Railroads and the Transformation of the Ante-Bellum Economy* (Cambridge: Harvard University Press, 1965), see maps 1 and 2.

6. Lee C. Soltow, *Men and Wealth in the United States, 1850-1870,* Forthcoming, Yale University Press.

7. Lee C. Soltow, "The Wealth, Income, and Social Class of Men in Large Northern Cities of the United States in 1860," Conference on Research in Income and Wealth, October 3-4, 1972, N.B.E.R., p. 6.

8. Computed from Schedule 1, *Eighth Census of the United States.*

9. U. S. Department of Labor, *Handbook of Labor Statistics, 1970,* p. 285.

10. *Ibid.*

11. Dorothy S. Projector and Gertrude S. Weiss, "Survey of Financial Characteristics of Consumers," Federal Reserve Technical Paper (Washington, D. C.: 1966), p. 110. The actual figure given there is $20,982 for December 31, 1962, but the Consumer Price Index is up about 75% since 1962.

12. Soltow, *Men and Wealth.*

VIII

THE GROWTH OF WEALTH
IN OHIO, 1800-1969

Lee Soltow

Ohio University

A description of the economic de-
velopment of Ohio should include a picture of long-run
growth of wealth or income in the state from the time of its
inception to the present. Fortunately, continuous yearly
series exist for Ohio in the form of aggregate property
valuation since 1826 and aggregate local and state property
taxes since 1800. These series will be combined in making
yearly per capita estimates of wealth from 1800-1969. The
clearly discernible trend when land was being settled
prior to 1855-60 will be contrasted to the trend since 1860
when there was relatively little more land available for
settlement. The per capita trend before 1860 is linear and
appears to have operated in a methodical fashion for many
decades. What might this mean to an average adult male
who was living in Ohio in this period? Would he experience
greater or smaller gains during the working years of his
life cycle than the long-run trend indicates? There certainly
are strong hints of what might have happened which may be
derived from the wealth-age patterns of individuals in 1850

and 1860. These are obtained from samples of the census of wealth of adult males in Ohio in this period. This paper is an analysis of the long-run trends and their ramifications in statistics of the censuses of wealth of individuals. It is often felt that little is known about economic growth before 1840 in the United States. This is because of the paucity of statistics for the period. Figures for Ohio can be a welcome addition to an understanding of early development, because the economic well-being of the people of Ohio can be contrasted to that of people living in the eastern part of the country.

Long-Run Trends

Estimates of wealth per adult male in Ohio will be made, ambitiously, for the entire span of years from 1800-1969. The reader may find that the figures prior to 1860 appear to be unreasonable; yet they are wealth estimates of the tangible evidence of material well-being. Economic growth for long periods of time probably can be measured more accurately using statistics of wealth rather than income. This is particularly true for the nineteenth century, when large portions of income were in the form of non-cash consumption. Saving, on the other hand, was largely visible in the form of tangible real and personal property in land, buildings, farm animals, business building, inventory, etc. Even intangible property held by people in Ohio might be visible in the sense that it represented ownership in tangible property somewhere in the state. Only cash, government property, and wealth of residents owned in other states might not be accounted for properly. The final results of the estimates are given in Chart 1, and we proceed to describe their derivation.

1. Total Estate, 1826-1969. A dollar valuation, presumably not much less than market value, was first placed on property in Ohio in 1826. This grand-duplicate figure con-

sisted of the value of land including houses, town lots including buildings, horses, cattle, pleasure carriages, and merchants' and brokers' capital. In 1831 the definition was broadened to include money loaned at interest and manufacturers' capital in the form of mills, foundries, distilleries, etc. Definitions were gradually broadened to include new forms of organization, such as public utilities. Since 1931 we have productive intangible property valued from capitalizing income at about 6 per cent. The valuation for the grand duplicate is perhaps not as reliable since 1935, when limits were placed on property tax rates and a new type of taxation was introduced in the form of the retail sales tax.

It is certainly admitted that not all forms of wealth are represented on the grand property duplicate. It is also admitted that assessed values rarely approximate market values and are usually much less than market values. But it is percentage growth rates that are important for us. Evidence can be presented to show that the grand-duplicate figures fairly represent long-run percentage growth in aggregate wealth. Estimates of Ohio's "true" value of wealth were made by the Census Bureau for nine years between 1850-1922. Grand-duplicate figures average between 50 and 60 per cent of these "true" values.

A further value problem is that re-evaluation of all property was not performed each year. Re-evaluation took place in 1826, 1835, 1841, 1847, 1854, 1861, 1871, 1881, and 1901 in the nineteenth century. This means that the grand-duplicate series plots as a step function, with one step usually representing a period of a decade. (The function would not be exactly flat since there were additions to the tax duplicate each year.) A trend line fitted to many steps might adequately reflect long-run trend. Some of the results of per capita growth per annum obtained from this procedure are:

	per capita growth rate in wealth
1826-1860	6.6%
1826-1870	4.9
1826-1900	2.8
1826-1934	2.3
1860-1969	1.5

There was a particularly large discontinuity arising with the re-evaluation of 1846, which probably has an undue influence. The overall rates do, however, show a clear demarcation in the trend before and after the Civil War. The rate of growth in the earlier period is three or four times that of the latter period. It was 2.0 per cent per annum for the period from 1826-1969, 1.5 per cent from 1860-1969 and 5.5 per cent from 1826-60. These figures do not give exact measurement, and one would like to find a more refined procedure.

2. Total Tax, 1800-1969. The annual revenue raised from property taxes climbed continuously from 1800 to the 1930's with but few exceptions. The expanding needs of local and state government necessitated additional resources almost annually. Revenues could be increased by increasing the tax rate on the grand-duplicate valuation and rates were much more likely to be increased in a steady fashion in the step-function years between re-evaluation of the duplicate.

A plotting of total tax per adult male adjusted for price increases, TT, reveals a very decided logarithmic trend from 1800 to 1860 and another after 1860. If data are adjusted to 1957-59 dollars and retail sales taxes are included after 1934, we have $\log TT = -49.1 + .0279t$, 1800

$$(.0008)$$

$\leq t \leq 1860$, $R^2 = .95$ and $\log TT = -12.1 + .0080T$, 1860

$$(.0002)$$

$\leq t \leq 1969$, $R^2 = .94$. These equations show growth rates in per capita taxes of 6.7 per cent prior to 1860 and 1.9 per cent after 1860. Retail sales taxes are included with property taxes after 1934, since the sales tax was introduced in 1935 in part because of limitations on property taxes. The constancy of total tax receipts per adult after 1860 is amazingly stable with trend lines fitted to the period from 1860 to 1900, 1860-1934, and 1860-1969 all yielding rates of about 1.9 per cent. One would expect these TT rates to be greater than those of grand-duplicate wealth, since government services have become an increasingly important part of our economy over time. This is particularly true in the case of all levels of education and services, strategic in local and state finance.

3. Relationship of Wealth and Taxes. The methodical increase in tax receipts from year to year makes it plausible that we smooth our grand-duplicate step function using TT. All we need is to establish the correlations between tax and wealth for the years after 1826. Let TE represent the grand-duplicate wealth per adult male in 1957-59 dollars and TT represent tax receipts per adult male in 1957-59 dollars. Least-square regression equations fitted to these scatter diagrams give log $TE_{1826-1870} = -.8672 + .7891TT$,
$$(.0486)$$
$N = 45$, $R^2 = .86$; log $TE_{1826-1900} = -.3722 + .7006TT$,
$$(.0276)$$
$N = 75$, $R^2 = .90$, log $TE_{1826-1934} = -.4623 + .7379TT$,
$$(.0234)$$
$N = 109$, $R^2 = -.90$; and log $TE_{1826-1969} = -.4572 + .7373TT$, $N = 144$, $R^2 = .93$. It is seen that the correla-
$(.0169)$
tions are high in spite of the step-function phenomenon in TE, and that the elasticity coefficients vary consistently from .70-.79. We can safely use the TT values from 1800-1825 in making estimates of TE for those years. This will generally be done with the 1826-1900 equation with its elasticity of .70. This will yield the most conservative estimate of the time trend in wealth. The TE values will be generated for all of the other years from 1826-1969 employing this conservative elasticity of .70. These $TE_{1826-1900}$ values are plotted in Chart 1.

195

Chart 1
Average Estate of Adult Males in Ohio, 1800-1969

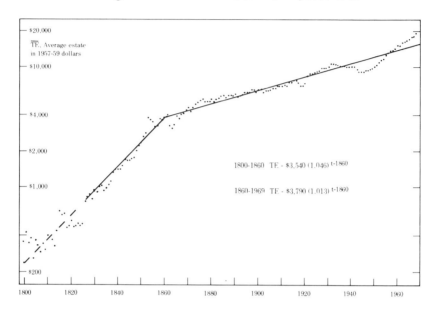

The above estimate is based on total state and local tax assessment figures from 1800-1935 and assessed valuation on the grand duplicate from 1826-1900. The tax and valuation figures were first adjusted for population and price changes in obtaining average tax, TT(year), and average estate, E(year). A linear correlation was next established of the form log E* = 1.6287 + .7006 log TT, using the data from 1826-1900. This equation was employed in conjunction with TT figures from 1819-1969 and resident-adjusted TT figures from 1800-1818 in obtaining average estate values. The TT values for residents only from 1809-19 were spliced into the series from 1819; the TT values for residents and nonresidents for 1800-1808 were then spliced into the data from 1809. The TT values from 1935-69 include not only property taxes, but retail sales and use taxes. The latter tax was inaugurated in 1935 because of the ten mill limitation on real estate tax collections beginning in 1935.

Source of data: Auditor of the State's reports, various years such as that found in *Acts of the State of Ohio*, Second Session of the General Assembly, Vol. II (Chillicothe) 1803, Auditor's Report: Dec. 7, 1803; invaluable are various collations appearing in the *Annual Report of the Ohio Commissioner of Statistics* beginning in 1857 and later appearing in the well-known annual volumes of *Ohio Statistics*. See particularly *Ohio Statistics*, 1893, pp. 661-3. Another valuable source is the *Annual Report of the Ohio Tax Commission*, 1934, pp. 128-9. Data from 1935-71 are in annual reports of the Department of Taxation, State of Ohio. Price indexes are from U. S. Department of Labor, *Handbook of Labor Statistics*, 1970, Table 120. Population data are from the *U. S. Census of Population*, various issues 1800-1970. Populations within a decade have been computed using the average annual percent of change in the decade. Some adjustments were made for 1800-1819 based on a population count of adult males in Ohio in 1807 and 1815 given in *Ohio Executive Documents*, 52D Session, Vol. 20, Pt. II (1856) p. 87.

4. Analysis of the Trends. Chart 1 indicates vividly the rate of growth of wealth in Ohio before and after the Civil War. There is no question that the trend lines differ. If logarithmic trend lines are fitted to the two segments of the chart, then $\log TE_{1826-1900} = -34.8 + .0195t$, 1800

$$(.0006)$$

$\leq t \leq 1860$ and $\log TE_{1826-1900} = -8.9 + .0056t$, $1860 \leq t \leq$

$$(.0001)$$

1969. These translate into growth rates of 4.6 per cent before the war and 1.3 per cent after the war. As stated previously, these are somewhat conservative estimates as chosen from:

Using	Growth rate		
	1800-1860	1826-1860	1860-1969
$TE_{1826-1870}$	.052	.059	.0146
$TE_{1826-1900}$	.046	.052	.0130
$TE_{1826-1934}$	.049	.056	.0137
$TE_{1826-1969}$	.049	.056	.0137

There are several interesting similarities between the estimates and values determined in other studies. First and foremost is the fact that Simon Kuznets found rates of growth per year for worker income in the United States to be .0138 from 1840-1960 and about .0141 from 1860-1960.[1] This rate is similar to that of our chart for the Ohio estimates after 1860 of .0130-.0146. It appears that the wealth trend in Ohio before 1860 would *not* be representative of its income trend. The very rapid increase in wealth means the wealth-income ratio in Ohio in early days was relatively low compared to that further east. Richard Easterlin has esti-mated that income per worker in Ohio climbed 2.0 per cent a year from 1840 to 1880. Our wealth figures show an increase of 3.9 per cent a year in this period. Thus the wealth-income ratio almost doubled in this time span.

Our Ohio series for total estate differs in several re-spects from that of Raymond Goldsmith's for reproducible tangible wealth for the United States. He finds real wealth per head increases at an annual rate of 2.2 per cent from 1805-50, 2.5 per cent from 1850-1900, and 1.3 per cent from 1900-1950.[2] The rate from 1900-1950 is in agreement with our Ohio estimate, but the 2.5 per cent rate from 1850 to 1900 is larger than our increase of 2.1 per cent in this period. The strong difference is before 1850, when Goldsmith's rate was 2.2 per cent for the United States and our Ohio rate was 4.5 per cent. It is noted that the Ohio figures, as contrasted to those of the United States, include the value of land which is both improved and unimproved.[3]

It is not unreasonable to consider the quantitative implications of growth obtained from a few gross calculations of land values in Ohio in 1800 and 1860. The census of agriculture reported the improved and unimproved acreage and cash value of farms in Ohio in 1860. From this we can compute the average value per acre as $33.12. The early price literature for Ohio indicates that land sold for about $1.00 or $2.00 per acre at the turn of the century for Ohio Company land and land in Hamilton County. If we use the $2.00 and $33.00 figures adjusted for price changes, the implicit growth rate is 5.9 per cent a year. This would be an estimate of wealth for farmers having the same size farms in each year. The average cash value in 1860 in Ohio of $33.12 was similar to that of $38.91 in Pennsylvania and $38.30 in New York. The corresponding figures in 1850 of $19.93, $27.33, and $29.00 for the three states indicate that values in the East were 50 per cent more than in Ohio. Surely the values in the East must have been many times those in Ohio in 1800.

There is another form of verification of the long-run trend for Ohio before 1860 which may be obtained from wealth averages of various age groups from the censuses of wealth in 1850 and 1860. If a particular age group were experiencing the Ohio trend before 1860 of 4.5 to 5 per cent a year, how might its wealth average, $W_{age, year}$, differ from that of another age group in the same year? It would seem that it should fully reflect the annual trend for a group one year older than another and that $\overline{W}_{age,year} - \overline{W}_{age-1,year}$ would be .045 or .050. We will find that it does just that.

Table 1

The Average Value of Real Estate Owned by
Adult Males in Ohio in 1850 and 1860

Age	1850 Age 20 in the year	Average real estate	Age	1860 Age 20 in the year	Average real estate
20-24	1845-49	$ 161	20-24	1855-59	$ 213
25-29	1840-44	412	25-29	1850-54	521
30-34	1835-39	501	30-34	1845-49	868
35-39	1830-34	1,081	35-39	1840-44	1,004
40-44	1825-29	1,116	40-44	1835-39	2,060
45-49	1820-24	1,213	45-49	1830-34	3,084
50-54	1815-19	1,607	50-54	1825-29	2,435
55-59	1810-14	2,171	55-59	1820-24	3,825
60 & up	-1809	1,805	60 & up	-1819	2,520
20-99		884	20-99		1,420

Source: Probability samples of size 10,393 in 1850 and 13,696 in 1860 and 9,823 in 1870 were drawn from Schedule 1 of the manuscripts of the United States censuses in those years. Ohio residents constituted about 8-9 per cent of these populations. The samples are further described in a book manuscript, *Men and Wealth in the United States, 1850-1870.* Procedures, definitions, and limitations are also described in Lee Soltow, *Patterns of Wealthholding in Wisconsin Since 1850* (Madison 1971).

The figures of Table 1 seemingly exude this trend. There is a methodical increase in the real estate average, $RE_{age,\ 1850}$, in going from those in their 20's to those in their 30's, 40's, and 50's. These are men who entered the labor force at, say, age 20 in the 1840's, 1830's, 1820's, and 1810's. The logarithms of the seven averages of Table 1 from 25-59 plot approximately as a straight line for 1850 with respect to age, yielding the ratio trend $RE = \$109 \ (1.055)^{age}$, $25 \leq age \leq 59$. The arithmetic straight line fitted to all data for Ohio is $RE = -836 + 47.7age$, $20 \leq age \leq 99$. This average increase for each age year of $47.70 can be expressed as a per cent of the average estate, $\overline{RE} = \$951$. This gives an apparent growth rate of 5.02 per cent an age year. When the age range is limited to 20-59, the rate is .067. Thus the 1850 wealth-age

199

gradient is at least as large as—and is probably larger than—the wealth-time gradient from 1800-1850 of .045 or more. Time is represented by age.

The reader may claim that the evidence of the relationship between time and age is weak, that it might be possible to have a strong wealth-age gradient with relatively little economic growth over time. Let it be said in rebuttal that there is evidence that states and territories further west than Ohio did not exhibit the strong growth rate in 1850. This is true for the state of Wisconsin, where there was really no gradient above age 30.[4] A study of the author's childhood county in western Iowa clearly indicates the same phenomenon. Here there was no population until 1853, a wealth differential between those 20-29 and 30-99 in 1860 and differentials between those 20-29, 30-39, and 40-99 in 1870. It is unfortunate that we have no wealth-age profile for Ohio for a year like 1830 or 1820. These may very well have shown definite leveling in wealth for those of age 30 or 40 or more.

Shifts in Wealth-Age Patterns

There is an aspect of the wealth-age curve as important as its gradient. This is the shift in the curve from one decade to the next. Table 1 indicates for the real estate values that the Ohio curve for 1860 lies above that for 1850 by about 50 per cent. The average real estate for all adult males in 1860 was 1.501 times that in 1850 when averages are corrected for price increases. This yields an average annual increase of 4.1 per cent. The change in real estate values between 1860 and 1870 should be adjusted for a price increase of 42 per cent. When this is done we find an average annual per cent of change of 1.4 per cent. This is phenomenal verification of the fundamental change in long-run trend shown in Chart 1. However, this is only for real estate values. It is possible to make a comparison between the wealth-age curves for 1860 and 1870 using the concept of total estate or real estate plus personal estate. Similar apparent growth of 4.5 to 5 per cent a year again appears, but the shift upward from 1860 to 1870 is at best 2.5 per cent when adjustment is made for price increases. There very definitely is a diminution in the shift of the wealth-age curve from 1850 to 1860, measured at an annual rate of 4.1 per cent, as compared to 1860 to 1870 when the rate was at most 2.5 per cent. This is certainly evidence that the long-run trend from 1800-1969 did not produce an immediate discontinuity at 1860. It was rather one of deceleration after 1850 which probably lasted for more than two decades.

The deceleration was one marked by a change from a position where time was equivalent to age at a rate of 4.5 per cent to one where age brought a 4.5 per cent rate but time decreased to a 1.3 per cent rate. There is rationale after 1870 for 4.5 and 1.5 per cent rates, since the population was increasing about 3 per cent a year. If those already in the labor force experienced 4.5 per cent gains while there was fresh injection of a propertyless class at age 20 amounting in numbers to 3 or 3.5 per cent of the population, then wealth per adult male might increase at rates roughly of .045–.030 = .015 or .045–.035 = .010. Why didn't this occur before 1850 or 1860? I would argue that there were two exceptional aspects. (A) The young man could much more readily acquire land before 1850 and enjoy the fruits of land clearance and capital gains. (B) The young or older men were likely to have been born in the East rather than in Ohio, to have moved from areas of relatively high wealth and perhaps to have brought some wealth with them, or to have received transfers or inheritances from those still in the East. These two effects will be discussed at length.

Passing of the Frontier in Ohio, 1825-1850

The period of settlement in the state lasted at best into the 1850's. The year of organization of each of the 88 counties is given by:

Organization year	Number of counties
1788-99	5
1800-09	25
1810-19	26
1820-29	11
1830-39	9
1840-49	9
1850-51	3
	88

Probably more revealing is the number of acres of assessed land in the state (owned by residents and nonresidents) which increased steadily from 1803 to the middle of the 1850's. It reached an aggregate of 25,000,000 acres in 1854 and remained at this level thereafter.[5]

	Acres assessed (millions)
1803	7.1
1810	9.1
1820	13.3
1830	15.8
1840	21.0
1850	24.0
1857	25.3
1871	25.4
1900	25.5

Population growth reached a peak early; the gain in the absolute number of adult males from 1830 to 1840 was actually greater than it would be again until 1870-80. This increase must have come in part from the opening of canals in Ohio. Lands near canals in the central part of the state went up relatively in assessed value. Railroads built in the 1840's enhanced land values in that decade by making it easier to ship goods. Population increases undoubtedly helped augment land values. These values in turn must have stimulated further migration as long as there was available land. It provided a strong statistical relationship before 1860. The general elasticity coefficient of average total estate with respect to adult-male population size for the 35 points between 1826 and 1860 was 1.34. It was .88 for the 110 points from 1860-1969 and was 1.01 for the entire interval from 1826-1969.

The density of population in a given area would be strongly related to land values and average wealth per person. Consider the densities and total estate owned for people in the 88 counties of Ohio in 1860.[6]

Persons per square mile	Number of counties	Adult-male Average wealth
20 & up	7	$2,630
16-19	10	2,321
12-15	28	2,314
10-11	15	2,078
8- 9	15	1,912
7- 8	9	1,805
0- 6	4	1,346
	88	

A county twice as dense as another enjoyed a differential in total estate of 30-33 per cent. It is not the mere increase in numbers of men but the activities of men which determine development. Population density may be but a proxy for this development. A distinction of importance for farm acreage was the proportion of it that was "improved" or cleared for grazing, grass, or tillage. The improvement could enhance the value of land more than increases in population. Consider the following equation determined from data for 562 counties in the northern states from Ohio to Iowa and Minnesota in 1860: log CV = -.9011 + .7588 log

$$(.0130)$$

I + .0994 log D, where CV is the cash value per acre in

$$(.0184)$$

the county, I is 100 times the proportion of reported land which is improved, and D is the density or population per square mile. It appears that development as measured by I is strategic. The ratio of density in Ohio in 1860 to that in 1826 was 3.7; the ratio for I is not really known but may have been about the same, as judged from assessed acreage figures. We account for more than a tripling of land values per acre from 1826-60 if 3.7 is substituted for I and D in the above least-squares equation. This amounts to a 3.5 per cent yearly increase in value even though it stems only from a cross-sectional study for 1860. This analysis indicates that activities of settlement were very lucrative indeed and probably explains a strong part of the extraordinary increase in wealth before 1860.

Wealth from the East

The rapid rise in average wealth in Ohio before 1860 could also be explained on the basis of movement of men and their wealth from the East. Improved communication and transportation surely would bring diminution in land value differentials due to distance barriers to eastern markets. Distance differentials would diminish over time on every occasion that there was an improvement in the road, canal, railroad, post or even telegraph systems. The average wealth in Ohio was substantially less than that in the nation in 1820. This disparity diminished so that Ohio's average was that of the nation by 1860 and 1870. The only firm information about this disparity before 1860 is for the census year of 1850. The sample described in Table 1 may be confined to data for native-born adult males residing in northeastern states and Ohio in 1850. The equation for real estate is RE $= -953 + 58$ A $- 261$ OR, where RE is
$$(16) \qquad (64)$$
the dollar wealth of the individual, A is the age of the individual, and OR is 1.0 if the individual is an Ohio resident and 0.0 if a resident of a northeastern state. The average wealth of Ohioans was 78 per cent of that of northeasterners for those born in the United States.[7] This disparity is about what one would expect if the growth trend for wealth in the United States before 1860 were about 1.5 per cent and that for Ohio were 4.5 per cent.

204

t	U.S. using $(1.015)^{t-1860}$	Ohio using $(1.045)^{t-1860}$	Ratio of averages
1860	1.000	1.000	1.00
1850	.862	.644	.75
1840	.742	.415	.56
1830	.640	.267	.42
1826	.602	.224	.37

It is conceivable that this scheme has some validity, although one cannot be certain about a 3 per cent differential.[8] Yet such a differential in capital accumulation may very well have been sufficient to draw men to Ohio.[9] The multiple regression equation developed from the sample of 1860 wealth data shows that Ohio residents did as well as those in the northeastern states.

The process of migration of native-born men from the East to Ohio ended when settlement of land was completed. Data on the Ohio-born population as a per cent of Ohio residents were obtained for 1860 and 1870 only and are shown in Table 2.

Table 2

The Nativity of Adult Males Residing in Ohio
in 1860 and 1870, Classified by Age

Age	Number of Ohio born as a proportion of the number of:			
	All adult males		Native-born adult males	
	1860	1870	1860	1870
20-29	.54	.71	.69	.86
30-39	.36	.51	.54	.79
40-49	.29	.34	.38	.51
50-59	.17	.30	.21	.42
60-69	.10	.27	.13	.35
70-99	.07	.12	.11	.14
20-99	.36	.49	.49	.67

Source: See Table 1.

205

The symmetry of the figures for those 20-49 in 1860 and those 30-59 in 1870 certainly leads one to believe that the percentage who were Ohio-born was about 30 in 1850, 36 in 1860, 49 in 1870, and 70 in 1880. We are further led to believe that the percentage was 5 in 1820, 10 in 1830, and 17 in 1840. The proportion of the native-born adult population in Ohio which was Ohio-born is probably the strongest indicator of a fundamental shift after 1860. This feeding of native-born into Ohio lost its impact by 1860 when half of native-born adults had lived in Ohio all of their lives.[10] It was the end of a saga of wealth accumulation greater than that of the national average.

The results of the 1850 census showed that Cincinnati had climbed almost to the same population size as New Orleans, and that it was far larger than Pittsburgh. A perspicacious chronicler of the times addressed himself to the question of how population and property values could have increased so dramatically in fifty years. Charles Cist traced the development of transportation and communication decade by decade from the river steamer to the stage coach and the "ponderous" Conestoga wagon to turnpikes and canals. He observed that by time measurement Cincinnati and Boston were closer together in 1851 than were Cincinnati and Columbus in 1841 because of the advent of the railroad and telegraph. He further observed that if land is "$50 in one place and 50 cents in another", and if food in the latter is cheap because it is a cereal region, then surely a man should not be deterred from moving to the region where he might accumulate capital gains.[11] Ohio provided this opportunity to accumulate wealth for half a century. The advantage of time was largely eliminated by 1860 as the land was settled and property values and wealth in Ohio reached those of the East.

GROWTH OF WEALTH IN OHIO, 1800-1969

1. Simon Kuznets, *Economic Growth and Structure* (New York, 1965) p. 305.

2. Raymond Goldsmith, "The Growth of Reproducible Wealth of the United States of America from 1805 to 1950", *Income and Wealth*, Series II, (Baltimore, 1952) p. 269.

3. The Federal Census Bureau made estimates of "true" value of wealth in Ohio from figures for assessed valuation decennially from 1850-1900 and for 1904, 1912, and 1922. A growth rate of 1.56 per cent a year is obtained when a semilogarithmic trend is fitted to the eight estimates from 1860-1922 after adjusting for population and price changes. Our estimates are about half those of the census averages, presumably because the census estimates are more comprehensive measures and are actual market values instead of assessed values. For a discussion of census estimates see Raymond Goldsmith, *Ibid.*, pp. 256-7. Figures on assessed and market values in Ohio in selected years are given in Manuel Gottlieb, "Building in Ohio Between 1837 and 1914," *Studies in Income and Wealth*, Vol. 30, Dorothy Brady, ed., (New York, 1966).

4. *Patterns of Wealthholding in Wisconsin*, p. 89.

5. It is possible to segregate land acreage into that owned by residents and non-residents of taxing districts for the years 1809-19. It is stated in Chart 1 that resident taxes only were used in developing the wealth series from 1800-1819. Points on the chart for these years would have been about 50 per cent higher if taxes of non-residents had been prorated among residents. The trend line from 1800-1860 would have shown a 4.0 per cent increase a year instead of the 4.6 per cent increase.

6. Aggregate total estate was reported for every county in 1860. See U. S. Census, *Statistics of the United States (Including Mortality, Property & c.,) in 1860* (GPO: Washington, 1866), p. 319.

7. The introduction of a qualitative variable accounting for the proportion who were farmers indicates that Ohio did as well as it did in part because it had more of its labor force in farming.

8. Raymond Goldsmith lists 2.2 per cent growth of reproducible tangible wealth in the United States from 1805-50. Horatio Burchard's series shows a 1.8 per cent rate between 1825-60. *Historical Statistics of the United States, 1789-1945*, Series A2.

9. It has been suggested that migrants moved west partly because of expectations rather than on "known and immediately realized gains in income". It seems that promise of rapid wealth accumulation counteracted attractions of income and consumption. See William N. Parker and Franklee Whartenby, "The Growth of Output Before 1840," *Studies in Income and Wealth*, Vol. 24, p. 211, in reference to a suggestion of Richard Easterlin.

10. Ohio-born in sizable numbers also moved further west. In both 1860 and 1870 the proportion of adult males born in Ohio living in Ohio was but 57 per cent. A contrast for 1860 is adult males born in Pennsylvania; 12 per cent lived in Ohio and 16 per cent lived further west.

11. Charles Cist, *Cincinnati 1851*, (Wm. Moore, publisher, Cincinnati, 1851), pp. 310-314. Other volumes were published in 1841 and 1859. See also Harry N. Scheiber, *Ohio Canal Era: A Case Study of Government and the Economy, 1820-1861*, Ohio University Press, 1969, pp. 198, 335.

IX

THE ROLE OF BANKS IN THE ECONOMIC DEVELOP- MENT OF THE OLD NORTHWEST

Donald R. Adams, Jr.

Southern Illinois University

I

   Few subjects in the ante-bellum development of the American economy have garnered as much attention as the banking system. Both modern scholars and contemporary writers have produced a substantial body of literature on the subject.

  Until very recently, modern scholarship had concentrated its interest on a few institutions (e.g., the First and Second Bank of the United States) or a specific event or set of events (e.g., The Jackson-Biddle Bank War or the Panic of 1837).

  Recent work by Cameron, Green, and others has focused on an aspect of the banking system which holds great interest for the economic historian; namely, the role of banks in the process of economic development.[1] Following that lead, this paper attempts to assess the contribution of commercial banking to the economic development of the Old

Northwest. We have confined our study to the years prior to 1860 on the grounds that the regional character of the five states comprising the Northwest territory had surely begun to break down by that date in the face of rapidly developing national markets.

Section II presents a brief narrative of ante-bellum banking in the Old Northwest. Section III develops a set of criteria with which to evaluate the impact of commercial banks on the development process. Section IV evaluates our findings and presents some conclusions.

II

The first paper-issuing institution west of the mountains was not properly a bank, but the Lexington Insurance Company, incorporated in 1802 with an authorized capital of $150,000.[2] The first banking institution in the Old Northwest appeared one year later. The Miami Exporting Company began operations in 1803 in Cincinnati, having acquired a forty-year charter to do business, and boasting an authorized capital of $500,000.[3] Originally formed to promote exports from the Ohio Valley, the lure of bank profits caused it to abandon all but its banking activities after 1807. Another early institution, the Bank of Detroit, appeared in 1806. Described as "a creature of Boston capitalists," this bank had an ambitious 101-year charter and an equally ambitious authorized capital of $1,000,000.[4] Neither of these great expectations was fulfilled, and the Bank of Detroit was legislated out of existence in 1808.

The decision not to recharter the First Bank of the United States in 1811 and a post-war migration of Settlers westward were both stimulants to the growth of state banking. While the paper issue of western banks was moderate in comparison to the eastern states in 1812, the issues of these banks increased considerably following the war and still more in 1817 when Ohio and Indiana increased their banking facilities. In this process of post-war expansion, the various states exercised a variety of institutional and legal arrangements.

Ohio opted for a system of regulated, privately owned commercial banks.[5] In general the Ohio system exhibited most of the flaws associated with private state banking. Among these were: lack of centralized control over bank reserves; periodic suspension of specie payment; inability of the state to enforce banking legislation and the continued existence of private non-chartered institutions. While many complained that such a system unduly proliferated the number of banks, the continued circulation of substantial amounts of foreign bank notes and the tendency of insurance companies and other non-bank firms to provide banking services cast considerable doubt on this assertion. The existence of dividends ranging from 8 to 15 per cent in the post-war years also belies this purported ease of entry.[6]

Indiana in 1816 and Illinois in 1821 chose to operate state-owned banking systems. Neither system survived the Panic of 1819 and its aftermath. While the second State Bank of Indiana, initiated in 1834, enjoyed considerable success, Illinois' banking system had the distinction of failing twice; once in 1825 and again in 1842.

Michigan chose still another option. Within two years of achieving statehood in 1835, a "general banking law" was passed which contained a key provision relieving banks of the responsibility of redeeming their notes in specie. A host of "wildcat banks" was the result. With the repeal of the general banking law in 1839, the number of banks in Michigan fell from twenty-eight in 1839 to two by 1843 and never exceeded seven in any year between 1843 and 1860. Thus, the Michigan experience represents the extreme case in terms of ease of entry for new banking institutions.

Wisconsin's commercial banking policy is in some respects the opposite extreme. Established as a separate territory in 1836, Wisconsin quickly chartered four banks. These institutions met with immediate disaster in the Panic of 1837, and none survived beyond the early 1840's. In effect, banks were prohibited in Wisconsin from 1841 until a constitutionally ordered referendum conferred on the legislature the power to charter banks in 1852. A "general banking law" was passed the same year and the first bank chartered in 1853.

During the absence of authorized commercial banks, the Wisconsin Marine and Fire Insurance Company, chartered in 1839, took up the slack. Almost immediately this company began issuing certificates of deposit redeemable in gold. These certificates, when loaned out by the company, circulated as money.[7] During the years of banking prohibition the circulation of the Wisconsin Marine and Fire Insurance Company grew from $19,747 to $1,470,235.[8]

Despite these differences in the approach to commercial banks among the states of the Old Northwest, it is possible to provide some generalizations concerning the experiences of the banking system as a whole.

The rapid growth of population and economic activity following the war led to an optimistic expansion of commercial banking in the Northwest. The banks were to perform two vital roles in this growth. First, they were to facilitate east-west trade by discounting the bills of exchange which arose in the export of western staples, and secondly, they were to provide longer term capital for land purchases, improvements to the land and other investment projects.

The disastrous price declines which heralded the Panic of 1819 began in 1818 and were particularly severe in the west.[9] By the midsummer of 1818 many western banks were in deep trouble. Depositors and holders of bank notes clamored for specie, and banks found the task of turning illiquid, real estate secured notes into specie well nigh impossible. Suspension of specie payment was the result for most banks. The largest single holder of state bank notes was the Bank of the United States, which delivered two crushing blows to the state banks in 1818. First the BUS announced that all agreements with state banks pertaining to rates of redemption would terminate on June 30, 1818, and further ordered its cashiers to accept as cash only specie and BUS notes. Secondly, the Cincinnati branch of the BUS was ordered to call for the balances due it from all state banks at the rate of 20 per cent each month.

The suspensions of 1818-19 placed state banks in a virtually untenable position. After February 20, 1817, the Secretary of the Treasury was directed to collect all dues in legal currency which included coins, notes on the BUS, treasury notes, and notes of specie paying banks.[10] Thus, suspension by state banks meant their notes were not accepted by tax collectors and land offices, which generally resulted in rapid depreciation. Refusal to suspend meant a rapid exhaustion of specie reserves as banks and individuals holding the notes of specie paying banks demanded gold and silver. To make matters worse, a sudden worsening in the international terms of trade produced a larger than normal deficit, and specie held by the BUS flowed eastward to satisfy commercial debts abroad.

Reaction to the events of 1818-19 varied. For most state banking systems the 1820's were years of retrenchment or liquidation. The soundest banks struggled to resume specie payments and restore the public's confidence, while the weakest collapsed.

Both state-owned systems in Indiana and Illinois failed during the early 1820's, as did many private banks in Ohio. In Michigan the Bank of Michigan survived the events of 1819 but remained the sole Michigan banking institution until 1827.

By the early 1830's several factors combined to bring about a renewed interest in banking. Not the least of these factors was the uncertain future of the Bank of the United States.

The events of 1832-39 left an indelible mark on the state banks of the Old Northwest. The period began with Jackson's re-election, which sealed the fate of the Second Bank of the United States and ended with financial collapse and economic depression.

The imminent demise of the BUS prompted all states to react. Ohio discussed a state bank but instead substantially expanded the number of chartered banks.[11] By 1835 Illinois had virtually completed the hapless task of liquidating the State Bank of Illinois, and in February of that year a second State Bank of Illinois was established in Springfield with six branches.[12] Both the Shawneetown Bank and the Bank of Cairo reopened, and the former became a special depository for federal funds received at the Shawneetown land office. Indiana chartered a new state bank in 1834 with headquarters in Indianapolis and ten branches. Depending as it did on the Cincinnati and Louisville branches of the BUS for credit and currency, the passing of the BUS posed a major problem for Indiana by the mid-1830's.

Wisconsin's first bank, the Bank of Wisconsin at Green Bay, was inherited from the territory of Michigan when Green Bay was included in the new Wisconsin Territory. Wisconsin quickly joined the bank expansion of the 1830's by chartering the Bank of Mineral Point and the Miner's Bank of Dubuque in 1836. Before any of these institutions could exert a considerable influence disaster struck. During 1837 all Wisconsin banks either suspended specie payment or failed. Launched as they were in the heated expansion of 1835-36, far from any supervisory body or rapid lines of communication, the collapse of these frontier banks is hardly surprising. The same fate awaited the fourteen new banks chartered in Michigan during 1835 and 1836.[13]

The events of 1836-37 have been the object of intense study by scholars for some time. Traditional accounts see a direct link between the failure to recharter the BUS and the subsequent financial panic and depression. The link,

213

as these accounts contend, was the over-expansion of state banks now freed from the control of the BUS. This expansion, complicated by the Deposit Act of 1836, the distribution of the federal surplus and the Specie Circular of July, 1836, overextended the banking system. When the panic struck in 1837, the banks were forced into a massive liquidation which ended with the general suspension of specie payments in the summer and fall of 1837.

Modern scholars have chipped away at the foundations of this traditional account to such a degree that the edifice seems in danger of toppling.[14]

Since 1832 the treasury had been depositing funds with various state banks and encouraging banks to treat federal deposits as a form of reserves by expanding loans gradually to offset the contraction of circulation by the Bank of the United States.[15] The treasury informed deposit banks that

> The deposits of public money will enable you to afford increased facilities to the commercial and other classes of the community, and the department anticipates from you the adoption of such a course . . . as will prove acceptable to the people and safe to the government.[16]

As of April, 1836, federal deposits were lodged in the following institutions of the Old Northwest.

Federal Depository Banks in
the Old Northwest, 1836

Franklin Bank (Cincinnati)	$ 244,048.12
Commercial Bank (Cincinnati)	395,175.82
Clinton Bank (Columbus)	328,127.52
State Bank of Indiana (Indianapolis)	1,377,949.98
Michigan Bank (Detroit)	1,070,820.03
Farmers and Mechanics Bank (Detroit)	703,675.25

Source: *Report of the Comptroller of the Currency*, House Documents, 44th Congress, 2nd Session, (1877), p. 200.

By the end of 1836 nearly $7,000,000 of treasury deposits were lodged in Northwest banks and 70 per cent of this total was held by four large institutions. Such a concentration ran counter to the treasury's desire to use federal deposits to stimulate the economy. Consequently, in June of 1836 Congress decreed that the treasury should select at least one deposit bank in each state which chartered banks and that no one bank could hold federal deposits in amounts greater than three-fourths of its paid-in capital. An amending act of July 4, 1836, gave the Secretary of the Treasury the power to transfer federal funds to "produce a due equality and just proportion" of deposits among the states.[17]

Compliance with the Deposit Act had the potential of placing a great strain on the banking system, particularly on those banks in which federal deposits were concentrated. It has been estimated that to comply with the law $18.3 million of the nearly $34 million of federal funds deposited in states banks would have to be transferred.[18] In addition to this transfer, another $12 million had to be distributed because $22 million in federal funds had accrued in depository banks between the passage of the act and its implementation. Thus, total transfers amounted to about $30 million. Despite this large sum, Temin has calculated that only five states lost public deposits between June and December of 1836 and that the total loss of all five states was less than $1.5 million.[19]

In the same month as the Deposit Act, the congress provided for the distribution of the federal surplus. The states were to receive the balance in the treasury in excess of $5 million as of January 1, 1837. This sum, nearly $37 million was to be distributed in four equal installments in January, April, July, and December of 1837. The federal surplus was being held in depository banks, and, depending on the regional concentration of these deposits, interregional transfers might be required. In fact, the total interstate transactions required for the payment of the first installment was only $1.4 million and for the second installment, $1.3 million.[20] The only two Northwestern states which lost funds in the distribution were Ohio and Indiana, and only Ohio banks were required to transfer funds outside of the Northwest.[21] In all, less than a quarter of a million dollars in federal funds left the Northwest as a result of these transfers.

The third major financial shock of 1836 occurred when the Specie Circular was issued in July of that year. The Circular stated that after August 15 only specie and Virginia land script would be accepted in payment for federal land.[22] The two-fold impact of this directive was to increase the demand for specie in the Northwest at the same time as it reduced the acceptability of state bank notes formerly used for land acquisition. Land sales accordingly declined.[23]

It is difficult to assess the impact of the Specie Circular, coming as it did hard on the heels of the Distribution Act and preparations for the distribution of the federal surplus. Recent scholarship has suggested that while the Specie Circular was intended as an anti-inflationary device, it may have had the opposite impact. The reduction in land sales which it triggered reduced federal revenue and the federal surplus which was to be distributed, but the same reduction in land sales may have shifted spending from land to other commodities. Initially, both prices and land sales dropped sharply, but prices recovered by mid-1838 and wholesale prices in Cincinnati were higher in 1839 than in 1837.[24] Banks experienced nearly a two-fold increase in specie reserves due largely to the fact that all land sales were now specie transactions. Thus, banks were able to expand loans without reducing reserve ratios.[25]

Declining land sales meant declining federal revenues, and by 1837 it was necessary for the treasury to draw upon deposit banks for about $20 million more than the banks received in government deposits.[26] In Indiana, federal deposits fell from over $2 million in 1836 to $576,277 in 1837 and disappeared by 1840.[27] In Ohio treasury deposits fell from $4,126,483 in January of 1837 to $384,906 in December of the same year. Deposits in Michigan banks, most of which were federal deposits, fell from $2,114,943 in 1836 to $342,760 in 1840.[28]

Subjected to the multiple strains caused by the Distribution Act, the distribution of the federal surplus, the Specie Circular, and the withdrawal of federal deposits, the commercial banks of the Old Northwest were on the brink of disaster in the Spring of 1837. The anti-bank sentiment of the early 1830's was about to produce some undesired consequences; namely, a collapse of confidence in banks as a whole.

Prices began to fall in 1837, and Northwest banks came under considerable pressure as the public attempted to reduce its holdings of bank money. The Summer of 1837 saw many banks in the Northwest suspend specie payment. The suspension of 1837 marked the end of the depository system, since the law excluded banks which suspended from receiving federal funds. The treasury withdrew funds from suspending banks by drawing on them for the third installment of the surplus distribution in July, 1837.[29]

In May, 1838, the Specie Circular was repealed and some pressure removed from the specie reserves of the banking system. Banks in both the East and West were preparing for resumption of specie payment set for August 13, 1838. While most eastern banks were retrenching and reducing obligations in anticipation of resumption, most banks in the Northwest continued to expand. This course of action probably reflected a belief that the distress of 1837 would be short-lived. Instead, it was the recovery which was short-lived, and between September, 1839, and February, 1843, prices underwent a decline comparable to those of 1819-21.[30]

News of eastern bank suspensions reached the Northwest in the Fall of 1839. Realizing the threat which their swollen circulation now presented, the banks of the Northwest

217

followed suit. Of those lucky enough to have survived the ordeal of 1837, nearly all succumbed after 1839.

A survey of the Old Northwest from the vantage point of the mid-1840's showed the banking system in shambles. Ohio, which boasted thirty-four banks and over $16 million in loans and discounts in 1839, was reduced to eight banks with less than $3 million in loans and discounts by 1844. By 1842 the state legislature in Indiana ordered the State Bank of Indiana to resume specie payment, but by 1844 loans and discounts were only a little over one-half of their 1839 level. The State Bank of Illinois went into liquidation in 1842 followed by the Bank of Illinois at Shawneetown in 1843. The state took possession of over $3 million in internal improvement bonds held by the banks, cancelled them, and burned them in the presence of the state legislature. None of Wisconsin's banks survived even the initial panic in 1837. Michigan, where banks could begin operations without the obligation to pay specie, started in 1837 with eleven banks and $564,275 in specie and ended in 1839 with twenty-eight banks and $290,058 in specie. The General Banking Act, which spawned the bank expansion, was repealed in 1839, but this action was largely academic. By the end of 1839 most wildcat banks had failed, and only three chartered banks and four banks organized under the general law remained.[31]

The expansion of banking in the Northwest was exceptionally slow for nearly a full decade following the dismal years of 1842-43. Only in the early 1850's did the loans and discounts, circulation and deposits of Northwestern banks reach levels attained in the late 1830's.[32] Once bank development got under way around 1851-52, it progressed rapidly except for a setback following the Panic of 1857.

III

Defining the functions of the commercial banking system in advance of assessing their role in the economic development of the Old Northwest is a necessary but risky undertaking. It is possible to stress the bank's role as a monetary agent whose bank notes and, to a much lesser degree, demand deposits were an important component of the money supply in the Northwest.

On the other hand, commercial banks form an important component of a broad group of institutions known collectively as financial intermediaries. Except for the First and Second Bank of the United States and some unauthorized lending institutions, commercial banks represented the dominant form of financial intermediary in the ante-bellum Northwest. Viewed as an intermediary, the role of the commercial banking system is that of transferring real resources (in the form of savings) from less pro-ductive uses to more productive uses (generally in the form of investment). In this process of intermediation banks may also enhance the efficiency (lower the cost) with which this transfer takes place—and also have a substantial impact on the final disposition or allocation of investment.

In the context of the growing economy this process of intermediation almost certainly involves a movement away from the financing of purely commercial transactions, which are short-term and liquid, in favor of acquiring long-term, less liquid assets often associated with the acquisition or improvement of land, the development of manufacturing, or the growth of social overhead capital.

Contemporaries and modern scholars alike have been quick to point out the fundamental conflict which arises in a commercial banking system which is, at the same time, the chief element in the creation of the money supply and the principal financial intermediary. As one scholar of American financial history has described the conflict: "a banking system based on 100 per cent reserves is perfectly stable . . . no bank money is created and there can be no effect on the price level; but it provides no capital accumulation, since it acts only to mobilize the savings of depositors. American financial history in one dimension can be viewed as a tug-of-war between those who want rapid accumulation and those who desire economic stability."[33] Not until the principal responsibility for monetary policy was assumed by the Federal Reserve System did commercial banks completely escape this dilemma.

Clearly, the most important function of the banking system when viewed as a monetary agent is the capacity to create money. In the Old Northwest banks relied almost entirely on bank note issue to perform this function. "Deposits," states Golembe, "except for federal deposits in certain of the banks, were of little quantitative importance and, in addition" (and perhaps more importantly) "were not a function of the lending operations of the bank."[34] Treasury deposits, which did loom large for some banks in some years were often treated as a form of reserves—a practice not discouraged by the Treasury.

Even individual deposits "were often in the form of special deposits by such people as pension officers or tax collectors." In some cases such deposits "were kept separate from other funds so that the depositor could receive back exactly the same currency he had left."[35] Specialized studies of state banking systems confirm this generalization. In Indiana, for example, "the use of deposit accounts as a credit function had practically no existence."[36] Thus, if we are willing to forego the controversy concerning the proper role of "near money" in the money supply, it is probably safe to conclude that the total supply of bank money in the Old Northwest can be roughly equated to the quantity of bank notes in circulation.[37]

The debate still rages on the proper role which should be assigned to the supply of money or changes in the money supply within economic theory and in the formulation of appropriate economic policy. Fortunately, we can narrow our concern to the role which the creation of bank money performs in the development process. This role can be subsumed conveniently under two broad headings: the passive role and the active role. The former concentrates on adjustments in the money supply which permit the process of economic growth and development to proceed smoothly, while the latter encompasses a number of "structuralist" hypotheses which assign a major role to monetarily inspired inflation and "forced" or "involuntary saving" leading to a transfer of real resources from savers to investors.

What we have termed the passive contribution of the banking system's purely monetary function has been characterized by one scholar as an increase in the population served by the money supply. As development occurs and greater specialization and division of labor appears in both production and consumption, additional monetary transactions are required between firms at different stages of the production process. Thus, more and more monetary transactions are needed for a given final output.[38] Patrick has described this passive role of banks and other financial intermediaries as "demand following." Thus, "the evolutionary development of the financial system is a continuing consequence of the pervasive, sweeping process of economic development."[39] To perform even this passive role effectively, most economists believe, the money supply should grow more rapidly than real output if development is to proceed free from excessive inflation or deflation.[40]

Available data permit some crude estimates on increases in the supply of bank money relative to population, income, and output. As a first approach, Cameron has suggested a measure of bank offices per 10,000 inhabitants.[41]

Cameron's rating system identifies ratios of over 1.0 as high, 0.5 to 1.0 as moderate, below 0.5 as low, and below 0.1 as very low. For the Northwest as a whole all ratios in Table 1 are below 0.5 and in one year, 1830, below 0.1. Figures for the United States as a whole indicate low or moderate densities over the same period. In all years for which data are available the densities for the Northwest are below the national average and in only one year and one state (Wisconsin, 1860) did the ratio exceed 1.0.

Perhaps a better measure of the population served by the money supply is contained in Table 2. Here we measure bank money (bank notes) per capita between 1820 and 1860. For the Northwest as a whole, bank money per capita increased between 1820 and 1860 but remained substantially below the average for the United States as a whole. Furthermore, in only one year and one state (Illinois, 1840) did bank money per capita in the Northwest exceed the average for the United States.

Estimating the changes in bank money with respect to total income and output is difficult and speculative. Some rough calculations are, however, possible and may be enlightening.

We note from Column 1 of Table 3 that income for the United States increased by about two and one-half times between 1840 and 1860. Column 2 indicates the appropriate absolute figures. The assumption made here is that during the early nineteenth century the movement of net national product and income was quite similar. We thus apply the NNP index to Easterlin's income estimate for 1840 to obtain the 1860 income estimate. Column 3 shows that the share of income accruing to the East North Central states (Northwest) increased from 12 per cent to 15 per cent between 1840 and 1860. Over the same period bank money in the Northwest increased 2.31 times. From columns 2 and 3 the implied increase in income in the Northwest was 3.16 times between 1840 and 1860. These figures indicate that income growth was substantially *greater* than the growth of bank money over the period in question. In absolute terms the ratio of bank money to total income fell from .086 in 1840 to .064 in 1860. Even if we consider bank notes and deposits, the ratio falls from .113 in 1840 to .088 in 1860. Gurley and Shaw contend that ratios of 10 per cent or less

Table 1

Bank Density
(Banks/10,000 Population)

	Ohio	Ind.	Ill.	Mich.	Wis.	NW	US	NW/US
1820	.344	.136	.363	-	-	.302	.319	.946
1830	.117	-	-	.316	-	.081	.255	.317
1840	.243	.189	.189	.471	.323	.239	.526	.454
1850	.287	.131	-	.125	-	.165	.353	.467
1860	.222	.274	.432	.053	1.392	.397	.496	.800

Sources: *Historical Statistics of the United States*, pp. 7, 13, *Report of the Comptroller of the Currency*, House Document 44th Congress, 2nd Session, pp. 195, 226-28.

Table 2

Bank Money per Capita
1820-60

	Ohio	Ind.	Ill.	Mich.	Wis.	NW	US	NW/US
1820	$2.07	$1.87	$ .94	$ -	$ -	$1.93	$3.72	.518
1830	-	-	-	-	-	-	4.70	-
1840	3.03	4.35	7.82	1.23	3.53	3.99	6.25	.638
1850	5.46	3.34	-	1.57	-	3.67	5.64	.650
1860	3.41	3.99	5.24	.29	5.71	3.90	6.57	.593

Sources: *Historical Statistics of the United States*, pp. 7, 13, *Report of the Comptroller of the Currency*, pp. 194, 227-29, Friedman and Schwartz, *Monetary Statistics of the United States*, (New York: Columbia University Press, 1970), p. 220.

Table 3

	(1) NNP(US)	(2) Income(US)	(3) Northwest Share of Income	(4) Northwest Bank Money
	(1840=100)			(1840=100)
1840	100	$1,103,000,000	12%	100
1860	253	2,790,590,000	15%	231

Sources:

Column (1) Davis, Easterlin, *et al. American Economic Growth* (New York: Harper & Row, 1972), p. 34.

Column (2) Richard A. Easterlin, "Interregional Differences in Per Capita Income, Population, and Total Income, 1840-1950," *N.B.E.R. Trends in the American Economy in the Nineteenth Century*, Volume 24, Conference on Research in Income and Wealth (Princeton: Princeton University Press, 1960), p. 47.

Column (3) Richard A. Easterlin "Regional Income Trends 1840-1950," in Harris (ed.) *American Economic History* (New York: McGraw-Hill, 1961), p. 535.

Column (4) *Report of the Comptroller of the Currency*, pp. 227-29.

generally prevail in poorer countries rising to around 30 per cent in the most advanced.[42] The ratio of money to income was moving in the opposite direction from what we would expect in a developing economy.

A final portion of the money supply should be briefly considered here. In addition to bank notes the public also held specie. It is, therefore, legitimate to ask whether or not there was an increase in this component of the money supply in the Northwest sufficient to offset the decline in bank money. While data for the Northwest is not readily available, Friedman and Schwartz do estimate the amount of specie held by the public for the United States as a whole. Rough estimates indicate that the public did indeed hold as money a greater proportion of the total specie supply in 1860 than in 1840. The proportion rose from around 58 per cent in 1840 to about 64 per cent by 1860.[43] More importantly, the total stock of specie grew from about $70-80 million in 1840 to about $235 million in 1860. Thus, specie held by the public grew from $35-45 million in 1840 to around $150 million in 1860. Depending on the initial importance of public specie holdings in the total money supply of the Northwest, this better than three-fold increase

224

in non-bank money might have been sufficient to offset the declining ratio of bank money to total income. Even if this were the case, however, any increase in the ratio of the money supply to income cannot be attributed to the activity of the commercial banking system.

On the whole, then, the commercial banks do not seem to have been an effective instrument in increasing the number of people served by the money supply or in raising the ratio of the money supply to income.

Turning to the "active" role of bank money in the development process it is helpful to identify some of the restrictions—self imposed as well as external—that diminished the banks' ability to expand the money supply.

Legal restrictions by the various states often limited the banks' ability to expand. Most state bank charters limited the note issue of banks to an amount equal to capitalization or some multiple thereof. If charters restricted banks to issuing a multiple of *paid-in capital*, as for example in Indiana, the common practice of starting operations with a great deal less than authorized capital served to further restrict note issue.

Another constraint was the passage of a variety of "free banking laws" during the 1850's. A common characteristic of these laws was a restriction on the total issue of bank notes and in some cases on the denominations allowed. In Ohio, banks chartered under the free banking law were required to deposit state or U.S. bonds equal to 60 per cent of their capital stock with the state auditor, who then issued notes equal in value to the securities deposited but not more than three times the bank's capital. Illinois banks were similarly constrained, and one indication of the inadequate circulation of bank money in that state was the need to pass legislation in 1853 making illegal the issuance or receipt for deposit any paper money other than bank notes. Wisconsin's free banking act, modeled after the New York act of 1838, required the deposit of approved securities with the state treasurer in exchange for bank notes. The situation in Wisconsin illustrates one difficulty with such laws. Wisconsin law limited the public debt to $10,000, thus most securities deposited in return for notes were from other states. A decline in the value of such securities would prompt the state comptroller to "call" for an increase in the bonds deposited *or* a decrease in outstanding notes. The comptroller made a 10 per cent call in 1854, and in 1860 the state issued a 2 per cent call on Missouri bonds and a 6 per cent call on Virginia bonds. In 1861 the state legislature was forced to prohibit future calls in order to prevent recurrent banking crises.

In a broader sense commercial banks were also restricted by the attitudes and official policies of those in power. According to one scholar "in no other sector of the economy, with the possible exception of foreign trade, have governments intervened so broadly, so consistently and with such telling effect—usually bad."[44] Official attitudes toward banking varied in intensity over time. Legislation ranged from ineffective and unenforced prohibitions against issuing small denomination bank notes to the literal prohibition of banking in Wisconsin from the early 1840's until 1852. Legislative or policy reaction to economic conditions was often swift and anti-bank. Bankers themselves often internalized those official prejudices and compounded the problem. For example "the experience of the 1840's convinced both bankers and the legislatures that regulated their activities that long-term loans were 'bad.' In the 1840's they may have been so, but the policies that grew out of that period severely restrained the activities of the banks long after the conditions of the 1840's had disappeared."[45] Data in Table 4 show little change in the reserve ratios of Northwest banks following the demise of the BUS and the end of the redemption policy.

It is also interesting to note from Table 4 that the reserve ratios of Northwestern banks compare quite favorably with the reserve ratios of all state banks. Indeed, with the exception of a few years in the mid-1830's reserve ratios

Table 4

Reserve Ratios

	(1) BUS (Western Branches)	(2) All State Banks	(3) Northwest Banks
1819	.198	.301	.416
1820	.970	.372	.243
1821	1.185	.403	.148
1822	1.189	.243	-
1823	1.413	.305	-
1824	.446	.296	-
1825	.774	.267	-
1826	.567	.243	-
1827	.247	.272	-
1828	.169	.261	-
1829	.217	.299	-
1830	.165	.249	-
1831	.101	.217	.246
1832	.213	.203	.207
1833	.166	.211	.209
1834	.191	.343	.413
1835	.226	.435	.433
1836	-	.265	.314
1837	-	.299	.417
1838	-	.303	.411
1839	-	.334	.330
1840	-	.309	.309
1841	-	.324	.283
1842	-	.339	-
1843	-	.572	.424
1844	-	.663	-
1845	-	.493	-
1846	-	.398	.297
1847	-	.333	.293
1848	-	.361	.305
1849	-	.380	.335
1850	-	.345	.322
1851	-	.313	.261
1852	-	-	.259
1853	-	.322	.260
1854	-	.290	.250
1855	-	.288	.232
1856	-	.303	.275
1857	-	.271	.216
1858	-	.479	.212
1859	-	.540	.196
1860	-	.403	.151

Sources:
Column (1) J. Van Fenstermaker, *The Development of American Commercial Banking* (Bureau of Economic and Business Research, Kent State University, 1965), pp. 246-247.
Column (2) *Ibid.*, pp. 66-67 through 1837. After 1837, *Report of the Comptroller of the Currency*, p. 205.
Column (3) Before 1835, Van Fenstermaker, pp. 197, 198, 209, 210, 222, 223. After 1835, *Report of the Comptroller of the Currency*, pp. 227-229.

in the Northwest banks were generally lower than those for all states combined. Thus, however restrictive we may judge the Northwestern banks to have been, they do not appear to have been, on the surface, any more restrictive than all state banks taken as a whole.

In addition to the redemption policy of the BUS, there is also the question of the reserve ratio of the BUS. If the BUS, particularly its western branches, followed a conservative note issue policy, then state banks in the Northwest would be forced to follow or face chronically unfavorable clearing balances. If, on the other hand, the BUS issued freely, then state banks could extend note issue and use BUS notes when the western branches tried to redeem state bank notes.[46] As Table 4 indicates, during the early thirties the reserve ratios of the BUS western branches were generally below those of the Northwest. This phenomenon may be explained by an overly restrictive note issue policy on the part of commercial banks, or the fact that the flow of BUS notes eastward prevented the state banks from accumulating BUS notes for redemption purposes. The preponderance of evidence suggests that if the state banks of the Northwest were overly cautious in their note issue policy, we should not attribute this to the restrictive policies of the BUS either in terms of its redemption policies or its own note issue policy. Indeed, in the eyes of some scholars the real value of the BUS may have been psychological. Its very existence and soundness may have instilled a degree of confidence which enabled all banks to operate *more* efficiently with lower reserve ratios.[47]

In addition to legal and institutional restrictions on the note issue policy of commercial banks, economic conditions in the Northwest also played a role. Rockoff has identified three characteristics common to the Northwest which operated against a more rapid expansion of loans and hence the money supply. They are: (1) an undeveloped capital market, (2) a serious portfolio problem, and (3) lack of confidence in the banking system.[48]

Because of underdeveloped capital markets, the cost of liquidating assets (in particular, long-term assets) on short notice was higher in the Northwest than in the Northeast, for example.

The uncertainty of capital markets should be reflected in the banks' portfolios of earning assets. Under conditions of uncertainty banks would normally strive to diversify their assets in order to produce a desirable balance between risk and uncertainty on one hand and high income producing loans on the other. Northwestern banks faced a situation in which most of their loans were based on land and improvements to the land or the production and export of agricultural surplus. The former were inherently long-term and illiquid and the latter risky and subject to a great short-run variation. Thus the inability to spread risks through diversification probably served as a check on the more rapid expansion of bank money.

The fear, if not the existence, of wide spread "wild-catting," particularly following the demise of the BUS, led to frequent "runs" or the fear of frequent "runs." Bankers thus intimidated might be reluctant to extend note issue to the degree that they might consider prudent in a less apprehensive environment.

On the whole, then, there is a variety of both economic and non-economic factors which help to explain what appears to be a rather restrictive policy of Northwestern banks in the provision of bank money. We should, however, keep in mind the following. First, while reserve ratios of Northwestern banks did not fall rapidly until the late 1850's, the supply of bank money did increase due to increasing specie reserves within the banking system. The supply of specie held by banks in the Northwest increased from $2,814,560 in 1835 to $4,080,114 in 1860. Over the same period bank notes in circulation grew from $6,493,071 to $27,007,910.[49] The real question is whether the high reserve ratios which persisted over most of the period can be justified in light of the developmental needs of the area and the extent to which this problem, in light of the similarity of reserve ratios for all state banks to those of the Northwest, was peculiar to the Northwest or one which characterized state banking as a whole.

Just as insufficient expansion of the money supply may act to depress price levels and perhaps output, so too a very rapid increase in the money supply may stimulate investment while lowering consumption. The structuralist view maintains that if the money supply increases more rapidly than output, and the real purchasing power of consumers declines, real resources *may* be released for investment purposes.[50] We stress the term "may," for consumers can thwart this process by increasing their consumption expenditures as a percentage of income—or by using some or all additional income they gain from expansion in the investment sector for consumption pur-chases.[51]

Lack of data on consumption, investment, and savings unfortunately makes a detailed discussion of the role of involuntary saving impossible. However, some rough and ready calculations may shed some light on the subject.

There were two periods of sustained price increases in the Northwest during the period under discussion, the first from 1834 through 1837 and a second, longer period from 1843 through 1857.[52] During the initial period of price increases, Berry's data for Cincinnati indicate a nearly 38 per cent increase in wholesale prices. Over the same period, the supply of bank money grew even more rapidly, increasing over 100 per cent. Since it is highly unlikely that income could have expanded at anywhere near the rate of the price increase, real purchasing power almost certainly declined during these years. Thus, the first period of price increases surely generated some involuntary saving.

Over the second span of years, 1843-57, prices rose by about 4.5 per cent a year and increases in the supply of bank money were in the neighborhood of 4.8 per cent per year. From Table 3 it appears that personal income grew at about 6 per cent per annum in current prices. Thus, unlike the former period, real income growth ruled out any forced saving.

A key element in the "forced" saving argument is that resources formerly devoted to consumption are transferred to investors. Commercial banks as intermediaries can play an important role in this process. Therefore, what is needed is some evidence that the banks of the Northwest were channeling increased resources away from consumer oriented activities to capital formation. Some evidence exists to suggest that this was the case. In Indiana, for example, total bank loans increased from $1,810,966 in 1835 to $3,264,072 in 1837. Over the same period Bills of Exchange (the type of loan more closely associated with consumption activity) fell in value from $376,175 to $374,956, and promissory notes (the type of loan most likely associated with capital formation) rose in value from $1,434,790 to $2,889,117.[53] The data on the State Bank of Illinois indicates a decline in bills of exchange from $1,106,000 in 1836 to $605,000 in 1837, while total loans increased from $2,045,000 to $2,954,000. Finally, the Bank of Illinois at Shawneetown held only 3.6 per cent of its total loans and discounts in the form of bills of exchange in 1837.[54]

Given the land fever which existed in these years, it is highly plausible that a large part of the increased lending for non-commercial transactions went into land or land related purchases. According to Golembe, however, "a sizeable part of the bank funds which went to speculators was expended not upon the purchase of land but upon improvements. . . ."[55]

On the whole, then, there does appear to be sufficient evidence to indicate some level of involuntary saving between 1835 and 1837 and further indications that some transfer of resources from consumers to investors took place.

Central to the problem of economic growth and development is the transfer of real resources from consumption to capital formation or alternatively from non-consumption (saving) to investment. In economic systems where groups of savers and investors differ, the process of capital accumulation involves both the acquisition of debt and the acquisition of financial assets. Financial intermediaries, such as banks, can greatly facilitate this process.

Self-finance does not generally promote a rapid capital formation growth rate, for while saving is a function of income, there is no guarantee that the distribution of income at any point in time need coincide with the distribution of entrepreneurial skills vital to the investment process.

External finance (the acquisition of debts and financial assets) can be direct or indirect. In the case of direct finance, the direct debt of deficit spending units is acquired by surplus spending units. If spending on capital formation is directly financed, debt tends to accumulate *pari passu* with wealth.[56] If debt accumulation and investment are to proceed more rapidly than the accumulation of wealth, then financial intermediaries are essential. Such intermediaries issue direct debt of their own, soliciting loanable funds from surplus spending units and allocating these loanable funds from surplus spending units among deficit units whose direct debt they absorb.[57] Even with financial intermediaries the growth of financial assets continues to equal the growth of debt, but "total debt, including both the direct debt that intermediaries buy and the indirect debt of their own that they issue, rises at a faster pace relative to income and wealth than when finance is either direct or arranged internally."[58]

The commercial banking system performs this intermediary function when it accumulates financial assets in the form of notes and discounts and issues its own indirect debt in the form of bank notes and deposits. Since demand deposits were not used extensively in the antebellum Northwest in the purchase of direct debt by banks, bank notes constituted the principal form of indirect debt.

232

Thus, to a large degree the effectiveness of commercial banks as intermediaries can be assessed by the rate at which the direct and indirect debt attributable to the banking system increased relative to income or wealth.

Again, only rough calculations are possible in estimating the ratio of debt to income in the Northwest. As we have observed, the indirect debt of the banking system (bank notes and deposits) declined in importance relative to income between 1840 and 1860. If we calculate the *total* debt attributable to the banking system the ratio of total direct and indirect debt to income is .549 in 1840 and .298 in 1860. Two things should be noted concerning the substantial decline in this ratio. First, the rather high ratio for 1840 is somewhat surprising. Gurley and Shaw estimate the ratio of total debt to GNP at about unity in 1900.[59] Secondly, according to the same authors "rapid output growth tends to shrink the financial ratio, while sluggish growth tends to inflate the ratio."[60] Thus, the high ratio of 1840 may, in part, reflect the downturn of 1837 through 1843, while the lower ratio in 1860 may be the result of the economic expansion from 1843 to 1857.

Central to the process of expanding total debt more rapidly than income or wealth is the impact which the intermediary must have on the portfolio decisions of ultimate savers. The latter group must be induced to hold assets in the form of the indirect debt of banks (bank notes and deposits) as opposed to tangible, non-financial assets. "The opportunity to hold financial assets of superior characteristics to inventories and specie as a store of wealth enables holders of such tangible assets to give them up for financial assets and for others to arrange the transformation of these freed tangible assets into a more productive form."[61] The portfolio aspect of measuring bank performance in this transformation process does not, therefore, deal with the composition of financial assets, but with the public's decision on whether to hold financial assets as opposed to real assets.

Only the slimmest evidence can be marshalled to investigate the success of banks in inducing the public to hold relatively more of its indirect debt. Lacking data on all tangible assets, we concentrate on the public's holding of specie as opposed to bank debt. Data from Friedman and Schwartz indicate an increase in the total supply of specie in the United States of about 260 per cent between 1835 and 1860.[62] Over the same period the supply of specie held by Northwest banks rose a bit over 40 per cent. Unless there occurrred an extremely large migration of specie from the Northwest to other parts of the United States, it seems reasonable to conclude that the public in the Northwest held a larger amount of specie relative to bank money as time went on. This is perhaps less true in the late 1850's when reserve ratios of Northwestern banks began to decline. At any rate there is little evidence to suggest that the banks enjoyed great success in persuading the public to hold *less* specie relative to bank debt. In fact, banks as a whole in the United States failed in this regard.

Another role performed by financial intermediaries is the allocation of finance. In its broadest context this role involves the division between consumption and investment, while in a narrower sense it deals with alternative investment projects. As a rule, nineteenth century commercial banks did not encourage loans for consumption purposes except in an indirect fashion through the discounting of bills of exchange for inventory accumulation by merchants. In the non-commercial area there is little evidence that banks were heavily involved in financing manufacturing enterprises. Two other areas, however, loom large in the banks' portfolios.

The first was loans for land purchases or improvements on the land, the second was internal improvements. It is difficult to generalize on the role of banks in the financing of land purchases and improvements since attitudes and legislation differed from state to state. Most state bank

234

charters contained some provision concerning the proportion of loans that could be secured by real estate. Nonetheless, Indiana was the only state of which it could be said that the entire banking system made a strong effort to avoid loans for the purpose of land speculation.[63] At the other extreme the State Bank of Illinois was allowed by its charter to create a fund of not more than $1,000,000 to be used solely for loans on real estate security of not more than five years duration.[64] In the latter case we may note that this amount represented between one-half to one-third of the State Bank of Illinois' total loans in 1836-37, the years when land sales reached a peak in that state. Another indication that the bank actually utilized this charter privilege is the increase in non-commercial loans from about 47 per cent of the banks' total loans in 1836 to around 80 per cent in 1837.[65]

For most banks, particularly in the frontier areas of the Northwest, lending for land speculation was attractive. With interest rates of money lenders running between 20-50 per cent and a lack of alternative loan opportunities, the temptation to expand loans on real estate security must have been great.[66] On the other hand, the long-term amortized loan or mortgage was not common in the early nineteenth century, which made bank borrowing somewhat less attractive to land buyers of modest means. Banks which did not lend extensively to the ultimate settlers of the land could still participate in land booms by serving as agents for non-resident capitalists or financing large scale speculators, who in turn could offer more favorable credit terms to potential farmers.[67] The Wisconsin Marine and Fire Insurance Company, which in fact operated as a bank, financed land purchases in still a different fashion. The company would purchase land directly from the government and then sell to settlers on a contract for deed basis.

As a group, the banks of Illinois, Wisconsin, and Michigan were most heavily involved in real estate transactions, particularly of a speculative nature.[68] It seems unlikely, however, that any banking system completely escaped the temptation to participate in the land fevers which periodically swept the Old Northwest.

A second major area of non-commercial lending for state banks was involvement in internal improvement projects. At first banks might become involved in the internal improvements mania by serving as agents in the transfer of funds from the East or from Europe to agents of the state. Only when these conventional sources of funds dried up did states borrow directly from banks.

In Ohio, where $6,101,000 was borrowed for canal construction between 1825-35, the banks were heavily involved.[69] Michigan banks had an early involvement with the railroads and many railroad charters in that state included banking privileges.[70] Indiana banks originally performed only a service function, while the state raised capital through bond sales, but here too the banks were eventually forced to loan directly to the state. By 1840 the State Bank of Indiana had 16 per cent of its total loans and discounts invested in internal improvement projects, while the State Bank of Illinois had more than one-half of its capital in the form of depreciating state internal improvement bonds.[71]

Illinois is perhaps the extreme example of the problems state banks encountered in their involvement with internal improvements. In 1837, the state of Illinois authorized increases in the capital stock of the State Bank of Illinois at Springfield and the Shawneetown Bank. The state was to purchase large shares of this additional bank stock. To do so the state's Directing Board of Fund Commissioners authorized the sale of $3,000,000 of 6 per cent Illinois Bank and Internal Improvement Stock. The scheme was that the state would purchase bank stock with its 6 per cent stock, use the dividends from the bank stock to service its bonds, and use whatever was left to finance internal improvements. The banks, of course, took advantage of this increased capital and expanded rapidly. By 1840 Illinois banks had the lowest density per unit of population of the Northwestern states and the highest ratio of bank money per capita, the highest ratio of bank money to income and the highest ratio of total bank debt to income in the Northwest. Also in 1840 Illinois banks resumed specie payment following the general suspension of 1839. Unfortunately, many neighboring states were late to resume specie payment, and Illinois banks were deluged with their notes for payment in specie which they did not possess. Nor did their large holdings of Internal Improvement bonds help, for by April of 1842 these bonds, which never sold at par except in the original purchase of bank stock, had fallen to 15 on the market. Both the State Bank of Illinois and the Shawneetown Bank failed in 1842, and in 1843 the state legislature voted to liquidate both. In all, Illinois banks had furnished the state with at least $1,000,000 in long-term loans for public works in addition to advancing money for ordinary expenditures which the state neglected while concentrating on internal improvements.[72]

Golembe estimates that during the late 1830's and early 1840's the states of Ohio, Indiana, Illinois, and Michigan expended about $40,000,000 on internal improvements. Roughly $8,600,00 or better than one-fifth of this amount was provided by state banks.[73] Since much of this capital was provided in periods when the normal source of funds were unavailable to the states, their importance should not be underestimated. Nor should the costs tò the community at large due to this involvement be minimized. In a period in which bank reserves could not be expanded to accommodate the desire of the public to reduce their holdings of bank money, heavy investment by banks in illiquid internal improvement securities can be reasonably questioned. Therefore, the long-run benefits of internal improvements must be balanced against the short-run disruptions of the economy due to bank runs and bank failures.

State banks also contributed to the development of the

Northwest by increasing the flow of loanable funds from areas with higher incomes which generated a higher volume of saving.

There seems to be little doubt that state banks played at least a limited role in attracting loanable funds from outside the Northwest. In Ohio in 1833 only $1,380,000 out of $4,730,000 in bank capital was held by residents of the state.[74] Perhaps three-fifths of the stock of the Bank of Michigan was owned by easterners, while funds for the establishment of the State Bank of Indiana came in large part from outside the state. Easterners were also heavy investors in the Bank of Illinois and the State Bank of Illinois.[75] It should be noted that this occurred in spite of charter provisions in some states which required sales of bank equity to residents before it could be offered to non-residents. Golembe uses 50 per cent as a working figure for eastern ownership of Northwestern banks.[76] To this figure we can add whatever foreign ownership existed. Since stock payments were generally only partial payments initially with the remainder payable at stipulated times or on a call basis, the result was a flow of capital from the east and Europe to the Northwest.

Developing regions, like developing countries, normally pass through a stage in which the importation of inventories and capital goods is greater than their capacity to export. Although higher western prices may have provided a stimulus for increased exports into the area, it is clear that a sizeable import surplus could not have been maintained for long unless somewhere there was a flow of funds sufficient to finance it.[77]

Financing an import surplus required a net capital inflow to the Northwest, and commercial banks often served as a focal point in maintaining this flow of investment. Eastern investment in western banks provided part of this flow. Government deposits in western banks, which were the result of land sales, formed another part. Another source in which banks played a lesser role was the direct investment in western land. Capital brought in by settlers and the expenditures of eastern capital by the state on various internal improvement schemes rounded out the sources of this capital inflow.[78]

Lending for strictly local commercial transactions probably formed only a small part of banking activity in the Northwest. Aside from internal improvements, land acquisition, and land improvement, the major commercial bank lending activity was with individuals engaged directly or indirectly in the export of the agricultural surplus of the Northwest Territory.[79]

IV

In this brief concluding section we face the difficult task of evaluating the role of the commercial banking system in the development of the Old Northwest.

Viewing the commercial banking system as a monetary agent, whose principle impact occurs via the money supply, the evidence seems to indicate a rather poor performance on the whole. As noted above, the ratio of bank money declined over the period investigated, and bank money per capita declined also. These results were not sensitive to the use of bank notes alone or bank notes and demand deposits, and there is little evidence except for a very brief period that significant involuntary saving was encouraged by the expansion of the money supply at a rate greater than that required for transactions purposes. .

Further evidence on the performance of banks as monetary agents can be mustered by rough estimations of the social savings attributable to the bank's function of substituting its credit (paper money) for commodity money. Using a technique developed by Stanley Engerman, it is possible to estimate the value of the resources saved as a percentage of output or income due to the issue of paper money by banks.[80] This technique involves some estimate of the reserve ratio of the banking system, the ratio of the money supply to income and the interest rate. All of these can be estimated from data available on the Old Northwest. While the calculations are relegated to a footnote, the results merit brief discussion.[81] Engerman estimated the social savings attributable to paper money for the decades 1839-48 and 1849-58 in the United States at 0.35 of 1 per cent of GNP and 0.43 of 1 per cent of GNP respectively. Similar calculations for the Northwest indicate social savings of 0.59 of 1 per cent of GNP in 1840 and .54 of 1 per cent of GNP in 1860.[82] It is first of all interesting to note that the estimate of social savings for the Northwest appear greater than those for the country as a whole. This is perhaps to be expected in a region where the economy is being monetized rapidly. Since the social savings appear to be higher in the Northwest, the cost to society of an insufficient expansion of the money supply were proportionately greater. In short, the opportunity for relatively significant social saving existed in the Northwest but banks failed to take full advantage.[83] One final point with respect to the social savings argument concerns the question of reserve ratios. Our calculations show that the reserve ratio of Northwestern banks decreased by around 50 per cent between 1840 and 1860 from approximately 30 per cent to about 15 per cent.[84] Given reasonable considerations of safety, it is hard to conceive of reserve ratios falling significantly below the level attained in 1860. Thus, there is some evidence that the failure of the money supply to increase more rapidly than it did was not entirely a result of high reserve ratios, but rather a consequence of too few banks.[85]

High dividends and profits plus large numbers of "irregular" or unchartered banks also seem to indicate a less than optimum number of banks in the Northwest. For example, the Bank of Indiana paid dividends of around 9 per cent per year during the late 1830's.[86] Golembe points out that the issue of irregular banks is somewhat counter cyclical to that of regular banks in the Northwest. This seems to indicate an attempt to increase the money supply when normal or regular banks were unwilling or unable to do so.[87]

The performance of commercial banks as intermediaries is even less clear-cut than their role as monetary agents. The banks clearly made some contribution to development in their role as intermediaries. Tangible assets were exchanged for the financial assets of banks. Land purchases and improvements were financed by some banks, and the flow of loanable funds to the Northwest was increased by the activities of banks. Banks did play a role in the financing of internal improvements, and to the extent that these improvements promoted development so too did the banks. Banks clearly were instrumental in maintaining the import surplus so necessary to the early development of any region.

Despite these valuable contributions we should keep in mind the fact that banks were at times not eager to perform their intermediary function in a fashion which favored long-run development. As Davis and North point out "despite the growing demands for longer term credits and loans to transportation and manufacturing enterprises, the commercial banks have steadily resisted these pressures."[88] At other times unrestrained bank expansion undermined confidence in the entire system and led to "runs," suspension, or both.[89] To the extent that such events interrupted the development process they were counter productive.

The lack of enthusiasm for developmental lending and the irregular behavior of banks can both be attributed in part to bank laws or charter provisions which were overly restrictive, contradictory, or based on ignorance of the functions of financial intermediaries.

Finally, it should be noted that the banking system of the Old Northwest was probably not unique in its failure to make an optimum contribution to the development process. Recent scholarship suggests that banking systems as inter-

241

mediaries are not highly essential to the growth process. Cameron suggests that banking, whether it developed competitively or monopolistically, did not generate high levels of saving and investment and in fact produced rather unimpressive results. "While there is as yet no definite proof that banking systems as intermediaries could not perform well if properly utilized, the evidence against them is mounting up."[90]

1. Rondo Cameron (ed.) *Banking and Economic Development* (New York: Oxford University Press, 1972). George D. Green, *Finance and Economic Development in the Old South* (Stanford: Stanford University Press, 1972).

2. R. C. Buley, *The Old Northwest*, V. I. (Indiana Historical Society, 1950), p. 567.

3. J. Van Fenstermaker, *The Development of Commercial Banking: 1782-1837* (Kent, Ohio: Bureau of Economic and Business Research, 1965), p. 166.

4. Buley, p. 569.

5. There were exceptions to this generalization. In 1816 the "Bonus Law" provided for the state to acquire some ownership in banks. This system was replaced in 1825 by a 2 per cent tax on dividends declared before the law and 4 per cent on all dividends after the law. The other exception was the formation of the State Bank of Ohio in 1845 which competed with private banks.

6. Thomas Berry, *Western Prices Before 1861* (Cambridge: Harvard University Press, 1943), p. 371.

7. T. A. Andersen, *A Century of Banking in Wisconsin* (Madison: State Historical Society of Wisconsin, 1954), p. 10.

8. L. B. Krueger, *History of Commercial Banking in Wisconsin* (Madison: University of Wisconsin, 1933), p. 48. It might be noted that by 1853 the circulation of the Wisconsin Marine and Fire Insurance Company exceeded that of the entire Illinois banking system.

9. Berry, p. 381.

10. Logan Esarey, *State Banking in Indiana 1814-1873*, Indiana University Studies, Indiana University, Bulletin X, No. 2, April 15, 1912, p. 223.

11. C. C. Huntington, "A History of Banking and Currency in Ohio before the Civil War," *Ohio Archaeological and Historical Publications*, Ohio Archaeological and Historical Society, Columbus, XXIV, 1915, pp. 37, 388-89.

12. The state started buying up the outstanding notes of the bank, and by January of 1832, $289,000 in notes had been redeemed and destroyed. By 1835 only $6,554.50 was outstanding.

13. Loans and Discounts doubled in Michigan between 1835-37. Van Fenstermaker, pp. 150-51.

14. Hugh Rockoff, "Money, Prices and Banks in the Jacksonian Era," *The Reinterpretation of American Economic History* (Fogel and Engerman, eds), (New York: Harper & Row, 1971), pp. 448-459, Peter Temin, *The Jacksonian*

Economy (New York: W. W. Norton, 1969); Richard H. Timberlake, "The Specie Circular and Distribution of the Surplus," *Journal of Political Economy*, LXVIII (April, 1960), pp. 109-17.

15. Harry N. Scheiber, "Pet Banks in Jacksonian Politics," *Journal of Economic History*, XXIII, No. 2, (1963), p. 198.

16. *Ibid.*, p. 199.

17. *Ibid.*, p. 203.

18. *Ibid.*, p. 205.

19. Temin, p. 134.

20. *Ibid.*, p. 132.

21. The first installment sent $33,000 from Ohio banks to banks in the Southwest and $80,000 to other banks in the Northwest. Indiana banks transferred $114,000 to other Northwestern banks. For the second installment the payments were identical. By the third installment, specie payment had been suspended and Ohio banks paid $150,000 to banks in the middle Atlantic states and Indiana banks once again transferred $114,000 to Northwestern banks. See Temin, p. 131.

22. Temin, p. 121.

23. See Smith and Cole, *Fluctuations in American Business, 1790-1860* (Cambridge: Harvard University Press, 1935), p. 55.

24. *Historial Statistics of the United States*, Bureau of the Census, Department of Commerce (Washington: Government Printing Office, 1957), p. 121.

25. Temin has argued that the failure of reserve ratios to decline following the demise of the BUS indicates no over-extension of the state banks. However, the increase in specie may have prompted banks to make dubious loans in lieu of allowing reserve ratios to increase.

26. Scheiber, p. 209.

27. Esarey, p. 258.

28. *Report of the Comptroller of the Currency*, Executive Documents of the House of Representatives, 44th Congress, Section Session, 1876-77, p. 229.

29. Scheiber, p. 210.

30. Berry, p. 454.

31. Alpheus Felch, "Early Banks and Banking in Michigan," *Pioneer Collection*, Pioneer Society of the State of Michigan, II (Detroit, 1880), p. 123.

32. Berry, p. 471.

33. Davis, Easterlin, Parker, *et al.*, *American Economic Growth: An Economist's History of the United States* (New York: Harper and Row, 1972), p. 355.

34. Carter Golembe, "State Banks and the Economic Development of the West," (unpublished Ph.D. dissertation, Columbia University, 1952), p. 58.

35. *Ibid.*

36. *Ibid.*

37. The "near money" problem involves the proper role which should be assigned to highly liquid financial assets, such as bonds or time deposits in the money supply.

38. Rondo Cameron, *Banking in the Early Stages of Industrialization* (New York: Oxford University Press, 1967), pp. 132-33.

39. Hugh T. Patrick, "Financial Development and Economic Growth in Underdeveloped Countries," *Economic Development and Cultural Change*, XIV No. 2 (January, 1966), p. 174.

40. Green, pp. 39-40.
41. Cameron, p. 297.
42. Gurley and Shaw, "Financial Structure and Economic Development," *Economic Development and Cultural Change* XV No. 3 (April, 1967), p. 261.
43. Friedman and Schwartz, *Monetary Statistics of the United States*, (New York: Columbia University Press, 1970), pp. 222-25.
44. Cameron, *Banking and Economic Development*, p. 9.
45. Davis, Easterlin, Parker, p. 350.
46. Rockoff, p. 456.
47. *Ibid.*, p. 457.
48. See *Ibid.*, pp. 455-56.
49. *Report of the Comptroller of the Currency*, pp. 227-29.
50. Note that the money supply will generally increase more rapidly than output because of the development process alone. Only increases over and above this rate would result in significant forced saving.
51. Green, p. 41.
52. See Berry, p. 425.
53. William F. Harding, "State Banks of Indiana," *Journal of Political Economy*, IV (December, 1895-September, 1896), p. 114.
54. Golembe, p. 109.
55. *Ibid.*, p. 123-124.
56. Gurley and Shaw, "Financial Aspects of Economic Development," *American Economic Review*, XLV (September, 1955), p. 518.
57. *Ibid.*, p. 519.
58. *Ibid.*
59. Gurley and Shaw, "Financial Structure and Economic Development," p. 258.
60. *Ibid.*, p. 260.
61. Patrick, p. 181.
62. Friedman and Schwartz, pp. 220-24.
63. Golembe, p. 134.
64. *Ibid.*, p. 157.
65. *Ibid.*, p. 106.
66. Allan G. Bogue, "Financing the Prairie Farmer," *The Reinterpretation of American Economic History* (New York: Harper and Row, 1971), p. 303.
67. *Ibid.*, p. 304.
68. Golembe, p. 135.
69. Berry, p. 412.
70. Golembe, p. 180.
71. Sharp, *The Jacksonians versus the Banks: Politics in the States After the Panic of 1837* (New York: Columbia University Press, 1970), p. 33.
72. Golembe, p. 187.
73. *Ibid.*, p. 187.
74. Huntington, p. 366.
75. Golembe, pp. 223-24.
76. *Ibid.*, p. 224.
77. *Ibid.*, p. 222.
78. *Ibid.*, pp. 222-30.
79. Ibid., p. 91.

80. Stanley Engerman, "A Note on the Economic Consequences of the Second Bank of the United States," *Journal of Political Economy*, LXXVIII (July/August, 1970), pp. 725-28.

81. Engerman's formulation is: $(1-S/M) \times (M/Y) \times (i)$ where S is total specie stock; M, the money supply; Y, income; and i, the rate of interest.

For 1840: $1-S/M = .691$; $M/Y = .086$; i assumed to be .10

1860: $1-S/M = .849$; $M/Y = .064$; i assumed to be .10

Thus social saving in $1840 = (.691) \times (.086) \times (.10) = .0059$

$$1860 = (.849) \times (.064) \times (.10) = .0054$$

82. Our use of the bank reserve ratio and the supply of bank money probably gives a more accurate estimate of the social saving due to bank money.

83. Note that any increase in the ratio of money to income would increase social savings still more.

84. If bank notes and deposits are utilized in this calculation, the reserve ratios are 24 per cent and 11 per cent respectively.

85. Recall that bank density/10,000 population was lower in the Northwest than for the United States as a whole in 1840, 1850 and 1860. See above, Table 1.

86. Esarey, p. 301.

87. Golembe, p. 210.

88. Davis and North, *Institutional Change and American Economic Growth* (Cambridge: University Press, 1971), p. 116.

89. *Ibid.*, p. 128.

90. J. G. Gurley, *American Economic Review*, LVII (September, 1967), p. 953.

245

X

PUBLIC CANAL INVEST-
MENT AND THE OPENING
OF THE OLD NORTHWEST

Roger L. Ransom

University of California, Riverside

I

In 1800, The Second Census of the United States reported that just over fifty thousand people lived in the territory of the United States lying roughly north and west of the Ohio River. Forty years later, the Sixth Census of the United States counted over two million people in the states of Indiana and Ohio alone; almost three million resided in the five states which were formed out of the "Old Northwest".[1] This rapid influx of people, which brought the share of the population living in Ohio and Indiana from less than 1 per cent of the nation's total at the turn of the century to almost 13 per cent by 1840, would not have occurred without major improvements in the transportation network of the country. These states were locked away from the markets on the Tidewater by the Appalachian Mountains. In 1820, producers in Ohio had no alternatives other than shipping their goods by wagon over tortuous roads of the mountain passes, or sending them down the long river route to New Orleans and then by sea

246

to the northeastern centers. Both routes were prohibitively expensive except for those people located along the Ohio River and its tributaries.

By the time a second peace with England was signed in 1814, the potential benefit which might develop from a transportation system directly connecting the Old Northwest and the Atlantic states was obvious to the most casual contemporary observer. All that remained to be worked out was how such an ambitious task was to be carried out. At least one serious attempt by private interests to breach the Appalachian barrier with water transportation had been made before the turn of the century.[2] However, the effort failed, and it became increasingly apparent that private capital alone was unlikely to shoulder the high risks and substantial costs involved in a trans-Appalachian water route. In 1808, Secretary of the Treasury Albert Gallatin put forward a bold proposal to use the federal government to finance a number of internal improvements.[3] His scheme, which included several water routes over the mountains, anticipated much of the subsequent investment in transportation over the next fifty years. Unfortunately for those interested in immediate construction of transportation improvements, Gallatin's suggestions floundered on the quibbling in Congress over the proper role of government support for such projects, and the evaporation of the federal surplus during the War of 1812.[4]

Nevertheless, the perceived benefits from a route to the west had increased enough by 1816 that DeWitt Clinton and his supporters were able to persuade the state of New York to construct a 363-mile canal from Albany to Lake Erie. The Erie Canal was a spectacular technological triumph demonstrating that canals could be built over long distances in unsettled areas. Perhaps equally important, it quickly proved to be an economic bonanza for the state of New York. Even before the first shipment from Buffalo reached New York City in 1825, revenues from the previously opened portions of the canal were paying for the interest costs on the entire project. Within a relatively short time the Erie became the principal transportation link between the tidewater and the growing economies of Ohio and Indiana.

The enormous success of the Erie produced a strong encouragement for other tidewater cities to compete with the northern route. Yet, despite the fact that both Philadelphia and Baltimore could find more direct routes to the Ohio River, the southern interregional canal routes failed to elicit the huge economic response of their northern neighbor. The Mainline Canal in Pennsylvania, constructed at a cost of over $16 million (compared to the seven million dollars invested in the Erie) was never able to bring more than a trickle of revenues to the state. An even less successful rival was the Chesapeake and Ohio Canal from Baltimore to the west, which was virtually a total loss.[5]

To those settling in the Old Northwest, the question of whether or not the canal systems of Pennsylvania and Maryland earned a normal return on their investment was hardly a matter for concern. Whatever the returns to particular projects, the interregional canals created a huge fall in transportation costs between the east and the Ohio Valley.[6] The effect of this decline in costs was to radically alter the terms of trade facing western farmers. Estimates of interregional trade flows by Kohlmeier [10] and Fishlow [4] leave no doubt that the opening of this "Northern Gateway" generated a large expansion of exports from the Ohio Valley by the late 1830's. Table 1 presents data regarding exports from the western states and traffic on interregional canals from 1835 to 1849. In 1835 the west sent about one-fourth of its 100,000 tons of agricultural exports to the east—all of it by canal. Fifteen years later, western shipments to the east had risen to over 500,000 tons, or 60 per cent of total exports from the region. The crucial role of the canals in carrying this trade is clear from Table 1; between two-thirds and three-fourths of the agricultural exports heading east used the Mainline or Erie Canals.[7]

Though the decline in costs due to the interregional canals represented the most dramatic shift in relative transfer costs, the appearance of more efficient transportation on the rivers in the west was an equally important factor in the early years. Between 1820 and 1840 the number of steamboats on the western rivers increased fivefold, and river rates on the Ohio and Mississippi Rivers had declined markedly.[8] This fall in rates from the Ohio Valley to New Orleans is reflected in the pre-eminent position of the southern market for western exports before 1840. Though the canals generated a far greater increase in traffic during the decade 1840-50, the Southern outlet for western products remained important at mid-century.[9]

Table 1

Western Exports Via the "Northern Gateway", 1835-49
(Thousands of tons)

Year	Total Western Exports	Exports Shipped To East	Total Via Canals	Percentage Via Canal
1835	102.2	23.4	23.4	100.0
1839	217.7	114.2	74.4	65.1
1844	435.6	263.0	164.5	62.5
1849	845.7	522.5	377.7	72.3

Source: Ransom [17], Table 1, p. 14.

II

Despite the great opportunity offered to western farmers by these lower interregional rates, the problem of getting products from farm to a secondary market near the terminus of a major transportation route remained formidable. Realizing this, the state governments of Ohio and Indiana undertook construction of a vast network of canals within the area of these states. In all, they invested approximately $20 million as a direct response to the opening of the Erie Canal.[10] The map shows the major projects constructed between 1825 and 1850. An indication of how great an effort this investment by the state represented is seen by the fact that funds for canal construction in 1840 equaled 3.7 per cent of personal income in Ohio and 4.8 per cent in Indiana.[11] Even allowing for the roughness with which the income and investment figures are estimated, it is clear that the effort to provide internal improvements in these states was considerable. The potential gains from these canals must have seemed large to the men who envisioned them as well as to the public who bought the bonds to finance them.

Yet, in spite of their promise and the enormous growth of the Ohio and Indiana economy, the economic performance of these canal ventures seldom justified this faith in their potential. Throughout the 1840's the canal systems in both states failed to pay their way; by the Civil War almost all of the state canals were either abandoned or leased to private users at a small fraction of their initial cost. The large investment by state governments in canals to open the Old Northwest placed an enormous strain on the state finances. In the mid-forties Indiana was faced with insufficient revenue to pay the interest on the state bonds and the strong possibility that the debt would have to be repudiated altogether. Though Ohio had sounder financing of her canal debt, additional taxes were required to cover the losses from the canal system.[12]

But what of the other benefits which were brought by the canal? The new transportation systems did, after all, greatly lower shipping costs into the interior. Even casual inspection of data on economic activity reveal that the "canal counties" invariably prospered relative to areas not served by the internal improvements. Such differences seem to lend support to arguments that, when the social

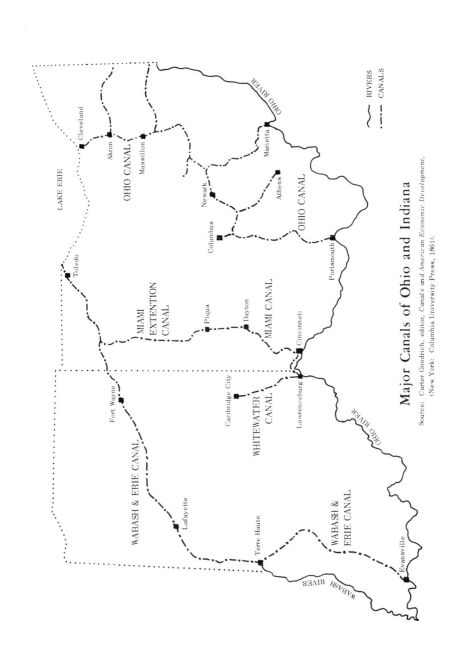

Major Canals of Ohio and Indiana

Source: Carter Goodrich, editor, *Canals and American Economic Development*, (New York: Columbia University Press, 1861).

RIVERS

CANALS

LAKE ERIE

OHIO RIVER

Cleveland

Akron

Massillon

OHIO CANAL

Newark

Athens

Columbus

OHIO CANAL

Portsmouth

Toledo

MIAMI
EXTENTION
CANAL

Piqua

Dayton

MIAMI CANAL

Cincinnati

Fort Wayne

Cambridge City

WHITEWATER
CANAL

Lawrenceburg

OHIO RIVER

WABASH & ERIE CANAL

Lafayette

Terre Haute

WABASH &
ERIE CANAL

Evansville

WABASH RIVER

return is fully considered, the canals did pay their way.[13] Such evidence must be used cautiously, however. The "gains" observed in canal counties might be only a reflection of the importance of *interregional cost changes*, not the result of gains from the intraregional canal. Given a strong impetus for expansion of exports due to the former changes, development located in the canal counties might have occurred in another area of the state with only slightly higher costs. Only the *net contribution* of the local improvement can be considered as a part of the social return to that project.

Figure 1

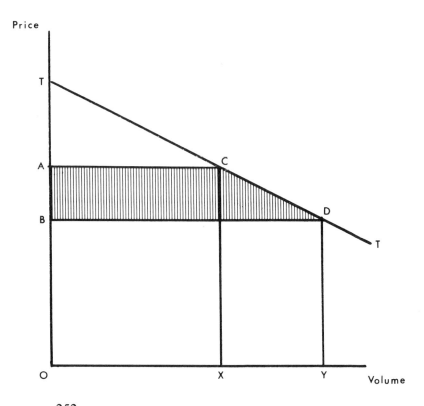

The problem, of course, is to untangle and measure the "economic rent" or "consumer's surplus" accruing to purchasers of canal services, once transportation costs have declined due to the canal. A simple diagrammatic representation of this "gain" can be seen in Figure 1. Suppose there is a demand curve TT for transport services showing the relation between the price of the service and the volume of traffic demanded (measured in ton-miles). The canal causes transport prices to fall from OA to OB, so the demand for transportation rises from OX to OY. The shaded area ABCD approximates the benefits which are received from the use of the transportation service, but not paid to the transportation agency in revenues. Because each shipper pays a single price (OB) for all units purchased, the transportation agency is unable to capture the "consumer surplus".

Unfortunately, the area ABCD cannot be directly measured. In fact, we usually observe only the price OB and quantity OY which exist with the canal route. Most attempts to estimate the "savings" from the canal involve a comparison of costs "with the canal" (i.e., OB in Figure 1), to those costs "without the canal" (i.e., OA in Figure 1). Since only the actual price and volume of traffic are known, this results in an estimate of social benefits which is an upper bound to the actual level. While this bias can be adjusted somewhat, most of the "social saving" estimates—to use Robert Fogel's expression—tend to create upward biased estimates of the social return. There remains a considerable controversy over the interpretation of this estimate in the evaluation of the canal (or rail) project's net worth.[14]

Whichever of the many estimating techniques is employed, quantitative measures of external benefits from canals invariably rest on two basic parameters. First is the magnitude of the cost differential between the canal and its closest competitors. The greater this cost advantage favoring the canal, the larger any potential savings to producers using the facilities must be. Second is the level of traffic which the canal was able to generate during its useful life. If canal traffic never in fact developed, then no matter how great the unit savings available may have been, we must conclude that the impact of these lower costs did not provide sufficient stimulus to economic activity to warrant the cost of the canal. While these points may seem obvious, they serve to remind us that the level of external benefits is likely to be highly correlated with the more traditional measures of canal performance —the level of traffic and toll revenues. The problem of evaluating the canal is further complicated by the need to look at these parameters not at a point in time, but over the entire life of the canal operation. If alternative transport systems appear which reduce the canal's cost advantage, then the associated benefits from the canal become smaller. Successful competition—as in the case of railroads bidding away canal traffic—lessens the impact of the canal over time. Though a promising venture in the beginning, the canal investment may have become economically inefficient due to changes in technology.[15]

With all this in mind, the success—and failure—of canals in providing economic gains to the Old Northwest will be approached in this essay by applying "cost-benefit" logic to the major canal projects undertaken by the states of Ohio and Indiana.

III

The Ohio Canal was unquestionably the most successful attempt to take advantage of the opportunity offered by the Erie Canal's lowering of interregional transfer costs. Finished in 1833, the 309-mile canal served the eastern portion of the state from Portsmouth on the Ohio River to Cleveland on Lake Erie. The optimistic predictions of the canal's builders seemed more than justified by the end of the 1830's. Throughout the 1840's revenues remained high, in spite of the economic slump at the outset of that decade. By 1850 the rapidly expanding level of traffic was exceeding 20 million ton-miles per year. Estimates of the external benefits, coupled with the toll revenues, are presented in Table 2.[16] The figures suggest that the annual return to the state remained around 10 per cent throughout the forties; a return well above prevailing rates in the capital markets.[17] Other measures similarly show the beneficial economic effects of the canal. By 1850, Akron, Massilon, Dresden, and Newark had all expanded as centers of agricultural processing related to the canal commerce.[18] The impact of the Ohio Canal on the state was clearly substantial. By extending the savings offered by the Erie Canal into the interior of eastern Ohio, the canal tapped a rich area of potential economic specialization in 1833. As the traffic and revenue patterns for the next two decades illustrate, this specialization did develop. It is reasonable to conclude that, without the canal, development of this region would have been retarded for some time.

The obvious success of the Ohio Canal provided strong arguments for those favoring the use of waterways to open

Table 2

Returns on the Ohio Canal, Selected Years 1836-55
(In Thousands of Dollars)

Years[a]	Toll Revenues	Traffic (Millions of ton-miles)	Social Return[b]	Total Return	Rate of Return on Investment[c]
1836-38	157	10.1	101	258	6.1
1839-41	277	15.6	255	532	12.5
1844-46	205	14.3	207	471	9.8
1851-53	203	28.9	178	504	9.0
1854-56	78	18.0	18	97	2.3

Notes:
  a. Figures are averages for years indicated.
  b. See text for a discussion of estimating procedures for social returns.
  c. Rate of return calculated on $4.25 million initial investment in the Ohio Canal.
Source: Ransom [18], pp. 1053, 1056.

the western portions of the state. When the state began the eastern trunk line in 1825, it was already thinking of a western counterpart northward from Cincinnati to link that commerce with the Great Lakes. By 1831 this project was well under way with the completion of the Miami Canal to Dayton. It was further developed as part of the Miami Extension Canal project with the additional canal mileage to Piqua in 1837. These original sections of the Miami Canal, which cost just under one million dollars, seemed a well conceived investment. Just as the Ohio Canal had tapped the "Northern Gateway", so the Miami Canal offered the Miami Valley cheap access to the expanding river commerce of Cincinnati. Unlike the Ohio Canal, however, the Miami Canal had only a minor effect in reshaping the trading pattern of Southern Ohio. Cincinnati remained primarily dependent on the River for her commercial activities, and the canal added only a minor impetus to that trade in the 1840's.

Nevertheless, for its size the canal did a fairly robust business. By 1840 some 40,000 tons of agricultural products were arriving at Cincinnati, and in 1847 (the peak year for Cincinnati arrivals) the total reached more than 45,000.[19] It appears as though the Miami Canal south of Piqua generated some eight million ton-miles of traffic in 1851, and perhaps half that level ten years earlier.[20] If the savings per ton-mile on the Miami Canal were approximately comparable to those of the Ohio Canal in the same period, then the canal would have generated about $50,000 annually in social returns.[21] Combined with the toll revenues, this implied that the Miami Canal produced a level of benefits ample to assure profitable operation in the 1840's. Though not nearly as important to the state's economy as the Ohio Canal, the project between Cincinnati and Dayton—and probably the extension to Piqua—seems to have been a sound investment.

Our discussion to this point suggests that—at least until 1835 or so—Ohio's decisions on internal improvements resulted in carefully planned projects with great economic potential. The five or six million dollars invested in these two waterways were paying handsomely within ten years.

However, as traffic expanded on the canals, a new form of transportation sought to profit from the growing commerce along the canal routes. As early as 1838 the Miami Canal had direct rail competition as far as Dayton; by the end of the fifties both Dayton and Cincinnati were linked to Lake Erie with through rail connections.[22] On the route of the Ohio Canal, the railroad construction was slightly slower, but by 1853 all major ports along the canal were linked by rail to Cleveland. Though the full impact of these developments were not apparent on canal returns until the mid-fifties, the speed with which the railroads drew traffic away from "profitable" waterways such as the Ohio Canal illustrates the superiority of the railroad by the end of the 1840's. Traffic on the Ohio Canal fell by more than one-half from 1851-52 to 1854-55; toll revenues fell by still more, and the "external benefits" were almost wiped out as a result of the cheap alternative of the railroad.[23] By the end of the decade, estimated returns on the Ohio Canal—even including indirect social benefits—were almost certainly negative.[24]

The emergence of the railroad at this time as a superior technology was not entirely unexpected. In the late 1830's rail advocates were already busy pointing out the obvious deficiencies of canal technology. Capital costs of construction were high; routes were relatively inflexible and confined to a narrow band around the canal; and speed of travel was hardly faster than by overland horse and wagon. If the potential for railroads seemed small in 1825 when the initial plans for the Ohio Canal system were formulated, such was not the case ten or fifteen years later.[25] Yet the canal enthusiasts continued to press their case, and their arguments carried the day. In 1835 Ohio launched an ambitious program of canal expansion which included not only a number of feeder canals for the Ohio

257

Canal route, but also the completion of the Miami Extension Canal from Dayton to Toledo. These decisions were made, of course, in the context of an expanding market for western produce and the proven success of earlier canal ventures. Despite considerable difficulties which were encountered in raising funds in the capital market, the western trunk line project was completed in 1841—at a cost of over six million dollars to the state. While it is easy to admire the perseverence and skill with which canal advocates managed to complete the state's commitment to western trunk-line canals, the simple truth remains that their triumph was an unmitigated economic loss for the people of Ohio.

Estimates for traffic on the entire route of the Miami and Erie Canals are presented in Table 3.[26] Only one-fourth of the total volume of 25.8 ton-miles shipped in 1851 was a result of the extension of the canal through to Toledo. Most of the export traffic generated to Cincinnati in that year came from the southern end of the canal; only the import traffic from Toledo traveled any distance on the canal, and the tonnages shipped were small. The bulk of

Table 3

Traffic on the Miami and Erie Canal, 1851

Canal Section[a]	Traffic to Terminus (Millions of ton-miles)	Traffic from Terminus (Millions of ton-miles)	Total Traffic (Millions of ton-miles)
Miami Canal	5.6	2.4	8.0
Miami Extension	3.0	3.7	6.7
Wabash & Erie	8.0	3.1	11.1
Total Traffic	16.6	9.2	25.8

Notes: Traffic volume estimated for each of the three sections:
Miami Canal: Between Dayton and Cincinnati.
Miami Extension: Between Dayton and Toledo (except Junction City traffic).
Wabash and Erie Traffic: Traffic entered as "clearing" or "arriving" at Junction City, on the Wabash and Erie Canal.
Source: Estimated from data in the Ohio Board of Public Works, *Annual Report* [14], p. 30.

Toledo's traffic for export came from the junction of the Ohio system with Indiana's Wabash and Erie Canal, not the interior of Ohio. Over 75 per cent of the arrivals at Toledo originated at Junction City. Barely a million ton-miles of traffic were generated North of Piqua on the Miami Extension Canal.[27] The small level of economic activity which did develop on this stretch of canal could surely have located elsewhere for only slightly higher costs inasmuch as transport savings from the canal were relatively minor. As an incentive to develop northwestern Ohio, the Miami Extension project failed. As a trunk line to connect Cincinnati and the Great Lakes it was no more successful. A generous estimate of the total volume of traffic in Table 3 suggests that the canal in 1851 generated about seven million ton-miles; the total was surely not that high throughout the decade, and most of it was concentrated at the southern end of the canal project.

IV

Indiana shared Ohio's dream of making Toledo a major port on the Great Lakes. The desirability of cheap transportation to link the Great Lakes and the Wabash Valley was apparent once the Erie Canal was opened. In the early 1830's, a canal appeared to be the obvious answer, and the existing Ohio plans for a western canal to Toledo seemed ideal for the Indiana needs. Planning for a canal from Evansville to Toledo began in 1828. Unfortunately, work on the project was not started until 1831 in Indiana and 1834 in Ohio. By 1843 the Indiana canal had only reached Lafayette and by 1847 Terre Haute.[28] Like the Northern section of the Miami Extension, the Wabash and Erie Canal suffered from incredibly poor timing. Conceived early enough to be supported by the canal enthusiasm of the mid-thirties, it was not finished in time to avoid either the crippling effects of the economic slump of 1839-43 or the disastrous effects of rail competition to Toledo, Cincinnati, and Cleveland in the early 1850's.

Indiana, to be sure, did expand rapidly in the decade 1840 to 1850. However it is difficult to attribute this growth to the Wabash and Erie Canal. Indeed, the expansion of activity makes the failure of the canal all the more striking. Even by the most generous estimate, the economic effects of the canal on northern Indiana were minimal. The Wabash and Erie route did contribute some 100,000 tons of agricultural shipments to Toledo (see Table 3). However, this is a rather modest level of activity when compared to the receipts of goods at Cincinnati from the Miami Canal or Cleveland from the Ohio Canal.[29] The reason for this low volume of traffic from Indiana is not hard to find. As early as 1838 a Boston merchant noted that it was fifty cents cheaper per ton to use the river and Southern Gateway from Lafayette than to use the canal to Toledo and east. Another observation at the same time claimed that the river-ocean route to New York cost about ten dollars per ton; via the canal it would cost twelve dollars per ton.[30] Lafayette was only two hundred miles by canal from Toledo—the northern end of the Wabash route. If the river could compete in 1838, the falling costs of both river and rail alternatives must have reduced the possible savings to producers using the canal to very low levels by the mid-forties. The canal did not reach Evansville until after 1850, and the section between that city and Terre Haute never generated significant traffic, while accounting for large losses in net expenses.[31]

The Wabash and Erie Canal north of Terre Haute cost Indiana more than four million dollars. The level of traffic and implied savings suggested by the discussion above could not have covered the costs involved in this investment. The expansion of production in Indiana seems to have been in response to the growing market for foodstuffs in the United States, and the extension of interregional transportation into the west generally. The Wabash and Erie Canal provided very little impetus to widening that market in Indiana. Producers in the northern parts of the state would, if the canal were not built, have located in other feasible areas of production in Indiana—along the Ohio River, the Wabash River, or the increasingly longer routes of railroad developing towards the end of the decade. The losses in terms of production foregone would have been small, and the costs from interest and capital charges from the canal investment could have been avoided.

V

The broad conclusion which emerges from a cost-benefit approach to the economic contribution of these canal projects is that none of them fully repaid the state its intial development. The Ohio Canal came closest, operating at a high level of revenues and traffic for some fifteen years. Portions of the Miami and Erie Canal were profitable for a time, but they accounted for less than one-sixth of the investment in the entire canal project. The Wabash and Erie was never economically viable. With the appearance of the Railroad in 1850, all of the canal ventures became unprofitable operations even when virtually all measures of direct and indirect benefits are considered.

Yet, to use this "positive net benefit" criteria to assert that the state investment was "wasted" in every case seems rash. A number of considerations need to be faced before reaching such a judgment. First, is it in fact reasonable to assume that the planners of the canal could accurately predict the rate of technological progress—specifically the rapid development of rail technology? Our answer, for at least the first phases of the Ohio canal construction, was unequivocally: *no, they could not.* The example of the Erie Canal and other eastern ventures—plus the early performance of the Ohio Canal itself—provided solid evidence on the ability of water transportation to provide efficient means of moving commodities over long distances. Railroads, by contrast, were relatively new and untested in the early thirties. On the later projects, such as the Miami Extension and Wabash and Erie Canal, our judgment suggests the states might have been more cautious. Both Indiana and Ohio appear to have made a serious error in judgment in pushing these projects to completion in the 1840's. Though planned when they might serve a useful purpose, neither project was finished soon enough to avoid serious problems which had been developing for some time. In most cases, the state expenditures after 1837 reflected an unwillingness by the canal commissioners to alter existing plans, many of which had become outdated. Still, this is far easier to conclude now than it was at the time. In effect, we are castigating the conservatism of canal advocates for not risking the new technology rather than the proven one.

A further question regarding the "cost-benefit" approach is the danger of ignoring the overall effects of the substantial fall in transportation costs because we are using a *partial analysis* of transport benefits. The fact that railroads did in fact reduce rates (by a much smaller fraction than the canals had earlier cut costs) causes our model of "savings" to conclude that the "worth" of the canal was reduced. The railroad expropriated the canal traffic and, adding some additional traffic, was able to shift the savings from reduced transportation from the canal to its own ledger. In so doing, the analysis makes the canals seem unnecessary.[32] But the initial savings effected by the canal are still there! What we observe is an excess capacity in transportation because the state decided to invest in a form of capital which was relatively long-lived and became obsolete. The contribution of the canal in its productive period should not be dismissed. After all, waterways provided the first impetus to expansion—and perhaps represented a necessary precursor to the later development of railroads.

The judgment regarding the appropriate technology, then, becomes one of timing. In this regard, it is important to consider the perceived cost and risk factors surrounding internal improvements during the first third of the nineteenth century. Canal and Railroad ventures at this time were both hazardous, involving large outlays of capital and uncertain payoffs. Had the state not built the internal water systems, would private capital have financed comparable transportation cost reductions? Would the private choice of technology have been superior to that of the state? A yes answer to both of these queries involves an exercise in counterfactual history which I believe stretches the imagination. The Old Northwest at the outset of the canal era was a largely unsettled region. One effect of the state's pledge to provide transport improvements was to encourage would-be immigrants to move to the new region confident that the terms of trade would improve. And they were not disappointed; the state fulfilled its commitment. The network of canals assisted many parts of the Old Northwest to expand production in response to a rising national market for their exports.

However, the role of canals must not be exaggerated by our exoneration of the men who decided to push ahead with risky ventures. To be sure, projects such as the Erie Canal which brought enormous cost reductions in interregional trade, were a necessary step for the economic growth of the Old Northwest. The benefits to this single project were probably sufficient to cover the losses of all its imitators in the Antebellum West. Nevertheless, the impact of canal technology on western growth was limited to a rather brief interval between the opening of the Ohio Canal and the advent of through connections of the western railroads by the mid-1850's. In those twenty-five years, canals brought about huge reductions in hauling goods both within the west and from the west to the tidewater. They substantially aided and encouraged the rapid settlement of the Old Northwest noted at the outset of this essay. They shared in the growth which meant that by 1850 home manufactures—once the mainstay of frontier farm production—had declined to trivial levels.[33] Finally, they

263

pioneered the opening of markets which allowed Indiana and Ohio in 1850 to account for 15 per cent of all corn and wheat produced in the United States.[34] However, the canals did not fundamentally alter the structure of the western economy as an agricultural export region. Most of the "manufacturing" in 1840 was to process the flow of agricultural exports to other markets. Farming remained the nucleus of the economy of Ohio and Indiana until after mid-century. Canals, in the parlance of development economics, promoted *extensive economic growth*. Factor inputs increased with the influx of people farming new lands, and output rose accordingly.

Life on a farm in the Old Northwest in the heyday of the "canal era" remained essentially an isolated, rural existence. It took the introduction of the railroad with its ability to move people and goods rapidly, together with the telegraph's revolutionary impact on the speed of information, to transform the Old Northwest into the young industrial society of the Civil War period. And canals, which had provided the initial impetus to the settlement of this vast region, were quietly retired amid the bustle of a new and very different era.

1. The population figures are taken from *Historical Statistics* [24], Series A-20 and A-134-39. The five states are: Ohio, Indiana, Illinois, Michigan, and Wisconsin.

2. The Inland Lock and Navigation Company attempted to connect the various rivers of northern New York into a water route from the Hudson to either Lake Erie or Lake Ontario in the late 1790's. The project was begun but never finished. For a full account of the early attempts to cut transportation routes through New York see Miller [12].

3. Gallatin [7]. Gallatin planned four trans-Appalachian routes and hoped to finance his scheme with the surplus in the Federal Treasury.

4. For an excellent summary of the Gallatin plan in the perspective of future developments, as well as its fate in Congress, see Goodrich [8], Chapter 2.

5. The problems of the Mainline as a competitor to the Erie are discussed in Ransom [17]. The C & O's inability to pay off its $11 million cost is well documented by Sanderlin [20], and Segal [22]. Rubin [19] has provided an excellent analysis of the dilemma facing Philadelphia and Baltimore as to how to meet the challenge of the Erie Canal in the late 1820's and 1830's.

6. Crude estimates of transportation costs before 1820 suggest that the Erie Canal and its imitators reduced shipping charges to the tidewater by a factor of ten (from $100/ton to $10/ton) as early as 1835; and both tolls and carrying charges fell thereafter. See Ransom [17], Scheiber [21], and Taylor [23] for observations of costs in the canal era.

7. The canals also dominated the westbound flow of imports from the tidewater. See Ransom [17], Table A-1, p. 30.

8. On the growth of western river traffic, see Hunter [9] and Berry [2]. A concise general summary of the statistics of Antebellum river commerce is in Fishlow[5].

9. Fishlow estimates that the southern route took 49 per cent of all foodstuffs in 1839, and this had declined to 31 per cent by 1853 ([4], p. 284).

10. Ohio spent $4.25 million on the Ohio Canal; $8.1 million on the Miami and Erie Canal; and another $3.2 million on various "feeder canals" for these two trunk lines. Indiana spent $4.6 million on the Wabash and Erie as far as Terre Haute (the eventual cost to the Ohio River exceeded $6 million), and $1.4 million on the Whitewater Canal.

11. The estimates are from Segal[22], p. 233.

12. See Benton [1] for a good discussion of the Indiana crisis of 1846-7. Scheiber[21] gives an excellent account of Ohio's financial problems.

13. Historians of the canals have frequently employed comparisons of data on population, occupational employment, and value of real estate to infer the benefits from canals. See, for example, McClelland and Huntington [11], Scheiber [21], Segel [22], and Neimi [13] on Ohio, and Benton [1] for the Wabash and Erie in Indiana.

14. Fogel first used the phrase "social saving" in his article on the savings from interregional rail shipments in 1890 ([6]). Most of the numerous comments and rejoinders which followed deal with the concept of social savings as a proxy for the social return to railroads. The most useful discussions for the present essay are those of: Fishlow [5], pp. 468-72; Ransom [15], pp. 371-73; Scheiber [21], pp. 391-97; and Segal [22], pp. 247-48.

15. The problem of technological obsolescence of the canals as the railroad developed poses problems in the evaluation of state investments. To the extent that some of the projects were constructed before the potential of the railroad was apparent, their contribution should be considered on the basis of their performance before the railroad. As we shall note below, a judgment regarding the future prospect of alternative systems cutting short the period of returns is seldom unambiguous.

16. The "social return" shown in Table 2 is the estimated "rent" which must have accrued to producers along the canal as a result of lower transport costs brought by water transportation (i.e., the area of ABCD in Figure 1). For a more complete discussion of the estimating technique see Ransom [18], pp. 1043-49.

17. The social returns estimate of Table 2 is probably downward biased. A simple estimate of savings, based on the volume of traffic in 1850 and a savings per ton-mile of 15c (the approximate "market" differential between canal and wagon travel), suggests benefits on the order of $1.5 million. However, such an estimate is highly biased upwards. The estimates of Table 2, considering only

shipments viable without the canal, imply an average social return per ton-mile of about $0.62 in 1850 and $1.63 in 1840. See Ransom [18].

18. Scheiber [21], chapters 8 and 9, provides the most complete discussion of this diverse development. Segal [22], pp. 236-37, and Neimi [13], pp. 507-508, analyze employment data to indicate the shift into manufacturing and commerce. Additional data on capital investment is in Ransom [16].

19. Scheiber [21], p. 202, Table 8.4.

20. See Table 3, below. Arrivals in 1845 were about half the total for 1851.

21. The estimates are at best ball-park guesses. Although volume on the canal doubled, the rent per ton-mile probably fell substantially with the appearance of rail alternatives. See note 16 above concerning the saving per ton-mile on the Ohio Canal.

22. The little Miami Railroad opened 38 miles of track to Dayton by 1838. By 1850, the Mad River and Lake Erie Railroad ran trains from Dayton to Sandusky. Direct rail connections between Cincinnati and Cleveland were completed not long after. See Scheiber [21] and Ransom [18] for additional discussion of railroads in Ohio to 1850.

23. Of the estimated $18 million in social returns from the Ohio Canal in 1854-56, two-thirds of that was from coal. Thus, the benefits to agricultural producers, which had comprised the bulk of returns throughout the 1840's, had practically vanished. (Ransom[18], p. 1053.)

24. Ransom [18], p. 1058.

25. See the discussion by Scheiber, who points out that the rail advocates were pressing their case as early as 1828 ([21], pp. 276-317). Rubin [19] points out that rail potential was seriously considered in the Pennsylvania debates of the late 1820's regarding the route of the Mainline. In fact, the 80 miles from Columbia to Philadelphia on the Mainline was completed with a railroad.

26. The estimates of Table 3 were constructed from aggregate tonnages reported by the canal commissioners in 1851 ([14], p. 30). The estimates assume that all clearings (or arrivals) at intermediate points are destined for (or originate from) the two terminal points of the canal. The average distance per ton of exports was just over 70 miles; that for imports just under 80 miles.

27. Computed from data provided in Ohio Board of Public Works [14], p. 30.

28. Benton [1] provides an excellent summary of the construction of the canal. About 70 miles of the project were in Ohio, connecting the Miami and Erie Canal to Toledo.

29. Cleveland in 1851 received 425,000 tons from the Ohio Canal; Cincinnati 180,000 tons from the southern parts of the Miami and Erie route which was, of course, a much smaller area served (Ohio Board of Public Works [14], p. 30).

30. Benton[1], p. 105.

31. Benton notes that there were never more than 33 boats used on this portion of the canal. By 1858 a serious move was underway to abandon the southern part of the canal entirely ([1], pp. 78-80).

32. That is, by attributing *all* the savings to *one* mode of transportation, a partial analysis can lead to conclusions that *neither* system was a huge benefit. The relatively "small" savings from canals illustrate the superiority of the

railroad; whereas a "low" social savings from the railroad suggests the limited improvement of rail over existing canal travel in the 1850's.

33. In 1850, the Census of Agriculture reported that home manufactures in Ohio were about 2.5 percent of all manufactures; in Indiana the percentage was approximately 8 ([25], pp. 791-96).

34. Estimated by DeBow [3], p. 177.

REFERENCES

1. Benton, Elbert J. *The Wabash Trade Route in the Development of the Old Northwest*, Baltimore: Johns Hopkins Press, 1903.

2. Berry, Thomas S. *Western Prices Before 1860*, Cambridge, Mass.: Harvard University Press, 1943.

3. DeBow, J. E. *A Statistical View of the United States . . . A Compendium of the Seventh Census*, Washington, D.C.: 1853.

4. Fishlow, Albert. *American Railroads and the Transformation of the Antebellum Economy*, Cambridge, Mass.: Harvard University Press, 1965.

5. ———. "Internal Transportation," Chapter 13 of Lance Davis *et al.*, *American Economic Growth: An Economist's History of the United States*, New York: Harper & Row, 1972; pp. 468-547.

6. Fogel, Robert W. "A Quantitative Approach to the Study of Railroads in American Economic Growth: A Report of Some Preliminary Findings," *Journal of Economic History*, XXII (June 1962).

7. Gallatin, Albert. "Report on Roads and Canals," *American State Papers*, Miscellaneous, I, pp. 724-41.

8. Goodrich, Carter. *Government Promotion of American Canals and Railroads, 1800-1890*, New York: Columbia University Press, 1960.

9. Hunter, Louis C. *Steamboats on the Western Rivers*, Cambridge, Mass.: Harvard University Press, 1949.

10. Kohlmeier, Arthur. *The Old Northwest as the Keystone of the Arch of the American Federal Union*, Bloomington: Principalia Press, 1938.

11. McClelland, C. P., and Huntington, C. C. *History of the Ohio Canals, Their Construction, Cost, Use and Partial Abandonment*, Columbus: 1905.

12. Miller, Nathan. *Enterprise of a Free People*, Ithaca: Cornell University Press, 1962.
13. Neimi, Albert. "A Further Look at Interregional Canals and Economic Specialization, 1820-1840," *Explorations in Economic History*, (Second Series), 7, (Summer 1970); pp. 499-520.
14. State of Ohio, Board of Public Works. *Annual Report for 1852*, Columbus: 1853.
15. Ransom, Roger L. "Canals and Development: A Discussion of the Issues," *American Economic Review*, LIV, (May 1965); pp. 365-76.
16. ———. "A Closer Look at Western Manufacturing," *Explorations in Economic History*, (Second Series), 8, (Summer 1971); pp. 501-508.
17. ———. "Interregional Canals and Economic Specialization in the Antebellum United States," *Explorations in Extrepreneurial History*, (Second Series), 5, (Fall 1967); pp. 12-35.
18. ———. "Social Returns from Public Transport Investment: A Case Study of the Ohio Canal," *Journal of Political Economy*, 78, (September/October 1970); pp. 1041-60.
19. Rubin, Julius. "Canal or Railroad?" *Transactions of the American Philosophical Society*, Vol. 51, Part 7, Philadelphia: American Philosophical Society, 1961.
20. Sanderlin, Walter S. *The Great National Project: A History of the Chesapeake and Ohio Canal*, Baltimore: Johns Hopkins Press, 1946.
21. Scheiber, Harry N. *The Ohio Canal Era: A Case Study of Government and the Economy*, 1820-1861, Athens, Ohio: Ohio University Press, 1969.
22. Segal, Harvey. "Canals and Economic Development," in Carter Goodrich (editor), *Canals and American Economic Development*, New York: Columbia University Press, 1962; pp. 216-48.
23. Taylor, George R. *The Transportation Revolution*, New York: Holt, Rinehart & Winston, 1951.
24. United States Bureau of the Census. *Historical Statistics of the United States, Colonial Times to 1957*, Washington, D.C.: 1960.
25. United States Census Office. *Seventh Census of the United States, 1850*, Washington, D. C.: Robert Armstrong, 1853.

XI

THE RAILROADS AND MIDWESTERN DEVELOPMENT 1870-90: A GENERAL EQUILIBRIUM HISTORY

Jeffrey G. Williamson

The University of Wisconsin

> . . . historical research deals with the past that was and not with the past that might have been. Moreover, I cannot see how one can know in exact quantitative terms . . . something that actually never happened. The result of such investigation is for me "as if" history, quasi-history, fictitious history—that is, not really history at all. (Fritz Redlich [1968].)

> It does require maturity to realize that models are to be used but not to be believed. (Henri Theil[1971].)

1. *"Social Savings" and General Equilibrium Analysis*

The "traditional" economic historian has rarely been satisfied with partial equilibrium analyses of nineteenth century American railroads. His interest has always been in evaluating the railroads as they interact with the whole framework of the American economy. Not only has he tended to think in general equilibrium terms (although never utilizing formal models), but the potential dynamic effects of the rails has always been his prime focus. Fishlow's impressive book on American ante-bellum railroads certainly follows in this tradition.[1] The key question central to Professor Fishlow's book is apparent from its title: what role did transportation play in transforming the structure of the American economy? The present paper raises the same question for the Gilded Age.

With the important exception of Fishlow, cliometricians have reduced the larger issues involving the rails as a force in American development to an exercise in partial equilibrium statics. Were the railroads an efficient investment choice? Even more than this query, the measure which has recently caught the historian's attention is the *social savings* of the railroads. Although this paper does not dwell on Professor Fogel's social savings computations,[2] a review of the concept may be useful in placing our own approach in perspective.

The social savings computation attempts to measure the resources saved by the introduction of a given investment or innovation. In essence, it measures the flow of benefits from a given project. Normally, economists relate this flow of benefits to the requisite costs (e.g., railroad construction) to derive a benefit-cost ratio or some other more sophisticated rate of return calculation on the investment project under consideration. If private and social costs and benefits diverge, the historian can evaluate *ex post* the extent of this gap and explore the necessity of government intervention. In addition, since decisions are based on imperfect information, the historian may also wish to evaluate the extent to which *ex post* experience fulfilled private or public decision-makers expectations. These are in fact some of the issues raised in Fishlow's research on the ante-bellum railroads. Professor Fogel's focus is somewhat different. First, Fogel relates the social savings of the railroads to gross national product rather than utilizing the social savings measures to compute rates of return or benefit-cost ratios. The

270

explanation for this procedure can be readily found in Fogel's initial query: Were the railroads indispensable to American development? Presumably, a ratio of the social savings produced by the interregional railroad network to gross national product of, say, 1 per cent implies a rejection of the "axiom of indispensability" since that gap represents less than one year's growth in GNP. Second, Fogel is not concerned with the marginal impact of an additional railroad venture but rather with the *total* impact of the railroad network in 1890.

This survey need not summarize the debate generated by Fogel's stimulating book,[3] but Fishlow's careful review of the social savings concept deserves our attention. First, the usual index number problem must be confronted. Given a (constant) cost differential between two modes of transport, does one use traffic volume at the time of introduction of the new mode or the volume under the old mode in computing benefits? If the cost differential is large and the derived demand for transport services relatively elastic, the index number problem may be significant. This effect can be readily seen in Figure 1 where we invoke the assumption of constant costs. (This assumption is maintained in Fogel's and Fishlow's work and is applied throughout the present paper as well.) Shall we define social savings as $[P_o - P_1] T'_1$, as Fogel does, or rather as $[P_o - P_1] T'_o$? A more important issue arises when the cost differential is large and the gestation period lengthy:

> Once beyond the confines of the individual project, and with a long interval between introduction of an innovation and measurement of its effect, the distortion becomes considerably more worrisome.[4]

The difference between $[P_o - P_1]T'_1$ and $[P_o - P_1]T_1$ may be large enough to render the first calculation questionable, or even worse, deceptive. Indeed, suppose the shift in the derived demand for transport services is induced by railroad investment itself! Fishlow was certainly concerned with these

Figure 1

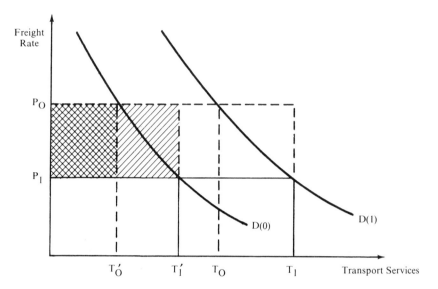

second-round effects, although he was unable to adjust for them:

> A final and very significant distortion in the calcula-
> tion of social saving derives from the existence of indirect
> benefits. Because there are second round effects of
> the initial reduction in transport costs, namely induced
> capital formation and expansion in other sectors, the po-
> sition of the demand schedule for transport services is
> not independent of movement along it.[5]

What are these second round effects? First, there are
the full general equilibrium comparative static effects
to consider. A fall in interregional transport costs gener-
ates production effects throughout the economy. In particular, the railroads fostered regional specialization and
interregional commodity trade. The concomitant resource
reallocation was complex. To understand it adequately,
a full general equilibrium framework which specifies ex-

plicit production and consumption conditions in all regions is required. The model developed in section 3 is one such candidate. Indeed, it was designed mainly to confront such general equilibrium effects.[6] Second, transport improvements may have dynamic effects over and above the comparative static resource re-allocation induced by the innovation. It may foster technical change in both industry and agriculture, and scale effects in industry. It may also induce greater rates of foreign in-migration either through the real income effect of the rails or, more importantly, by the shift to more labor-intensive economic activities. Railroad construction itself as well as the agricultural activity fostered by declining transport costs were both relatively labor-intensive activities. As such, their relative expansion should have had favorable effects on real wages, employment and thus in-migration. Finally, the railroads may also induce more rapid rates of capital accumulation. A full discussion of the capital formation effect is, however, postponed to sections 3 and 5 where the dynamic effects of the rails are given theoretical and quantitative content.

The discussion in this introduction should suffice to point out the limitations of a partial equilibrium evaluation of an innovation of such pervasive importance as the railroads. Only general equilibrium analysis can give us insight into historical events of this magnitude. Furthermore, some effort, however primitive, must be made to understand their potential dynamic effects as well. These are the issues which the remainder of this paper confronts.

2. The Railroads and the Midwestern Terms of Trade

The discussion up to this point has focused exclusively on the economic impact of the rails on late nineteenth century America. Yet the approach taken in this paper is considerably different from that of Professors Fishlow and Fogel. Fishlow, Fogel, and other researchers have devoted much of their research efforts to documenting the *effective transport charges* for railroads and other competing modes. As a reading of the railroad literature will attest, documenting these transport charges (whether measured as "shadow prices" or rates actually paid) is fraught with difficulty.

American economic historians unanimously agree that railroad freight rates fell sharply from 1870 to 1890. In spite of this unanimity, there have been few attempts to construct continuous real transport cost series relevant to interregional trade within the American economy. The difficulties in constructing such series become immediately apparent in a reading of Robert Higgs' recent attempt.[7] Professor Higgs takes *quoted* nominal freight rates on key agricultural products and deflates these rates by the prevailing prices of corn [*sic*], cotton [*sic*], and wheat. The resulting measures yield crude indices of the movements in the percentage by which farm gate prices diverge from urban market prices. His indices for wheat and especially corn *do* fall significantly from 1870 to 1890. They are not without wide short run variance, but the long run decline is unmistakable and pronounced. True, if these series are extended to the mid 1890's, the long run trend is far less clear. Yet even these estimates present interpretive difficulties. Railroad rates are of interest to us *only* to the extent that they account, at least in part, for spatial commodity price differentials. Now it is well known that *quoted* nominal transport charges often had little relation to actual or effective rates.[8] Furthermore, farmers had to pay a multitude of charges for shipment to the nearest rail connection with trunk lines to Chicago as well as for storage and hauling. Given these difficulties, we have departed from the conventional approach and have instead constructed explicit measures of regional commodity price differentials. Elsewhere we have constructed time series for these percentage price differentials between Iowa and New York City.[9]

These percentage rate differentials, $Z_A(t)$, clearly embody more than simply railroad rates on the long haul itself, but they more appropriately capture the issues raised in the literature: What was the impact of converging regional commodity prices on American development? We do not view as improper a restatement of this more general query to the narrower question: What was the impact of the railroads on American development during the late nineteenth century? Nevertheless, this literary license should be made absolutely clear.

These percentage regional commodity price differentials are displayed in Figure 2. The $Z_A(t)$ series refers to rates on eastern grain trade, while the $Z_I(t)$ series refers to those

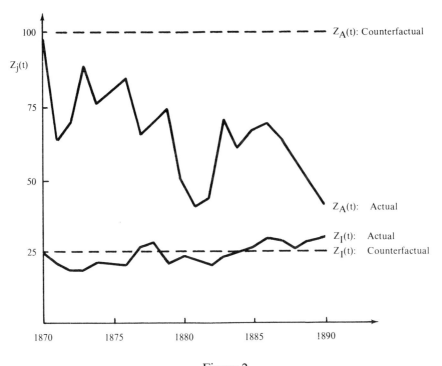

Figure 2

on western industrial goods trade. Two distinct characteristics of these $Z(t)$ series are immediately apparent. First, Z_A always exceeds Z_I since agricultural goods are high-bulk and low-value. Second, while Z_A declines sharply from 1870 to 1890, Z_I does not. Over the period as a whole, Z_I was relatively stable, although it is true that the industrial goods' freight rates were lower after 1870 in all years but two prior to 1885. They are higher thereafter. The differential behavior of Z_A and Z_I is at the heart of the railroad issue. Much of the historical regional specialization patterns, real wage behavior, and experience with capital-deepening in nineteenth century America can be explained by the variance in commodity terms of trade across sections. Convergence in these regional commodity price relatives must in large measure be associated with transport improvements in general and the railroads in particular, but these improvements had far greater effects on some commodities than others. The prices of midwestern agricultural and industrial products can be related to those in the East by the expressions

$$P_{AW} = (1 - Z_A) P_{AE},$$

$$P_{IW} = (1 + Z_I) P_{IE}.$$

Thus, the relative price of agricultural commodities in the Midwest as a ratio to that in the East can be reduced to

$$\frac{P_{AW}}{P_{IW}} \bigg/ \frac{P_{AE}}{P_{IE}} = \frac{1 - Z_A}{1 + Z_I} < 1.$$

The *relative* price of agricultural goods in the Midwest is always below that of the East. If *both* Z_A and Z_I fall over time, the midwestern terms of trade converge to the eastern terms of trade. But if Z_I *rises* while Z_A is falling, the convergence is retarded: indeed, should Z_I rise sufficiently it may offset the effects of the fall in Z_A entirely. Clearly, the historian cannot analyze the historical impact of grain freight rates independent of rates on industrial goods.

The counterfactual experiment performed in this paper can now be explicitly stated: How would the economy have developed over these two decades had these commodity price differentials remained constant at 1870 levels? We are *not* exploring a counterfactual world in 1890 which might have appeared had the railroads been eliminated as a transport mode. This—Fogel's—counterfactual world is very different from our own. We are instead imposing on the economy a counterfactual world of stable "transport rates" after 1870. By our reckoning, Z_A declined by 50 per cent over the two decades while Z_I was roughly stable. Thus, Z_A in 1890 was historically one-half of its counterfactual level. Actual historical experience with regional price differentials may be rationalized either by an appeal to an historical deterioration in the railroads' monopolistic tariff setting power, or by an appeal to declining real costs in supplying railroad service associated with increasing returns or technological improvements,[10] or by forces external to the railroad sector entirely. We are not concerned with causes of these "rate" movements but rather with their implications. These are presented in Figure 3. Since we shall be taking the East coast commodity price relatives as determined by world market conditions, these changing transport rates had an impact on the midwestern terms of trade only.[11] In the counterfactual world of stable transport charges, the relative price of industrial (agricultural) goods would have been far higher (lower) in the Midwest. Furthermore, the actual historical improvement in relative farm prices in the Midwest would not have been achieved in the counterfactual world: instead, the relative price of farm products in the Midwest would have fallen from 1870 to 1890, as in fact it did in East coast markets.

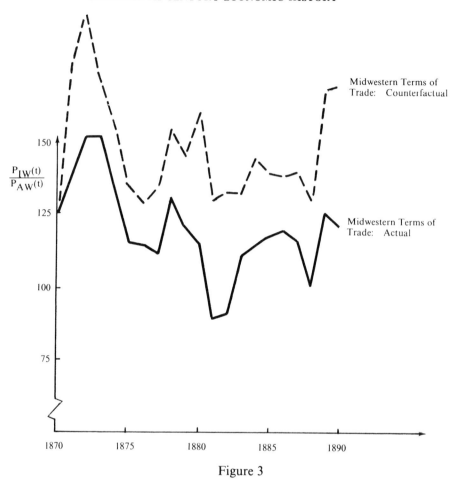

Figure 3

How would the counterfactual economy have compared with actual experience up to 1890? What was the impact of transportation improvements on the transformation of the American economy during the Gilded Age? An answer to these or any other questions posed of this period will be forthcoming only if an explicit model of the American

278

economy is developed, one which is relevant to the queries posed. The next section is devoted to that task.

3. A Model of American Regional Growth During the Late Nineteenth Century

3.1 Introduction to General Equilibrium Analysis

The model used in this study can best be understood if we first explore a simpler general equilibrium system, one which is representative of those recently applied to problems in economic history. The discussion in this section relies extensively for this purpose on the papers by Professors Jones and Hueckel.[12]

Consider a regional economy producing agricultural and manufactured commodities. Let agricultural goods be used only for consumption purposes,[13] and furthermore assume that these commodities dominate workers' expenditures. Let manufactures be used for both consumption and investment purposes. We also impose the conventional assumptions of pure competition, full employment and constant returns to scale. Furthermore, we invoke the "small country" assumption where commodity prices are given exogenously to the region and trade flows are determined residually; e.g., domestic demand conditions serve only to determine external trade volumes. Thus, the model is completely supply oriented. Finally, let the regional resource endowment be given exogenously. There are three primary factors of production: labor (used in both sectors), capital (used in both sectors), and land (used only in agriculture). The following notation will prove helpful:

$Q_A =$ agricultural output,
$Q_I =$ industrial output,
$R \ =$ land stock,
$L \ =$ labor force,
$K \ =$ physical stock of homogeneous machines,
$P_A =$ price of agricultural commodities,

279

P_I = price of industrial commodities,
d = rents (value marginal product of land),
w = wage rate (value marginal product of labor),
r = rate of return on capital (value marginal product of capital).

Full employment requires that

$$a_{RA} Q_A = R,$$

$$a_{KA} Q_A + a_{KI} Q_I = K,$$

$$a_{LA} Q_A + a_{LI} Q_I = L,$$

where a_{ij} is the amount of the ith factor necessary to produce the jth output. The a_{ij} are variable and respond to changes in relative factor prices. In equilibrium, factor payments exhaust total value of output, so that prices and unit costs will be equated:

$$a_{RA} d + a_{LA} w + a_{KA} r = P_A,$$

$$a_{LI} w + a_{KI} r = P_I.$$

To summarize, factor stocks are given exogenously, as are commodity prices and production technologies. The latter are described by the technical response of a_{ij} to factor input price ratios. Factor prices, income and output distribution are all determined endogenously in the system.

To illustrate the potential of such a model for historical research, consider only two key endogenous variables which are of special interest to the economic historian: (i) the real wage or workers' standard of living (in terms of food-stuffs) and (ii) industrialization as measured by the share of agricultural output in total constant price GNP. The system of simultaneous equations can be solved so that real wages and the output mix can be expressed in terms of exogenous variables and parameters describing the economy's structure:[14]

$$[1a] \quad w^* - P_A^* = \frac{1}{\Delta} \left\{ \left[\theta_{KA} \frac{\lambda_{KI}}{\lambda_{LI}} \lambda_{LA} \sigma_{L,R} - (\theta_{RA} + \theta_{KA}) \lambda_{KA} \sigma_{K,R} - \theta_{RA} \lambda_{KI} \sigma_I \right] \right.$$

$$\left. x(P_A^* - P_I^*) + \theta_{KI} \theta_{RA} \left[K^* + R^* \left(\frac{\lambda_{LA} - \lambda_{KA}}{\lambda_{LI}} \right) \right. \right.$$

$$\left. \left. - \frac{\lambda_{KI}}{\lambda_{LI}} L^* \right] \right\},$$

$$[2a] \quad Q_A^* - Q_I^* = \frac{1}{\lambda_{LI}} (R^* - L^* - \lambda_{LI} a^* {}_{RA})$$

$$+ \frac{1}{\Delta} \left\{ \left[\lambda_{KA} \sigma_{K,R} \left(\frac{\lambda_{LA}}{\lambda_{LI}} \sigma_{L,R} + \theta_{KI} \sigma_I \right) \right. \right.$$

$$\left. + \theta_{LI} \frac{\lambda_{LA} \lambda_{KI}}{\lambda_{LI}} \sigma_I \sigma_{L,K} \right] (P_A^* - P_I^*)$$

$$- \left[(\theta_{KI} - \theta_{KA}) \frac{\lambda_{LA}}{\lambda_{LI}} \sigma_{L,R} + \theta_{KI} \theta_{RA} \sigma_I \right]$$

$$\left. \left[K^* + L^* \left(\frac{\lambda_{LA} - \lambda_{KA}}{\lambda_{LI}} \right) - \frac{\lambda_{KI}}{\lambda_{LI}} L^* \right] \right\},$$

where $\Delta = \left[(\theta_{KI} - \theta_{KA}) \frac{\lambda_{KI}}{\lambda_{LI}} \lambda_{LA} \sigma_{L,R} + (\theta_{LI} - \theta_{LA}) \right.$

$$\left. \lambda_{KA} \sigma_{K,R} + \theta_{RA} \lambda_{KI} \sigma_I \right].$$

In these equations, θ_{ij} is the distributive share of factor i in sector j, λ_{ij} is the share of an input i used in the jth sector, $\sigma_{i,k}$ is the elasticity of substitution between a pair of inputs in agriculture, and σ_I is the elasticity of substitution in industry. An asterisk represents a percentage change in a variable: e.g., a positive value for $(w^* - P_A^*)$ implies that real wages tend to rise in response to a small percentage change in some exogenous variable of interest. Finally, Δ is assumed positive since only in that case does

281

the production possibility curve "bulge outwards" as in Figure 4 where equation [2a] is reproduced in a more familiar graphic context.

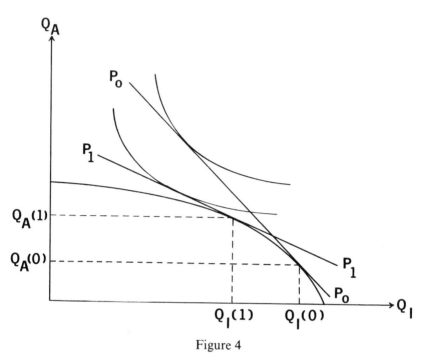

Figure 4

The production possibility curve is drawn where technology and resource endowment are fixed. Given relative commodity prices, the output mix is determined endogenously. The figure replicates the standard result that a relative expansion in Q_A takes place in response to an increase in the relative price of agricultural goods. To put it another way, any exogenous force (such as railway development) which raises the relative price of farm products in this regional economy will inhibit industrialization and foster agricultural expansion. In terms of [2a], $(Q_A^* - Q_I^*)$ must be positive. This result is readily forthcoming from

282

[2a] if it is rewritten for fixed endowments $(K^* = L^* = R^* = O)$ as in [2b]:

[2b] $$Q_A^* - Q_I^* = -a_{RA}^* + \frac{1}{\triangle} \left\{ \left[\lambda_{KA} \sigma_{K,R} \right. \right.$$

$$\left(\frac{\lambda_{LA}}{\lambda_{LI}} \sigma_{L,R} + \theta_{KI} \sigma_I \right) + \theta_{LI} \left. \frac{\lambda_{LA}\lambda_{KI}}{\lambda_{LI}} \sigma_I \sigma_{L,K} \right]$$

$$\left. (P_A^* - P_I^*) \right\} .$$

Since $\triangle$ is positive, and $a_{RA}^* \leqq 0$, then $(Q_A^* - Q_I^*) > 0$. Although the analysis is the same, the explicit statement in [2b] has an obvious advantage over the graphical analysis in Figure 4: it is susceptible to *empirical* investigation and thus can supply a precise answer to historical questions relating to tariff policy, world market conditions or interregional transport costs, all of which have an influence on $(P_A^* - P_I^*)$.

To take another example of the use to which these models may be put, consider an issue of concern to Turner and Habakkuk:[15] the importance of "land availability" in determining American real wages. In equation [1a], take $(P_A^* - P_I^*) = 0$, $K^* = L^* = 0$, but $R^* > 0$. Under these assumptions, [1a] collapses to [1b]:

[1b] $$w^* - P_A^* = \frac{1}{\triangle} \left\{ \theta_{KI} \theta_{RA} R^* \left(\frac{\lambda_{LA} - \lambda_{KA}}{\lambda_{LI}} \right) \right\} .$$

Thus real wages tend to be higher given the presence of a "frontier" if the proportion of the American labor force employed in agriculture exceeds the proportion of the American capital stock employed there: e.g., if agriculture is more labor intensive than industry. Otherwise, real wages may fall. Furthermore, [1b] can tell us by how much they would be raised if the parameters appearing in that expression can be estimated.

The economic system we have been exploring thus far is identical with the comparative static model used in the present paper to describe the Midwest in the late nineteenth century, *with two important exceptions*: (i) Since our interest is in the empirical application of this model, factor price equalization between sectors cannot be assumed since it was at no time achieved. The general equilibrium model discussed above assumes full mobility of capital. One reason why factor price equalization fails to appear in history is because capital is "putty-clay". Reapers cannot be converted into spindles overnight, and thus there is no reason to assume full mobility except for analytical convenience. Instead, the model developed in section 3.2 assumes that capital once in place is fully *immobile*. Only new investment can shift the relative employment of the midwestern capital stock and that takes time. Furthermore, our model of regional growth contains limitations on intersectoral financing of new investment by the introduction of a financial market which operates subject to positive transaction and information costs. Two borrowing rates (and net rates of return on capital) prevail in the Midwest to reflect this disequilibrium: a farm mortgage rate and an industrial bond rate. Labor migration off the farm to urban employment is also inhibited by uncertainty and information costs so that farm and urban wages need not be equalized in the short-run.

(ii) As it now stands, the comparative static analysis briefly developed above bears little resemblance to American sectional history, since changes in factor returns in the Midwest generated an immediate factor supply response. Consider the real wage expression [1a] once again. Cliometricians utilizing such models presumably feel that a comparative static experiment which holds resource endowments fixed while raising the relative price of agricultural goods is useful in understanding the impact of, say, declining interregional transport costs on real wages in the Midwest. Suppose, however, that the real wage itself influences $\overset{*}{L}$? Is comparative static analysis very helpful in this case? After all, higher real wages in the Midwest induced westward migration. In addition, higher return to western capital induced investment inflows from eastern financial centers.

It follows that the Midwest cannot be treated in isolation. Rather, the Northeast must be explicity introduced into our comparative static model, since interregional factor mobility is clearly an important aspect of American regional development. The model developed in section 3.2 treats this regional interdependence of factor markets explicitly. Having expanded the model to include two interdependent regional economies, we then are presented with the opportunity to introduce transport costs on interregional commodity trade and the railroad issue can be confronted directly.

The applications of general equilibrium models to problems in economic history have another weakness.[16] Even if we exclude a *foreign* migration response to American real wages (the "pull" of employment conditions), and exclude a *foreign* investment response to rates of return on American capital as well, can the dynamic effects associated with exogenous changes in the land stock, world prices, or transport costs be ignored in our two-region economy? Certainly not. However primitive, some theory of resource growth and technological change must be appended to the model. Comparative static analyses which identify the historical impact of exogenous variables on income distribution, factor prices, and output mix are of limited usefulness if these endogenous variables have an impact, in turn, on rates of capital formation, labor supply growth, or technological progress.

These introductory remarks set the stage for the remainder of this section. The model is presented verbally whenever possible. Those readers wishing a formal presentation of the model are encouraged to turn to Appendix A where it is presented in detail.

3.2 The Model Described in Detail[17]

It should be stressed at the outset that our interest is restricted to the interdependent development of the American Midwest and Northeast. The South is excluded from our analysis. In census terminology, the Midwest includes the East North Central and the West North Central states, while the East includes the New England and Middle Atlantic states. According to Easterlin's 1880 regional estimates, the sum of our East and West accounted for 62 per cent of the American labor force and 75 per cent of income.

The degree to which the East and West were specialized is revealed in Easterlin's figures. Fully two-thirds of the eastern (commodity producing) labor force was engaged in non-agricultural activity in 1880. As a consequence it seems reasonable to treat the Northeast as completely specialized in "industrial" products, commodities that may be used for both investment and consumption purposes. The East is characterized as producing industrial goods for local use and for export to the West; furthermore, eastern industrial goods must compete with foreign goods in both regional markets. The Midwest, on the other hand, is not fully specialized. It concentrates to be sure on the production of farm products for local consumption, and for export both to the East and to European markets. Yet an industrial goods sector does exist in the West, the output of which satisfies a portion of local consumption and investment demands.

The production process in each sector is described by a continuous, twice-differentiable, single-valued function. Agriculture utilizes land, labor, and capital in production, while manufacturing requires labor and capital only. We continue to treat capital as "putty-clay". Once capital goods are employed in a given production process, they cannot be transferred for use in another sector. Production is subject to constant returns to scale and diminishing marginal rates of substitution. An impressive amount of accumulated evidence on American production conditions suggests that the elasticity of substitution may be fairly close to unity in both agriculture and manufacturing.[18] By appealing to these results, a Cobb-Douglas specification is adopted in both regions, while exogenous rates of total factor productivity growth are allowed to diverge between sectors and regions.

Since our concern is with long-run full employment, cycles in factor utilization rates are ignored. Furthermore, we invoke the conventional assumption that marginal product pricing rules are satisfied in all regions and sectors of the economy. Note, however, that this assumption does not require factor price equalization between regions or sectors. Indeed, we shall see below that interregional and intraregional factor market disequilibrium is a distinctive characteristic of our economy.

With constant returns to scale and common efficiency levels how can the industrial sector co-exist in the two regions? The answer, of course, is to be found in the protective effect of interregional transport costs. This explanation has a venerable tradition in nineteenth century American economic historiography, and use is made of it here by the introduction of commodity price differentials between regions. Per unit transport costs incurred in interregional trade are treated like exogenous tariff rates. The rate on western foodstuffs shipped East is denoted by $Z_A(t)$ and the rate on eastern industrial goods shipped west by $Z_I(t)$. Clearly, Z_A and Z_I need not be equal: in fact, we have already seen in section 2 that Z_A exceeds Z_I by large measure during the late nineteenth century. Finally, although these rates are determined exogenously,

287

they are allowed to decline over time. Indeed, the purpose of this paper is to evaluate the impact of declining transport costs on regional specialization, trade creation, migration, and per capita income growth.

In the regional factor income equations, $T_E(t)$ and $T_W(t)$ represent revenues generated from the transportation sector. No explicit production function is introduced for transport activities: transportation costs are introduced exogenously. This specification is consistent with Fogel's and Fishlow's treatment, since they assume constant costs in the transport sector. Furthermore, we assume that transportation costs fully exhaust regional commodity price differentials. Revenue from transport activities must generate factor payments in the two regions. Thus, for example, revenue from West-East trade is expressed as

$$T_W(t) = Z_A(t) \left\{ D_{AE}(t) + Ex(t) \right\} ;$$

that is, the freight rate times the volume of western grains exported to the East and abroad. Similarly, transport revenue from East-West trade can be expressed as the freight rate times the volume of Eastern and imported industrial products shipped West.

Foreign imports of industrial consumption and investment goods are valued at Eastern (landed at port) prices. Similarly, exports of grain products from the West must first be transported to Eastern ports and thus are valued f.o.b. at grain prices prevailing in Eastern markets. Furthermore, the external trade balance is assumed to be zero. The Eastern price ratio, $P_{IE}(t)/P_{AE}(t)$, is given exogenously by world market conditions. It could be argued that American grain exports had a significant impact on the prevailing world price. That possibility is ignored, and instead the world demand for American grains is assumed to be perfectly elastic;[19] similarly, the supply of industrial import goods is also taken to be perfectly elastic. We interpret the historians' emphasis on "lagging export markets" for American farm products as an exogenous deterioration of international farm products' prices, rather than as a low rate of external demand expansion for U.S. grains in foreign markets. Relative prices in the West are jointly determined by changing world market conditions and interregional transport costs. In section 2, it was noted that $Z_A(t)$ declined far more rapidly than $Z_I(t)$; thus, the relative grain price in the Midwest behaved quite differently over time than did the Eastern terms of trade.

To complete the static system, some migration decision rules must be formulated which are capable of replicating some key characteristics of American regional development. George Borts has found, for example, that even during twentieth century American experience regional wage differentials have increased in spite of heavy interregional migration.[20] Borts attributes the result in large measure to the high population reproduction rate in low wage areas. For our period, the region of "high reproduction rates" is the *East* since that labor force is continually augmented by significant amounts of immigration from Europe. This is also a region of low *real* wages. A disequilibrium framework will make it possible to observe current wage differentials of considerable magnitude over very long periods of development. The more important issue, however, relates to the behavior of *real* wages since it is the real wage which influences migration behavior. The difficulty arises in constructing an appropriate cost-of-living deflator. In the migration specification which follows, we make a simplifying assumption which appears to have considerable empirical relevance. Regional cost-of-living differentials are produced when the expenditure bundle is significantly weighted by the presence of non-traded services or by bulk commodities with high transport costs. The evidence

289

suggests that the variance in regional prices of foodstuffs was a key determinant of regional cost-of-living differentials in the nineteenth century. Given that evidence, we shall assume that regional wage rates deflated by a cost-of-living index dominated by food prices are the real income variables relevant for migration decisions.

The following formulation of migration behavior is adopted. The gross migration rate from the ith to j^{th} region is $m_{ji}(t) = M_{ji}(t)/L_i(t)$ and, as in classical migration theory, the determinants of $m_{ji}(t)$ are expected net real income differentials. For simplicity, a one period model is hypothesized which excludes migration costs. Thus, $m_{ji}(t)$ is determined solely by the expected East-West real wage differential, $\tilde{w}^*(t) = \tilde{w}_E^*(t) - \tilde{w}_W^*(t)$, as in Figure 5.

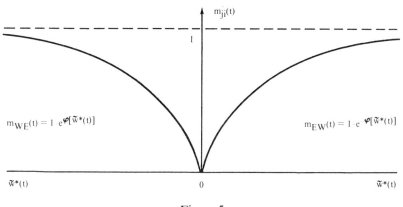

Figure 5

Suppose further that potential migrants determine $w^*(t)$ by reference to actual past wage differentials subject to an adjustment parameter. In this formulation, money wage differentials of considerable magnitude may be observed over very long periods of history in spite of massive western "settlement". These differentials may be attributed to persistent cost-of-living differentials or they may be explained by a national labor market continually subjected to major shocks and, as a result, in persistent disequilibrium. (Intersectoral migration within the West, e.g., migration off the farm, is treated in much the same fashion.)

Davis and others have argued that nineteenth century barriers to interregional capital mobility were significant. Now capital market imperfections may reflect nothing more than positive information costs, but in any case these costs are likely to have been very large for a young economy undergoing land-augmenting extensive development, and an effort must be made to capture them in our model.

Gross returns to (physical) capital in a given region or sector can be decomposed into

$$r_j(t) = [i_j(t) + \delta] P_{I_j}(t),$$

so that interest payments and depreciation requirements per unit of capital investment exhaust the *real* gross returns to physical assets at the margin. Investors outside of a region of plant location receive interest on the value of their investment less a transaction cost, a term discussed at greater length below when interregional capital markets are analyzed. In early phases of midwestern growth, the region relied heavily on Eastern financing, and thus in 1870 Western assets claimed by Eastern interests (accumulated by past financing) were relatively large while Eastern assets claimed by Westerners were negligible. It follows that Western regional product must have exceeded its regional income by net factor income payments to financial interests in the East. This result surely tended to reinforce Western dependence on net inflows to finance railroad development, land clearing, or industrial expansion. In any case, we shall also assume that all interregional financial intermediation is performed in the East and returns to such intermediation accrue to Eastern capitalists.[21]

291

Let τ be a fixed per unit search or information cost incurred with an intersectoral transfer of claims. The *net* interest rate on assets held outside the jth region is $[i_j(t) - \tau]$; that is, the effective interest rate facing the Eastern investor contemplating investment in the West is the Western rate less the per unit payment to inter-mediaries. Following the spirit of most work on financial intermediation by economic historians, we shall take τ as given by existing institutional arrangements. To be explicit, the volume of intersectoral flows is assumed to have *no* impact on τ, and furthermore the model does not consider the resource cost of intermediation nor does it confront the problem of optimal resource allocation be-tween financial intermediation and other activities. Fi-nally, note that if τ is positive, then it follows that even in equilibrium, where $i^*_W(t) - i^*_E(t) = \tau$ and interregional financial flows cease, the discrepancy between regional interest rates (and, of course, gross rental rates) may be quite pronounced.

Let $\phi_{ji}(t)$ denote the fraction of region i's gross sav-ings allocated to gross capital formation in the jth region. Analogous to the labor migration specification, the ex-pected East-West interest rate differential, $i^*(t) = i^*_E(t) - i^*_W(t)$, determines the interregional transfer subject to τ as in Figure 6. As the expected Western interest rate departs

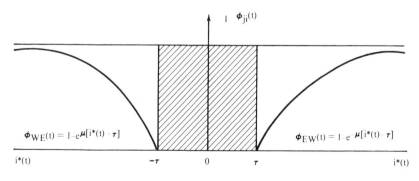

Figure 6

292

from the Eastern rate an increasing share of Eastern gross regional saving is allocated to Western capital formation and all of Western savings are reinvested there. The Western *intra*regional financial market is explained by a mechanism symmetrical to that formulated above for the interregional financial market. Thus, a differential may also appear between western industrial "bonds" and farm "mortgages".

Our model can now be completed with the addition of the remaining dynamic equations. Labor force growth is determined by the rates indigenous to each region as well as by the inflow of European migrants:

$$L_E(t) = n_E(t)L_E(t-1) + m_{EW}(t)L_W(t-1) - m_{WE}(t)L_E(t-1)$$

$$+ M(t),$$

$$L_W(t) = n_W(t)L_W(t-1) + m_{WE}(t)L_E(t-1) - m_{EW}(t)L_W(t-1).$$

In effect, constant labor participation rates are assumed so that the more abundant historical evidence on natural rates of population growth can be utilized. The regional rates, $n_E(t)$ and $n_W(t)$, are exogenous but they are not assumed constant. Since they are estimated from historical demographic data, they reflect declining rates observed in both regions over the period. $M(t)$ denotes the actual European in-migration flows recorded annually over the period. Migration to the West by European immigrants is viewed here as a two-stage process, since these flows first augment the eastern labor force. Eastern workers and new European immigrants are treated as perfect substitutes. The observed rate of regional labor force growth is therefore determined jointly by regional labor migration functions, and by these exogenously determined natural rates of growth and European migration flows.

It is generally agreed both in fact and in theory that "land" augmentation requires complementary investment. Martin Primack has shown just how important these investments were to the nineteenth century expansion of

293

American agriculture.[22] They involve land clearing, farm construction, fencing, drainage and irrigation. The real problem, however, relates to land clearing and preparation. Not long ago, Peter Kenen[23] made an interesting theoretical contribution which captures these conditions. Kenen proposed production functions utilizing factor service flows from labor and land stocks, but these stocks are unproductive until "improved" by a series of investments like those itemized by Primack in the case of land. Kenen is suggesting that we treat the production of "improved acres" in much the same way that we treat capital-goods production, and in the nineteenth century they both were highly labor intensive activities. In fact, interregional financial flows to the West were in part used to increase the rental value of land holdings at the frontier (either by *new* lands cleared or by the improved value of old lands). At this stage, our treatment of land augmentation will be far less sophisticated and more akin to recent applications of general equilibrium analysis to historical problems. That is, our proxy for land utilization is Tostlebe's improved land acreage series, and the exogenous rate of expansion in the land stock declines over time reflecting the gradual "closing of the frontier."

The most difficult task now remains. What determined the aggregate savings rate in the American economy in the late nineteenth century and thus the rate of capital formation? On this most important issue economic historians are uncertain. In fact, one of the least understood but most interesting aspects of United States development was the secular rise in the gross savings rate in the mid-nineteenth century. Our focus, however, is the period beginning 1869-78. Davis and Gallman present four series on the gross savings rate:[24] (i) in current and in 1860 prices; (ii) including and excluding agricultural clearing. Since our model explicitly includes only *purchased* capital inputs in western agricultural activity, the relevant series is the gross savings rate excluding agricultural clearing. In current prices, this measure of the gross savings rate rises from 0.18 to 0.20 between 1869-78 and 1894-1903.

What specification on the macro savings decision is historically most relevant for our period? In his discussion of the Civil War episode where gross savings rates in constant prices rose markedly, Temin suggests that the declining price of producer durables explains a large part of the rise but offers no other explanation.[25] For the period following 1869, we have basically three hypotheses suggested by the literature: (i) the role of the "rate of interest," (ii) the impact of income distribution, and (iii) a naive Keynesian specification. Differential savings rates according to the functional source of income are common in the growth literature and have long been a cornerstone in the historical literature as well. Yet we have only the sketchiest evidence on savings behavior by income groups or sectors in nineteenth century America. An *a priori* case has often been made that optimizing consumers will save more at higher interest rates. Yet there is very little empirical evidence which supports this proposition, and an equally plausible theoretical argument can be made which suggests an inverse relation. The economic historian places great emphasis on bank and non-bank intermediation as a means by which aggregate national saving is raised, yet there is little empirical evidence or compelling theoretical argument in favor of this proposition.[26]

Given the absence of a resolution of both the theoretical and historical debate on the determinants of aggregate national savings, we are forced to tread a˙ neutral path, albeit a path well trod by growth theorists. The savings rate is assumed equal across sectors and regions, and furthermore, it is allowed to assume the values actually estimated by Davis and Gallman. This certainly reduces our ability to explain American growth, since the exogenously determined savings rates hardly imply an explanation of the historical movements in current price investment shares. But even if the gross savings rate were assumed constant, would this necessarily imply a constant rate of capital accumulation even if the depreciation rate is fixed? The answer to this question is a resounding negative. Indeed, one prime contribution of modern growth theory has been to show how capital formation rates tend to diminish over time with fixed savings rates.[27] Define the aggregate capital stock as K(t), gross investment as I(t), the depreciation rate as δ, S as aggregate savings and $\bar{s}$ as the fixed savings rate. Then the rate of accumulation can be decomposed into

$$\frac{\dot{K}(t)}{K(t)} = \frac{I(t) - \delta K(t)}{K(t)} = \frac{I(t)}{K(t)} - \delta$$

$$= \frac{S}{P_I(t)} \cdot \frac{1}{K(t)} - \delta = \bar{s}\left[\frac{GNP(t)}{P_I(t)K(t)}\right] - \delta ,$$

where $P_I(t)$ is the current price of capital goods. In both theory and historical fact the capital-output ratio rises with accumulation thus generating a diminished *rate* of accumulation over time. Note that the rate of capital stock growth tends to decline over time even if the savings rate out of current income is constant. On the other hand, should $P_I(t)$ decline relatively over time, then it follows that I(t) will grow at rates exceeding GNP. More simply, from a fixed savings pool more investment goods can be purchased at lower capital goods' prices and, as a result, more rapid rates of accumulation will be forthcoming. This is precisely the effect Temin documents for the period 1849-58 to 1869-78 when the current price s(t) rose far less markedly than the constant price. In summary, we are in fact assuming that the price and income elasticities of demand for producers' durables are unity.

4. Rewriting American Sectional History, 1870-95

4.1 Establishing the Model's Plausibility

In the preceding section, a model of American regional development was constructed and its assumptions defended. Like all models, it is a simple representation of complex reality; in this case, the American economy[28] undergoing growth and structural change in the late nineteenth century. Yet the model does satisfy Fogel's prerequisite "efficiency" test, since it requires a minimum amount of parametric information.[29] This section hopes to show that efficiency and simplicity have been purchased at small cost. The model appears to retain the key elements of the American economy necessary to yield insight into many crucial questions of the period raised by economic historians. The proof, however, is in the eating.

Does the model reproduce history or does it instead generate fiction? Is the model capable of rewriting American economic history during the decades following the 1860's? In Appendix B, a detailed quantitative description of the American economy in 1870 is presented. Given these initial conditions and the estimated parameters, our model of regional growth can now tell a very precise quantitative story. That is, it makes precise predictions regarding key endogenous variables over the subsequent twenty-five years. Is the story purely fiction or does it closely conform to the facts? Are the simulated GNP per capita growth rates fairly close to those documented for the American economy by Gallman? Do predicted real wages for eastern manufacturing coincide with Lebergott's historical series? Does the model predict a rate of farm mechanization consistent with the evidence collected by Tostlebe, Kuznets, Rogin, and others? Is the predicted rate of industrialization consistent with observed experience? Does the model produce for the Midwest declining real farm mortgage rates, rising land values, stable yields

and rising farm income consistent with their actual behavior from the 1870's to the 1890's?

4.2   *Fact or Fiction? An Explanation of Late
        Nineteenth Century American Development.*

In section 5 our model will be used to explore the impact
of interregional transport cost conditions on midwestern
development from 1870 to 1890. The results will only be
as accurate as the underlying model. This is true, of
course, of any analytical history. The main motivation,
then, for the detailed numerical analysis reported in this
section is our concern with establishing the empirical
plausibility of our model. Only then can we turn with confidence to counterfactual analysis.

The model makes quantitative predictions on numerous
endogenous economic variables. Given space limitations,
this paper reports results only for the most important of
these and ones for which we have relatively detailed
historical documentation.[30] The present section explores
our success in rewriting the economic history of these
twenty-five years only as it appears in the behavior of (i)
aggregate GNP per worker, (ii) measures of structural
change as reflected in employment distribution by region
and sector, (iii) wages and the national labor market, (iv)
farm mortgage rates, and (v) farm yields, farm income
and farm land values in the Midwest.

4.2.1   *Macro Growth Performance: Gross National
          Product Per Worker.*

We begin with an examination of the aggregate per
worker productivity measures. The basic historical series
which we wish to explain is the Gallman index of gross
national product (in 1860 prices) per member of the labor
force. The aggregate output per worker series reported
in Table 2 are overlapping decade averages, converted to
an arbitrary 1870 base. First consider the long period

298

performance documented in Table 1. The conformity between the model and the Gallman index is remarkably
close. Over the thirty years 1869/78-1899/1908, the
Gallman data imply an average per annum growth rate
of 1.47 per cent, while over the same period the model
predicts 1.49 per cent. In addition, the model continues to
perform extremely well when the period is bisected into
shorter fifteen year movements, 1869/78-1884/93 and
1884/93-1899/1908, as in Table 1. The retardation in American growth rates from the early 1870's to the mid 1890's is

Table 1

Long Period Per Annum Growth Rates of GNP Per Worker,
1870-1908

Period	Gallman	Model
1869/78-1884/93	1.71%	1.69%
1884/93-1899/1908	1.24	1.29
1869/78-1899/1908	1.47	1.49

Source: See notes to Table 2.

Table 2

Indices of GNP Per Member of the Labor Force
1870-1908

Average Period	Gallman	Model
1869-78	100.0	100.0
1874-83	114.4	105.3
1879-88	126.5	116.7
1884-93	129.0	128.5
1889-98	130.2	138.8
1894-1903	140.9	149.6
1899-1908	155.2	156.1

Source: GNP in 1860 prices from R. Gallman, "Gross National Product in the United
States, 1834-1909," *Output, Employment, and Productivity in the United States After
1800* (New York: NBER, 1966), Table A1, p. 26. Labor force calculated from S. Lebergott,
Manpower in Economic Growth: The United States Record Since 1800 (New York: McGraw-
Hill, 1964), Table A-1, p. 510.

well known, and a plausible model should be capable of repro-
ducing this important facet of American nineteenth century
development.[31] Up to the late 1880's, the Gallman per annum
growth rate is 1.71 per cent (1.69 per cent in our model);
during the subsequent fifteen years terminating in the
middle of the first decade of the twentieth century, the
Gallman per annum growth rate is 1.24 per cent (1.29 per
cent in our model). Thus we have further confirmation
of the model's plausibility, since it predicts a major
retardation in GNP per capita growth replicating an important characteristic of late nineteenth century American
development.[32]

4.2.2 Wages and the Labor Market.

Some of the best historical information available for
testing the plausibility of our model relates to factor
markets and input prices. One of the most extensive, and
consistent, annual wage series is Lebergott's annual earnings of non-farm employees in 1914 dollars. Since the
current dollar earnings data is dominated by observations on eastern industries, and since the price deflator
is largely based on New York prices, the index is concep-
tually identical to our eastern industrial wage rate, $w_E(t)$.
There is one significant difference, however, between
Lebergott's real annual earnings index and $w_E(t)$. Lebergott's series refers to *employed* workers before 1900:
only after 1900 is he able to adjust for the effects of
unemployment on average annual earnings. The model, on
the other hand, assumes full employment; wages are fully
flexible and bear the brunt of labor market adjustment.
On these grounds alone, the predicted wage series is likely
to exhibit far greater short run instability.

Table 3 and Figure 7 confirm our expectations on the
real wage's short run instability, since the predicted
(eastern) industrial wage displays far more variance

around the trend than does Lebergott's series. Yet, the long term movements are surprisingly similar. From a common base in 1870 to the period 1890-95, the Lebergott unadjusted index rises to 2.15 while $w_E(t)$ increases to 2.29. However the model is unable to capture adequately the sharp cyclic retardation during the 1890's. It *does* record the rapid expansions in the early 1870's and the 1880's. It also reproduces the decline during the mid-late 1870's. Nevertheless, while real industrial earnings were relatively stable from 1890 to 1895 (and unemployment rates as high as 10 per cent), the model predicts a major

Figure 7: Trends in Industrial Earnings,
1870-1895

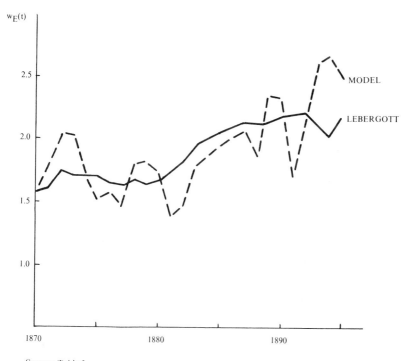

Source: Table 3.

Table 3

Trends in Real Wages, 1870-1895

Year	Real Annual Earnings of Non-Farm Employees: Lebergott		Model $w_E(t)$
	1914 dollars	Index	
1870	$375	1.570	1.570
1871	386	1.616	1.777
1872	416	1.742	2.047
1873	407	1.705	2.035
1874	403	1.687	1.714
1875	403	1.687	1.545
1876	393	1.645	1.562
1877	388	1.625	1.481
1878	397	1.663	1.792
1879	391	1.637	1.819
1880	395	1.654	1.728
1881	415	1.737	1.390
1882	431	1.805	1.473
1883	459	1.922	1.778
1884	478	2.002	1.863
1885	492	2.060	1.943
1886	499	2.089	2.018
1887	509	2.131	2.053
1888	505	2.115	1.878
1889	510	2.136	2.351
1890	519	2.173	2.321
1891	525	2.199	1.713
1892	527	2.207	2.063
1893	505	2.115	2.552
1894	484	2.027	2.662
1895	520	2.178	2.519

Source: Lebergott, *Manpower*, Tables A-17 and A-19, pp. 524 and 528.

rise in $w_E(t)$. Overall, however, the model appears to predict this crucial variable fairly well.[33]

The model has been shown to replicate one detailed historical wage series, that for eastern industrial workers. Does it perform as well for farm labor and industrial employment in the Midwest? The most effective way to answer this question is to use the scattered data reported in Lebergott's research to construct measures of wage relatives over the long term. These relatives are presented in Table 4. Lebergott's estimates of daily wages

302

Table 4

Measures of Labor Market Disequilibrium, 1869-1900

4.A Regional Labor Markets

Region	Year		
	1869 (daily)	1880 (daily)	1890 (daily)
Common Laborers:			
New England	$1.56	$1.28	$1.49
Middle Atlantic	1.58	1.27	1.45
Northeast (E)	1.57	1.27	1.47
East North Central	1.58	1.30	1.51
West North Central	1.55	1.43	1.48
Midwest (W)	1.57	1.36	1.50
(1870 = 100)			
Midwest ÷ Northeast	100	107	102
Model $\bar{w}_W(t)/w_E(t)$	100	119	109

4.B Industry-Farm Wage Differentials in the East North Central

Sector	Year			
	1869/70	1879/80	1889/90	1899/00
Iron and Steel, Annual Earnings Full Time Equivalent	$506	$416	$560	$579
Farm Laborers Average Monthly Earnings with Board	16.94	15.48	15.92	16.90
Iron and Steel ÷ Farm Laborer (1869/70=100)	100	89	117	114
MODEL $w_{IW}(t)/w_{AW}(t)$ (1870=100)	100	93	118	115

Source:
Table 4.A is calculated from Lebergott, *Manpower* Table A-2, 54.
Table 4.B is from *ibid.*, Tables A-29 and A-23, 545 and 539.

for common laborers in the Northeast and Midwest are reported in Table 4.A for 1869, 1880, and 1890. The regional wage relatives derived from Lebergott's data are to be compared with the model's predictions on the average midwestern wage relative to the northeastern wage. The model reproduces the historical experience with regional wage differentials (in current prices) without exception; it does equally well for the industry-farm wage differential in the Midwest (Table 4.B). The midwestern wage rises relative to that of the Northeast during the 1870's and declines thereafter, so much so that the midwestern laborer has a lower (money) wage by the turn of the century. It appears that the model is quite capable of capturing American experience with regional wage differentials and, by inplication, must reproduce farm wages and midwestern industrial wages with an effectiveness equal to that of the eastern industrial wage.

4.2.3   Changes in Economic Structure.

Thus far, the plausibility of our model of late nineteenth century American development has been evaluated in terms of aggregate growth performance and labor market behavior. It is, of course, essential that the model pass these critical tests to make the framework a serious candidate for historical analysis. Based on this evaluation alone, the model appears to command far more attention than we would devote to a "simple paradigm" of historical growth. Yet, many of the issues raised in the historical literature deal with the sources of industrialization, urbanization, and regional expansion during the late nineteenth century. To evalute the plausibility of the model in these dimensions, we now turn to its predictions on the regional and sectoral distribution of labor inputs over time: fact or fiction?

Table 5 displays three key measures of factor use in the American economy which have always been the focus of historian's interest in and of economist's concern with industrial development. The first of these is the share of industrial (nonfarm) employment in the midwest itself. The second is the share of the American (more precisely, the aggregate of the northeastern and midwestern) labor force employed in the Midwest. The third measures the relative importance of nonfarm employment in total employment.

The Perloff data on the nonfarm employment share is given only at Census dates. The absolute increase in industry's share is almost 7 percentage points up to 1890: in contrast to conventional historical accounts, hardly a noteworthy industrialization performance. The model predicts a rate of industrialization up to 1895 exactly the

Table 5

Sectoral Employment Distribution, 1870-95

Year	L_{IW}/L_W		$L_{AW}+L_{IW}/L$		$L_{IW}+L_{IE}/L$	
	Perloff	Model	Perloff	Model	Perloff	Model
1870	0.241	0.240	0.654	0.649	0.507	0.507
1875	-	0.260	-	0.633	-	0.535
1880	0.274	0.258	0.656	0.650	0.524	0.518
1885	-	0.240	-	0.630	-	0.521
1890	0.329	0.273	0.632	0.635	0.576	0.538
1895	-	0.329	-	0.631	-	0.576

Source: H. Perloff et al., Regions, Resources and Economic Growth, (Baltimore: Johns Hopkins Press, 1960), Chapter 12.

same, although the 1890 figure is somewhat lower. Although the figures are not presented here, the historical data suggests that the major period of industrialization prior to World War I is not the Gilded Age: rather, the majority of the employment shift took place after 1890! The model replicates this characteristic of United States growth very well: both the historical and the simulated series show three-quarters of the employment shift from 1870 to 1910 occuring in the last two decades.

The industrialization experience *within* the Midwest is considerably more dramatic, but the relative rates over time are comparable to those for the United States as a whole. Perloff documents an increase in the midwestern nonfarm employment share of 8.8 percentage points up to 1890, while the simulation records an identical increase by 1895. Finally, we note that the model also successfully replicates the changing distribution of the labor force by regions. The 1870's are years of minor increases in the American labor force share employed in the Midwest, while the 1880's record a significant reversal in this trend.

In summary, the model's ability to account for American industrialization and regional employment shifts is impressive. Utilizing the simple framework developed in section 3 we are able to reproduce, and thus understand, American experience with structural change in the post Civil War period quite adequately. Apparently, a more complex model is unnecessary for understanding economic performance over these twenty-five years. Can the same be said for the midwestern farm sector?

4.2.4 *The Farm Mortgage Rate.*

A midwestern farm mortgage rate series is displayed in Table 6. The series is for Iowa, but other midwestern states exhibit comparable trends. These historical farm mortgage rates are adjusted by commodity price movements. It is well known that if the price level is known with perfect certainty to be changing at an annual rate, $p(t)$, then the real rate of interest, $r(t)$, can be related to the *nominal* (quoted) rate, $i(t)$, by the expression

$$r(t) = \frac{i(t) - p(t)}{1 + p(t)} \quad .$$

Thus, the appropriate farm mortgage rate prevailing in the Midwest is the real rather than the nominal rate, and Table 6 embodies these adjustments where $p(t)$ is computed as an average rate of change in the Warren-Pearson index over the preceding five years. The adjustment is critical for an understanding of the operation of American financial markets and farmers' discontent, as well as for the evaluation of our model's empirical plausibility.

Table 6

Trends in Real Farm Mortgage Rates, 1870-1900

Year	Farm Mortgage Rates in the Midwest	
	Actual	Model
1870	.169	.160
1875	-	.122
1880	.123	.096
1885	-	.072
1890	.077	.057
1895	-	.048
1900	.040	.038

Source: The historical rates are for Iowa. In the original source they are quoted in nominal form. J. Bowman, "Trends in Midwestern Farm Land Values, 1860-1900," (unpublished doctoral dissertation, Yale University, 1964), Table II, Chapter III, III-14.

There seems little doubt that our model replicates this aspect of American financial history quite well. From 1870 to 1895, farm mortgage rates fell by remarkable proportions in the Midwest. Coupled with the rise in farm labor costs, this relative price movement played a key role in fostering the rapid rate of farm mechanization observed there.[34] The model closely predicts the magnitude of the precipitous fall. Iowa (real) farm mortgage rates fell from 16.9 to 7.7 per cent by 1890, a remarkable decline of 9.2 percentage points. The predicted farm mortgage rate declines from 16.0 to 5.7 per cent, a comparable fall of 10.3 percentage points. The correspondence is even closer by 1900. Once again, the model reproduces the behavior of a key endogenous variable surprisingly well.

4.2.5   Farm Yields, Income, and Land Values
in the Midwest.

Between 1870 and 1900, the model predicts a very moderate yield improvement of 14.9 per cent in the Midwest. Compare this with the historical evidence. Parker and Klein document a rise from 1869 to 1899 of 10.2 per cent for wheat in the Corn Belt states and 4.4 per cent in the West as a whole.[35] Not only are these secular trends adequately captured by the model, but turning points are reproduced as well. Again for wheat in the Corn Belt states, the Parker-Klein yield index rises from 1869 to 1889 and declines to 1899. Simulated yields exhibit comparable movements: they rise up to the mid 1880's, are stable to the mid 1890's, and decline sharply thereafter. Do these yield trends imply stability in farm income and thus cause for farm discontent? Not in the Midwest at least.

Measures of midwestern average labor productivity growth in agriculture are available, and they confirm the revisionist view of farm performance during this period of farmers' protest. Although the results are not presented here in tabular form, the model predicts the following midwestern farm performance from 1879 to 1899: in constant relative prices, farm income grows at an annual rate of 1.44 per cent. Compare this predicted performance with actual historical experience. Fogel and Rutner have estimated the per annum growth of real agricultural income per worker for the North Central region as 1.5 per cent over the same two decades.[36] The conformity between the predicted rate of 1.44 per cent and the observed rate of 1.5 per cent once again confirms the plausibility of our model. Note that this performance closely approximates that for the economy as a whole, negating any absolute or even relative farm deterioration thesis. Note further that this rapid growth performance in midwestern agriculture is not shared elsewhere in American agriculture: comparable statistics for the North Atlantic and the South are 0.2 and 0.9 per cent, respectively. One of the anomalies of this period of American economic history is that a continuous state of agrarian discontent coincided with impressive secular improvements in farm land values (positive capital gains). The evidence collected by Tostlebe, presented in Table 7, indicates the magnitude of the increase in Midwestern land values over the three decades following 1870, from $17.10 to $30.50 per acre (in 1910-14 prices). If we treat land as an asset with a permanent income (rental) stream over time, then land values will be determined by $V(t) = d(t)/r(t)$. The model determines rents, $d(t)$, endogenously. Given the Cobb-Douglas production function specified for the farm sector, land's marginal physical product can be expressed as $\beta_R Q_{AW}/R$ where β_R is a stable parameter and Q_{AW} is an endogenous farm output variable. Since midwestern

Table 7

Midwestern Land Values, 1870-1900

Year	Bowman (1860 Prices)			TOSTLEBE (1910-14 Prices)	Model (1910-14 Prices): V(t) Index at		
	Iowa	Illinois	Minnesota	Midwest	Current	$\frac{0}{1/3 \Sigma d(t)}$ $t = -2$	$\frac{0}{1/7 \Sigma d(t)}$ $t = -6$
1870	$21.60	$28.80	$19.54	$17.1	$12.3		
1875	-	-	-	-	13.4	$12.9	
1880	24.50	33.90	20.82	18.4	18.4	18.4	$18.4
1885	-	-	-	-	26.9	29.6	28.7
1890	36.30	53.90	30.40	30.0	34.2	30.4	32.9
1895	-	-	-	-	39.7	30.4	32.3
1900	55.30	62.20	38.80	30.5	46.3	28.5	24.6

Source: J. D. Bowman, "Trends in Midwestern Farm Land Values, 1860-1900," (unpublished doctoral dissertation, Yale University, 1964), Appendix Table A-2, Col. (4), 95 ff. Bowman's figures refer to wheat farms only. A. S. Tostlebe, *Capital in Agriculture: Its Formation and Financing Since 1870* (New York: NBER, 1957), Tables 6 and 9, 50-51 and 66-69. The model results are derived from the expression $V(t) = d(t)/r(t)$, and two variants allowing for price expectations: one includes the two preceding years and the other, six preceding years. In all cases, $V(t)$ is the current (real) farm mortgage rate.

agriculture was surely competitive, the annual gross rental price should be equated to the value of the annual service flow from land: i.e.,

$$d(t) = P_{AW}(t)\, \beta_R\, \frac{Q_{AW}(t)}{R(t)}.$$

The behavior of land rents over time can thus be composed into

$$\dot{d} = \dot{P}_{AW} + \dot{Q}_{AW} - \dot{R}.$$

The last two terms represent the movement in yields over time which we have already seen to be negligible up to 1899. How, then, do we account for booming land values over the same period? Must we appeal to irrational speculation?

Three land value series are presented in Table 7, one using current net rents, one using the expected rental rate based on the average net rents over the past three years, and one which uses the past seven years in generating expectations. The justification for the use of average lagged rents comes from Chambers' research. Some time ago, Chambers explored the determinants of farm land values for the first two decades of the twentieth century.[37] Net cash rents per acre were excellent predictors of farm land values in Chambers' study (applied to a period of real interest rate stability), but only when projected rents were based on the experience of the last seven to ten years. Table 7 presents similar calculations for the simulated data on the late nineteenth century. Although each of the predicted land value series exhibits a signifii-cant upward movement during these three decades, their short run behavior varies considerably as does the magni-tude of the long run improvement. The "best" V(t) predic-tion is produced using the three year average. For that series, V(t) rises between 1880 and 1900 from $18.40 to

310

$28.50 per acre, remarkably close to the Tostlebe figures (from $18.40 in 1880 to $30.50 in 1900).

The model accurately predicts the boom in land values in the 1880's and the somewhat more moderate rise in the 1870's. These results do not leave much of the movements in land values to be explained by "land monopolization" and "irresponsible speculation." Instead, the key to booming land values during an era of yield stability is simply the remarkable fall in midwestern farm mortgage rates.

5. The Railroads and Midwestern Development During the Gilded Age

Having established the empirical plausibility of our model of late nineteenth century American development, we can now return to the issues raised early in this paper. That is, our model includes exogenous interregional transport cost variables and replicates American economic development between the 1860's and the 1890's very closely. We can now experiment with that model. How would America in general, and the Midwest in particular, have developed over these two decades had interregional transport rates remained constant at their 1870 levels? In what ways would the counterfactual simulated history have differed from the "actual" simulated history?

5.1 The Railroads and Economic Growth: Dynamics.

In the introductory remarks to this paper, we emphasized that the traditional literature on the nineteenth century railroads stresses dynamic effects. There are numerous hypotheses which identify potential dynamic links between the railroads and economic growth. Consider the most prominent of these: capital formation rates.

The Keynesian tradition lays considerable stress on railroad activity as a key determinant of income growth in the late nineteenth century. Railroad construction itself

311

was, after all, a large share of U.S. net capital formation: in two peak periods, 1870-1874 and 1880-1884, the share of net railroad investment in total net capital formation was 34 and 17 per cent respectively.[38] Had net investment been lower in the absence of new railroad construction, presumably aggregate demand would have been negatively effected and income growth suppressed by departures from full capacity utilization. The conventional multiplier would assure a magnification of this impact, but the railroad literature stresses instead direct interindustry backward linkages. It had always been assumed that expansion of railroad capacity, as well as maintenance of that capacity, had a strong impact on supplying industries—in particular, the iron and steel industry.[39] Fogel has carefully examined this "backward linkage" thesis and found it wanting.[40] In any case, we have found that our full employment neoclassical model was quite adequate in accounting for American long run growth performance. It was not found necessary to introduce monetary variables or the possibility of departures from full capacity to account for late nineteenth century growth patterns. Thus, we feel reasonably confident in ignoring the Keynesian tradition as a means of exploring the dynamic effect of the rails through capital formation rates.

The dynamic effects of the rails are introduced in two ways in our model, both of which conform to the neoclassical tradition. First, by fostering interregional trade and specialization the railroads tend to raise the marginal value product of all agricultural inputs in the Midwest. In consequence, the average productivity of capital is raised in midwestern agriculture. That is, the capital-output ratio tends to fall in the midwestern farm sector. The impact does not stop there, of course, since forces are set in motion economy-wide in response to rate of return differentials and eventually the capital-output ratio tends to fall in all sectors. This effect was briefly discussed in section 3 where the rate of capital formation was decomposed into

$$\frac{\dot{K}(t)}{K(t)} = \bar{s} \left\{ \frac{GNP(t)}{P_I(t)\,K(t)} \right\} - \delta = \left[\bar{s} \Big/ P_I(t) \right] \left\{ \frac{GNP(t)}{K(t)} \right\} - \delta.$$

The once-over rise in GNP induced by the rails has the added dynamic effect of raising capital formation rates. From the initial capital stock, GNP is increased and thus even if the savings rate, $\bar{s}$, is constant, total savings are increased and consequently capital formation rates are raised.

There is an additional impact on capital formations rates as well. Note the two terms in front of the average product of capital in the above expression: i.e., $\bar{s}\big/P_I(t)$. The railroads tended to raise farm prices *in the Midwest.* In addition, they tended to lower capital goods prices, $P_{IW}(t)$, there as well, at least up to 1885. Thus new physical capital goods available for net investment would tend to increase given a fixed savings rate out of current income. This effect was discussed above, but it may be helpful to present it graphically in Figure 8.

We do not insist that these are the *only* dynamic links between the railroads and American economic growth, but by exploring the quantitative impact of these within our historical model of American development we hope to enrich our understanding of the potential importance of these dynamic effects. The research by cliometricians up to this point tends to minimize the dynamic effects of the rails, and the analysis in the present section may offer some guides regarding the extent to which the importance of the rails has been underestimated in the partial equilibrium analysis of earlier work. If the dynamic effects tentatively estimated appear to be powerful, then economic historians who view the approach embedded in the model developed in section 3 as too restrictive may be goaded into presenting alternative general equilibrium models of

Figure 8

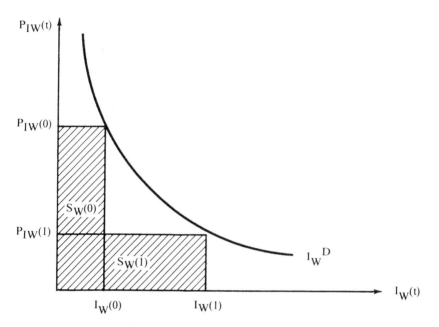

American development which introduce an explicit role for the rails. That is certainly the prime intent of this paper.

Table 8 dispells any doubt regarding the magnitude of these dynamic effects in the late nineteenth century. The table compares the "actual" growth performance of the American economy between 1869-1878 and 1884-1893 with that which would have taken place in a counterfactual world of constant transport costs during the Gilded Age. The differences are significant indeed.

In 1870 prices, GNP per worker would have grown at a rate of 0.68 per cent below that which was in fact achieved. Similar results are forthcoming when 1910 price weights are used: e.g., a gap of 0.77 per cent. One source of the lower growth performance in the counterfactual world

314

Table 8

The Impact of the Railroads on Economic Growth,
1869/78 to 1884/93

Growth Rates	Actual	Constant Transport Costs
GNP per worker in 1870 prices	2.49%	1.81%
GNP per worker in 1910 prices	2.33	1.56
Capital Stock	6.06	5.06
Midwestern Capital Stock	7.17	6.33

Note: Growth rates computed between averages for 1869-78 and 1884-93.

without declining interregional transport rates lies with capital formation experience. For the United States as a whole, the rates of capital stock growth would have been lower by 1 per cent in the counterfactual world.

The findings displayed in Table 8 do not adequately take account of the comparative static effect of the rails on output, since the majority of the rate declines took place early in the period and the growth rates in Table 9 are computed from an initial base averaged over the years 1869 to 1878. Table 9 may be more helpful in this regard. Gross national product would have been lower in 1871 by 9 per cent in the absence of transport improvements! The

Table 9

Railroad "Social Savings", 1871-90

Year	GNP in 1870 Prices		Social Savings $[(1)-(2)] \div (1)$
	Actual (1)	Constant Transport Costs (2)	
1871	321.2	293.0	0.09
1880	521.3	440.5	0.16
1890	776.6	614.4	0.21

Note: These "savings" ignore intraregional gains.

magnitude of the "social savings"—the percentage departure between actual and counterfactual GNP levels—increases over time as transport costs continue their decline and in addition as dynamic influences are brought into play. By 1890, the "social savings" share in actual GNP would have been 21 per cent. The "axiom of indispensability" cannot be accepted (or rejected) on the basis of such an estimate, but it certainly casts doubt on the partial equilibrium calculations presented thus far in the historical literature. Furthermore, the conventional literature has always been concerned with the impact of the *decline in transport costs over time* (primarily induced by the rails) rather than in the relative superiority of the railroads in 1890. The impressive growth performance of the American economy during the Gilded Age is indeed closely related to the interregional and intraregional transport improvements achieved from the Civil War decade to 1890. To ignore them is to miss a key factor accounting for the rapid growth in America during this period.

5.2   *Trade Creation and Midwestern Industrialization: Statics.*

The comparative static effect of the railroads on the structure of the late nineteenth century economy is straightforward. The impact of the assumed constant 1870 interregional transport costs on the Midwest is summarized in Figure 9 where the analysis is equivalent to the imposition of a deterioration in the terms of trade for a "small" country. The counterfactual relative prices facing the Midwest reflect the absence of interregional transport improvements. It was seen in section 2 that without transport improvements the relative price of farm products would have been far lower in the Midwest after 1870. The result would have been a relative contraction of the farm sector and, under normal local demand conditions, a reduction of grain exports from the Midwest. Given demand

Figure 9

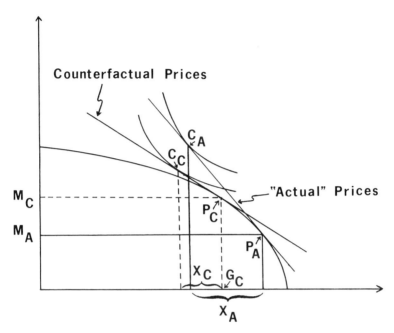

conditions in the East and the terms of trade prevailing there,[41] eastern consumption of western foodstuffs would remain unchanged. Consequently, the reduction in grain exports from the Midwest would be fully passed on as an equivalent reduction in grain exports from the United States: e.g., from East coast ports to Europe. This qualitative analysis then raises two issues relevant to late nineteenth century American and midwestern industrialization. (i) What was the likely *magnitude* of these comparative static effects? (ii) Are the dynamic effects sufficiently powerful *to offset*, eventually, the estimated comparative static effects? This second question follows from the analysis of section 5.1. Since the absence of transport improvements after 1870 would have lowered capital formation rates, the relative price of labor (although still rising) would have risen at a lesser rate up to 1890. Thus

317

the growth of those sectors utilizing capital-intensive production methods would have been suppressed as a result. That is, the dynamic effects suggest that industrialization rates would have been lower under the counterfactual regime of no transport cost changes since industry is more capital-intensive. Would the positive comparative static or the negative dynamic effects dominate over the two decades?

Table 10 supplies an unambiguous answer to this question. The share of agricultural value added in U.S. commodity output would have been far lower in 1890 had no improvements in interregional transport costs taken place during the Gilded Age. The implications are clear. *Declining interregional transport costs had a very powerful negative influence on American industrialization during the Gilded Age.* This is hardly a conventional conclusion, since most economic history texts argue the opposite: they focus entirely on (apparently weak) backward linkage effects of the railroads rather than on forward linkages and transport costs. The result can be documented in another way. In Table 11, we present the industrial labor force share in the total labor force for both the Midwest and America as a whole. The experiments reported there show that the Midwest industrial employment share in 1890 would have been .427, rather than .273, had no transport improvements taken place after 1870. The comparable actual and counterfactual figures for the U.S. as a whole are .637 and .538, respectively. No doubt revision of our model specifications and parameter estimates would alter these results somewhat, but the *magnitude* of the gap is so large as to require enormous revisions to affect significantly our findings.

The railroads inhibited industrialization during the Gilded Age, but this conclusion must not be confused with quite a different statement documented in section 5.1: the railroads fostered economic growth during the same period.

Table 10

The Impact of the Railroads on the
Output Mix of the American Economy, 1870-90

Year	Share of Agriculture in Commodity Output		Share of Agriculture in GNP		Share of Transport and Communications in GNP	
	Actual	Constant Transport Costs	Actual	Constant Transport Costs	Actual	Constant Transport Costs
1870	.433	.433	.358	.358	.173	.173
1875	.449	.393	.375	.340	.164	.134
1880	.460	.343	.400	.319	.130	.070
1885	.437	.328	.371	.301	.152	.082
1890	.393	.247	.355	.252	.096	.074

Table 11

The Impact of the Railroads on
Employment Distribution, 1870-90

Year	Midwestern Industrial Labor Force Share: L_{IW}/L_W		U.S. Industrial Labor Force Share L_I/L	
	Actual	Constant Transport Costs	Actual	Constant Transport Costs
1870	.240	.240	.507	.507
1875	.266	.311	.535	.564
1880	.258	.334	.518	.568
1885	.240	.364	.521	.600
1890	.273	.427	.538	.637

This clarification may be unnecessary to some readers. But it should prove sobering to those economic historians who insist on using indices of employment distribution and the like as measures of economic development.

5.3   *The Farmer: Midwestern Land Values, Rents, and Yields.*

We have seen in the previous section the great importance of interregional transport costs to the relative expansion of the farm sector. The present section examines midwestern agriculture in more detail. In the absence of declining transport costs, would land rents have undergone the mild rise up to 1890 which is observed in fact? If instead land yields and rents would have exhibited stability, would land values have undergone a far milder improvement as well? How much of the enormous rise in midwestern land values can be attributed to the rails, improved farm gate prices, and thus net cash income per acre?

Table 12 supplies some answers. First, quantum yields on the average midwestern farm would have undergone no rise whatever up to 1890 in spite of continued total factor productivity growth. It seems clear that the rapid historical increase in capital equipment per acre is able to account for some of the mild increase in actual yields, but since the impact of farm mechanization is to save labor rather than land, the marginal increases in land yields would have been absent under a counterfactual world of transport cost stability. Second, land rents as a result also would have exhibited remarkable stability up to 1890. Third, does this imply different counterfactual behavior for land values? Much to our surprise, the answer is in the negative! It was established in section 4.2, of course,

Table 12

The Impact of the Railroads on Land Values, Rents and Yields in the Midwest, 1870-1890 (1870=100)

Year	Land Values		Rents		Yields	
	Actual	Constant Transport Costs	Actual	Constant Transport Costs	Actual	Constant Transport Costs
1870	100	100	100	100	100	100
1875	138	141	109	100	105	98
1880	190	217	118	100	113	100
1885	279	227	127	109	125	102
1890	353	351	127	100	126	98

that declining farm mortgage rates explain most of the land value increases rather than an improvement in net cash income per acre. Nevertheless, one would have thought that zero growth in land rents would have reduced the land value "boom" significantly. This apparent paradox is explained quite simply: farm mortgage rates decline far more rapidly in our counterfactual world of constant transport costs. It should suffice to point out that higher farm equipment prices in the counterfactual regime up to 1885 inhibits mechanization and the introduction of labor-saving devices on the farm. In fact, while the capital-labor ratio increases from 1870 to 1885 by 2.9 times in the actual simulation, it rises by only 2.3 times under constant transport costs and thus high equipment prices. (In 1890 the multiples are 3.4 and 2.8 respectively.) This in turn implies a lower demand for farm credit and thus an even more rapid decline in farm mortgage rates. It appears that the diminished rise in land rents would have been offset by an accelerated decline in farm mortgage rates: the net result would have been a similar trend in land values. In summary, the farmer failed to receive a double blessing from the freight rate declines during the Railway Age. While rents, yields and farm income all rose in the Midwest as a result of the interregional transport cost reductions, land values apparently were only marginally influenced if at all.

5.4   Off-Farm Migration, Real Wages, and Labor Market Disequilibrium.

Although the historical literature is primarily concerned with the impact of the railroads on output levels and industrial structure, the process by which these end results were achieved may be of interest as well. How were off-farm migration rates affected by the rails? Did interregional transport improvements significantly influence westward migration rates, or was the impact felt primarily within the Midwest itself? Did the rails have a pronounced impact on the regional and sectoral wage structure? A comparative static equilibrium model like the one presented in section 3.1 cannot confront these issues, since it normally assumes instantaneous and costless factor mobility. Since our more realistic model of historical growth introduces constraints on factor mobility, it can more readily give some insight into the *process* by which new equilibrium conditions were achieved over time in the American economy.

Table 13 reports the estimated impact of the rails on farm employment. Had no interregional transport improvements taken place after 1870, the farm labor force would have been some 21 per cent smaller by 1890, just two decades later. Note, however, how the reduced farm em-

Table 13

The Impact of the Railroads on Midwestern
Employment and Migration, 1870-90

Year	Farm Labor: $L_{AW}(t)$		Midwestern Labor Force: $L_W(t)$	
	Actual	Constant Transport Costs	Actual	Constant Transport Costs
1870	49.3	49.3	64.9	64.9
1875	54.1	50.8	73.7	73.7
1880	61.4	55.1	82.7	82.7
1885	69.9	58.3	91.9	91.7
1890	73.4	57.7	100.9	100.6

Year	Off-Farm Migration Rate: $M_{IA}(t)$		East-West Migration Rate: $M_{WE}(t)$	
	Actual	Constant Transport Costs	Actual	Constant Transport Costs
1870	.000	.000	.003	.003
1875	.000	.015	.003	.003
1880	(.008)	.013	.004	.003
1885	(.001)	.015	.005	.004
1890	.022	.044	.003	.003

ployment would have affected the labor market elsewhere in the American economy. The *total* midwestern employed labor force would have been no different under the counterfactual conditions! The midwestern industrial sector apparently could have fully absorbed the "displaced" farm labor force so that the total midwestern labor force and the westward migration rates would have been almost exactly the same. *The conclusion is inescapable: our tentative findings suggest that although the rails had an important impact on agriculture in the Midwest, migration from the East was only marginally influenced by the subsequent regional trade creation.* The explanation for this apparently bizarre result can be found in Table 14. Real wages in western urban centers were strongly *suppressed*, relative to those in the East, by interregional transport cost declines up to 1890. The farm price gains to midwestern farmers were losses to Midwest urban labor. Typically, the economic historian focuses on the western employment creating effects associated with railway development and the consequent expansion of Midwest farming. What he fails to appreciate, however, is the symmetrical rise in food prices in western urban

Table 14

The Impact of the Railroads on Wages, 1870-90

Year	Real Eastern Wage: $\tilde{w}_E(t)$		Regional Real Wage Differential: $\frac{(100\,\tilde{w}_W(t)}{\tilde{w}_E(t)}$		Midwest Industry Agriculture Wage Differential: $(100)\,w_{IW}(t)/w_{AW}(t)$	
	Actual	Constant Transport Costs	Actual	Constant Transport Costs	Actual	Constant Transport Cost
1870	.975	.975	144.7	144.7	100.0	100.0
1875	1.048	1.002	160.4	160.9	86.3	94.9
1880	1.383	1.320	138.5	132.7	92.8	117.7
1885	1.472	1.346	143.8	146.9	109.8	113.7
1890	1.957	1.752	115.8	125.2	118.9	140.8

323

centers. To the extent that foodstuffs loom large in urban workers' budgets, the food price rise produced a marked improvement in the relative real wage in the East. The *net* inducement to migrate West, was, as a result, negligible. Table 14 documents that the *real* wage differential between West and East would have been only 2 per cent higher under constant transport costs by 1885. Only as late as 1890 does a significant difference between the actual and counterfactual regional wage differentials appear.

The offsetting cost of living effect on real wage differentials is far less pronounced *within* the Midwest. As a result, the employment impact of transport improvements has a much more impressive influence on the midwestern wage differential between industry and agriculture, and, as a result, on off-farm migration rates to midwestern urban employment. The off-farm migration rate is reported in Table 13 and the farm-industry wage differentials in Table 14. In the interests of brevity, consider only one year, 1890: in the counterfactual world of constant transport costs, the industry-agriculture wage differential would have been higher by some 18 per cent, and the off-farm migration rate double what it was in fact. Obviously, *urbanization in the Midwest was sharply curtailed by the interregional transport improvement during the Railway Age.*

6. *Summary and Disclaimers:*
   The Tasks of Cliometric History.

This paper has presented a fresh examination of the impact of the rails on the American economy during the Gilded Age. Our findings contrast sharply with the conventional literature, including the more recent contribution by Professor Fogel. First, "social savings" from interregional transport improvements is estimated to be larger than Fogel's by a factor of twenty. Had no interregional transport cost improvements taken place between 1870 and

1890, gross national product (in 1870 prices) would have been lower by some 20 per cent. This 1890 figure is the result of two mutually reinforcing effects: (i) the comparative static losses from diminished interregional and international trade and (ii) the dynamic effects associated with the rails. Physical capital formation rates would have been considerably lower under a counterfactual world of no transport cost improvements, in both the East and the Midwest. In consequence, we estimate that GNP per worker (1870 prices) growth rates would have been lower by about six-tenths of a percentage point per year over the two decades as a whole.

Second, declining interregional transport costs during the Gilded Age had a powerful negative influence on American industrialization, especially in the Midwest. The interregional and international trade creating effects were such as to inhibit, rather than foster, industrialization. Industrialization did take place during the Gilded Age, but it was hardly impressive and, furthermore, it would have been far more pronounced had interregional transport improvements been absent. This result is to be contrasted with the (now defunct) Rostow thesis which, by concentrating attention exclusively on backward linkages, argues that the railroads played an important role in fostering American industrialization. Although Rostow's focus was on the ante-bellum period, his position commonly appears in historical accounts of the post Civil war period. The hypothesis is rejected in the above pages where powerful forward linkages have been found to have seriously inhibited industrialization.

Third, the mild rise in midwestern yields and rents can be explained in large measure by transport improvements after 1870. Yet they provide no explanation for the boom in land values up to 1890. This apparent paradox is resolved by appealing to the indirect impact of the rails on the capital market. Without rails, midwestern farming would have expanded at far lower rates and as a result this sector's demands for external credit would have diminished. The net result would have been lower farm mortgage rates by 1890, and thus land values would have risen sufficiently on this account to offset the negative influence on yields and rents. Finally, our findings suggest that migration from the East to the Midwest was only marginally influenced by the rails. The impetus which the rails gave to farm employment via trade creation was fully satisfied by migration within the Midwest itself. Midwestern urbanization was inhibited by transport improvements during the Railway Age, but the expansion of eastern cities was not.

These results are only as accurate as the underlying model. This is true of any analytical economic history. As a result, the critical reader must carefully weigh the plausibility of our analysis at each of three crucial steps. First, is the counterfactual appropriate? Has the assumed decline in interregional relative commodity prices been accurately estimated? Can all of this decline be attributed to the rails? Is the interregional transport cost differential in 1870 larger than the railroad-no railroad cost differential estimated by Fogel in 1890? Second, is the full static general equilibrium model properly specified and estimated? No sensitivity analysis is presented in this paper due to the large number of parameters in the system. The task would require more computer resources than are presently available to us. Yet given the magnitude of the estimated effects presented in the above pages, it seems unlikely that our results would be seriously affected by even major revisions in the parameters.[42] Third, are the dynamic influences in the model appropriately specified? We feel somewhat less confident on this point and, as a result, anticipate sharp criticism from practitioners of the cliometric art. If a better understanding of the dynamic effects of the rails is forthcoming from such criticism, our modest efforts will have been amply rewarded.

Appendix A

Formal Statement of the Model

In constructing our model of American regional development, the following notation is used:

Endogenous Variables

$Q_{IE}(t)$:   Eastern output of industrial goods
$Q_{IW}(t)$:   Western output of industrial goods
$Q_{AW}(t)$:   Western output of agricultural goods
$K(t)$:   Total capital stock
$K_{IE}(t)$:   Eastern capital stock in industry
$K_{IW}(t)$:   Western capital stock in industry
$K_{AW}(t)$:   Western capital stock in agriculture
$K_{IEE}(t)$:   Eastern industrial capital stock owned by Easterners
$K_{IEW}(t)$:   Eastern industrial capital stock owned by Westerners
$K_{IWW}(t)$:   Western industrial capital stock owned by Westerners
$K_{IWE}(t)$:   Western industrial capital stock owned by Easterners
$K_{AWW}(t)$:   Western agricultural capital stock owned by Westerners
$K_{AWE}(t)$:   Western agricultural capital stock owned by Easterners
$I_{IEE}(t)$:   Gross investment in Eastern industry, financed by Easterners
$I_{IEW}(t)$:   Gross investment in Eastern industry, financed by Westerners
$I_{IWW}(t)$:   Gross investment in Western industry, financed by Westerners
$I_{IWE}(t)$:   Gross investment in Western industry, financed by Easterners
$I_{AWW}(t)$:   Gross investment in Western agriculture, financed by Westerners

327

$I_{AWE}(t)$:   Gross investment in Western agriculture, financed by Easterners

$L(t)$:   Total labor supply

$L_{IE}(t)$:   Labor supply in the East (all in industry) $= L_E(t)$

$L_{IW}(t)$:   Labor supply employed in the Western industrial sector

$L_{AW}(t)$:   Labor supply employed in the Western agricultural sector

$Y_E(t)$:   Eastern income

$Y_W(t)$:   Western income

$w_E(t)$:   Eastern wage rate (nominal)

$w_W(t)$:   Western wage rate (nominal)

$r_E(t)$:   Rate of return on Eastern (capital) assets

$r_W(t)$:   Rate of return on Western (capital) assets

$d(t)$:   Land rental rate

$\phi_{EW}(t)$:   Percentage of Western savings flowing to East

$\phi_{WE}(t)$:   Percentage of Eastern savings flowing to West

$\phi_{IA}(t)$:   Percentage of farm savings flowing to Western industry

$\phi_{AI}(t)$:   Percentage of Western "urban" savings flowing to agriculture

$D_{AW}(t)$:   Consumption demand for agricultural goods by Westerners

$D_{IW}(t)$:   Consumption demand for industrial goods by Westerners

$D_{AE}(t)$:   Consumption demand for agricultural goods by Easterners

$D_{IE}(t)$:   Consumption demand for industrial goods by Easterners

$m_{WE}(t)$:   Rate of migration from East to West, as a percentage of Eastern population

$m_{EW}(t)$:   Rate of migration from West to East, as a percentage of Western population

$\hat{m}_{IA}(t)$: Rate of farm to non-farm migration, as a percentage of farm labor force in West

$\hat{m}_{AI}(t)$: Rate of non-farm to farm migration, as a percent of Western industrial labor force

$i^*(t)$: Expected interest rate differential, West minus East

$\tilde{w}^*(t)$: Expected real wage differential, West minus East

$\tilde{w}_W(t)$: Western real wage

$\tilde{w}_E(t)$: Eastern real wage

$T_E(t)$: Revenue generated from Eastern transportation sector

$T_W(t)$: Revenue generated from Western transportation sector

$D_{AD}(t)$: Total domestic consumption demand for agricultural goods, East and West

$D_A(t)$: Total demand for agricultural goods, East, West, and Export

$EX(t)$: Quantum agricultural exports

$EXVAL(t)$: Value of agricultural exports, from Eastern ports

$IM(t)$: Quantum imports of industrial goods

$IMVAL(t)$: Value of industrial good imports, into Eastern ports

$P_{IW}(t)$: Price of industrial goods in Western markets

$P_{AW}(t)$: Price of agricultural goods in Western markets

$P_{IE}(t)$: Price of industrial goods in Eastern markets

$P_{AE}(t)$: Price of agricultural goods in Eastern markets

$R(t)$: Land stock in the West

$M(t)$: European in-migration

$A(t)$: Total factor productivity in Eastern industry

$A'(t)$: Total factor productivity in Western industry

$B(t)$: Total factor productivity in Western agriculture

$Z_I(t)$: Transport rates on East-West trade in industrial goods

$Z_A(t)$: Transport rates on West-East trade in grains

$COL_E(t)$:   Cost-of-living index in the East
$COL_W(t)$:   Cost-of-living index in the West

Production Conditions

[1] $Q_{IE}(t) = A(t)[K_{IE}(t)]^{\alpha_K}[L_{IE}(t)]^{\alpha_L}, \quad \alpha_L + \alpha_K = 1$

[2] $Q_{IW}(t) = A'(t)[K_{IW}(t)]^{\alpha_K}[L_{IW}(t)]^{\alpha_L},$
$\alpha_L + \alpha_K = 1$

[3] $Q_{AW}(t) = B(t)[K_{AW}(t)]^{\beta_K}[L_{AW}(t)]^{\beta_L}$
$R(t)^{\beta_R}, \quad \beta_K + \beta_L + \beta_R = 1$

Full Employment, Capital Accumulation,
and Labor Force Growth

[4] $K(t) = K_{IE}(t) + K_{IW}(t) + K_{AW}(t)$

[5] $K_{IE}(t) = K_{IEE}(t) + K_{IEW}(t)$

[6] $K_{IW}(t) = K_{IWW}(t) + K_{IWE}(t)$

[7] $K_{AW}(t) = K_{AWW}(t) + K_{AWE}(t)$

[8] $K_{IEE}(t) = I_{IEE}(t) = (1-\delta)K_{IEE}(t-1)$

[9] $K_{IEW}(t) = I_{IEW}(t) + (1-\delta)K_{IEW}(t-1)$

[10] $K_{IWW}(t) = I_{IWW}(t) + (1-\delta)K_{IWW}(t-1)$

[11] $K_{IWE}(t) = I_{IWE}(t) + (1-\delta)K_{IWE}(t-1)$

[12] $K_{AWW}(t) = I_{AWW}(t) + (1-\delta)K_{AWW}(t-1)$

[13] $K_{AWE}(t) = I_{AWE}(t) + (1-\delta)K_{AWE}(t-1)$

[14] $L(t) = L_{IE}(t) + L_{IW}(t) + L_{AW}(t)$

[15] $L_E(t) = n_E L_E(t-1) + m_{EW}(t)L_W(t-1) - m_{WE}(t)$
$L_E(t-1) + M(t)$

[16] $L_W(t) = n_W L_W(t-1) + m_{WE}(t)L_E(t-1) - m_{EW}(t)$
$L_W(t-1)$

[17] $L_{AW}(t) = L_{AW}(t-1) \left\{ n_W(t-1) - \hat{m}_{IA}(t-1) \right.$
$\left. - \dfrac{m_{WE}(t-1)L_E(t-1)}{L_W(t-1)} - m_{EW}(t-1) \right\}$
$+ \hat{m}_{AI}(t-1)L_{IW}(t-1)$

[18] $L_{IW}(t) = L_{IW}(t-1) \left\{ n_W(t-1) - \hat{m}_{AI}(t-1) \right.$
$\left. + \dfrac{m_{WE}(t-1) - L_E(t-1)}{L_W(t-1)} - m_{EW}(t-1) \right\}$
$+ \hat{m}_{IA}(t-1)L_{AW}(t-1)$

[19] $L_W(t) = L_{AW}(t) + L_{IW}(t)$

Income and Factor Pricing

[20] $Y_E(t) = \{r_E(t)K_{IEE}(t) + i_{AW}(t)P_{IW}(t)K_{AWE}(t) +$
         $i_{IW}(t)P_{IW}(t)K_{IWE}(t) + [\tau + \delta]P_{IE}(t)K_{IEW}(t)\}$
         $+ w_E(t)L_{IE}(t) + T_E(t)$

[21] $Y_W(t) = \{r_{IW}(t)K_{IWW}(t) + r_{AW}(t)K_{AWW}(t)$
         $+[i_E(t)-\tau]P_{IE}(t)K_{IEW}(t) + \delta P_{IW}(t)K_{AWE}(t)$
         $+\delta P_{IW}(t)K_{IWE}(t)\} + w_W(t)L_W(t)$
         $+ d(t)R(t) + T_W(t)$

[22] $w_E(t) = P_{IE}(t)\,\alpha_L\,\dfrac{Q_{IE}(t)}{L_{IE}(t)}$

[23] $w_W(t) = P_{IW}(t)\,\alpha_L\,\dfrac{Q_{IW}(t)}{L_{IW}(t)}$

[24] $w_{AW}(t) = P_{AW}(t)\,\beta_L\,\dfrac{Q_{AW}(t)}{L_{AW}(t)}$

[25] $r_E(t) = P_{IE}(t)\,\alpha_K\,\dfrac{Q_{IE}(t)}{K_{IE}(t)}$

[26] $r_W(t) = P_{IW}(t)\,\alpha_K\,\dfrac{Q_{IW}(t)}{K_{IW}(t)}$

[27] $r_{AW}(t) = P_{AW}(t)\,\beta_K\,\dfrac{Q_{AW}(t)}{K_{AW}(t)}$

[28] $d(t) = P_{AW}(t)\,\beta_R\,\dfrac{Q_{AW}(t)}{R(t)}$

[29] $P_{IE}(t)I_{IEE}(t) = sY_E(t) - P_{IW}(t)\,|I_{IWE}(t) + I_{AWE}(t)|$

[30] $P_{IE}(t)I_{IEW}(t) = s\phi_{EW}(t)Y_w(t)$

[31] $P_{IW}(t)I_{AWW}(t) = S_{AW}(t)\,[1-\phi_{IA}(t)] + S_{IW}(t)\phi_{AI}(t)$

[32] $P_{IW}(t)I_{IWW}(t) = S_{IW}(t)\,[1-\phi_{AI}(t)] + S_{AW}(t)\phi_{IA}(t)$

[33] $I_{AWE}(t) = |I_{IWE}(t) + I_{AWE}(t)|\left\{\dfrac{P_{IW}(t)I_{AWW}(t)}{S_{AW}(t) + S_{IW}(t)}\right\}$

[34] $I_{IWE}(t) = |I_{IWE}(t) + I_{AWE}(t)|\left\{\dfrac{P_{IW}(t)\,I_{IWW}(t)}{S_{AW}(t) + S_{IW}(t)}\right\}$

[35] $\quad S_{AW}(t) = sP_{AW}(t)Q_{AW}(t)$

[36] $\quad S_{IW}(t) = s \ |Y_W(t) - P_{AW}(t)Q_{AW}(t)|$

Transport Costs

[37] $\quad P_{IW}(t) = Z_I P_{IE}(t), Z_I > 1$

[38] $\quad P_{AE}(t) = Z_A P_{AW}(t), Z_A > 1$

Capital Markets

[39] $\quad \phi_{EW}(t) = \max \ |0, 1 - e^{-\mu[i^*(t)-\tau]}|$

[40] $\quad \phi_{WE}(t) = \max \ |0, 1 - e^{\mu[i^*(t)-\tau]}|$

[41] $\quad \hat{\phi}_{IA}(t) = \max \ |0, 1 - e^{-\mu[i^*(t)-\tau]}|$

[42] $\quad \hat{\phi}_{AI}(t) = \max \ |0, 1 - e^{\mu[i^*(t)-\tau]}|$

Consumer Demand

[43] $\quad D_{AW}(t) = L_W(t) \left\{ d_1 \left[\dfrac{(1-s)Y_W(t)}{L_W(t)} \right]^{d_2} \left[\dfrac{P_{AW}(t)}{P_{IW}(t)} \right]^{d_3} \right\}$

[44] $\quad D_{IW}(t) = \dfrac{(1-s)\,Y_W(t) - P_{AW}(t)D_{AW}(t)}{P_{IW}(t)}$

[45] $\quad D_{AE}(t) = L_E(t) \left\{ d'_1 \left[\dfrac{(1-s)Y_E(t)}{L_E(t)} \right]^{d_2} \left[\dfrac{P_{AE}(t)}{P_{IE}(t)} \right]^{d_3} \right\}$

[46] $\quad D_{IE}(t) = \dfrac{(1-s)\,Y_E(t) - P_{AE}(t)D_{AE}(t)}{P_{IE}(t)}$

Labor Migration

[47] $\quad m_{WE}(t) = \max \ |0, 1 - e^{\varphi\tilde{w}^*(t)}|$

[48] $\quad m_{EW}(t) = \max \ |0, 1 - e^{-\varphi\tilde{w}^*(t)}|$

[49] $\quad \hat{m}_{AI}(t) = \max \ |0, 1 - e^{\varphi\hat{w}^*(t)}|$

[50] $\quad \hat{m}_{IA}(t) = \max \ |0, 1 - e^{-\varphi\hat{w}^*(t)}|$

Real Wages and Interest Rates

[51] $\quad \tilde{w}_E(t) = \dfrac{w_E(t)}{COL_E(t)}$

[52] $\quad \tilde{w}_W(t) = \dfrac{\bar{w}_W(t)}{COL_W(t)}$

[53] $\quad \bar{w}_W(t) = \dfrac{w_{AW}(t)L_{AW}(t) + w_{IW}(t)L_{IW}(t)}{L_W(t)}$

[54] $\quad \tilde{w}^*(t) = \tilde{w}^*(t-1) + b \ \{\tilde{w}_E(t) - \tilde{w}_W(t) - \tilde{w}^*(t-1)\}$

[55] $\quad \hat{w}^*(t) = \hat{w}^*(t-1) + b \left\{ \dfrac{w_{IW}(t)}{P_{AW}(t)} - \dfrac{w_{AW}(t)}{P_{AW}(t)} - \hat{w}^*(t-1) \right\}$

[56] $\quad i_E(t) = \dfrac{r_E(t)}{P_{IE}(t)} - \delta$

[57] $\quad i_{IW}(t) = \dfrac{r_{IW}(t)}{P_{IW}(t)} - \delta$

[58] $\quad i_{AW}(t) = \dfrac{r_{AW}(t)}{P_{IW}(t)} - \delta$

[59] $\quad i^*(t) = i^*(t-1) + (1-\epsilon) \ \{i_E(t) - \bar{i}_W(t) - i^*(t-1)\}$

[60] $\quad \bar{i}_W(t) = \dfrac{i_{AW}(t)K_{AW}(t) + i_{IW}(t)K_{IW}(t)}{K_{AW}(t) + K_{IW}(t)}$

[61] $\quad \hat{i}^*(t) = \hat{i}^*(t-1) + (1-\epsilon) \ \{i_{IW}(t) - i_{AW}(t) - \hat{i}^*(t-1)\}$

Foreign Sector and Market Clearing Equations

[62] $\quad D_{AD}(t) = Q_{AW}(t) - EX(t)$

[63] $\quad D_{AD}(t) = D_{AW}(t) + D_{AE}(t)$

[64] $\quad D_A(t) = D_{AD}(t) + EX(t)$

[65] $\quad Y(t) = Y_E(t) + Y_W(t)$

[66] $\quad s = \{P_{IW}(t) [I_{IWE}(t) + I_{IWW}(t) + I_{AWE}(t)$
$\quad\quad + I_{AWW}(t)] + P_{IE}(t) [I_{IEE}(t) + I_{IEW}(t)]\} /$
$\quad\quad Y_E(t) + Y_W(t)$

[67] $\quad IM(t) = \dfrac{IMVAL(t)}{P_{IE}(t)}$

[68] $\quad EX(t) = \dfrac{EXVAL(t)}{P_{AE}(t)}$

[69] $\quad IMVAL(t) - EXVAL(t) = 0$

Transport Service Sector

[70] $\quad T_E(t) = \gamma T(t)$

[71] $\quad T_W(t) = (1-\gamma)T(t)$

[72] $\quad T(t) = Z_A(t) \ \{D_{AE}(t) + EX(t)\}$
$\quad\quad + Z_I(t) \ \{D_{IW}(t) + I_W(t) - Q_{IW}(t)\}$

333

APPENDIX B

Initial Conditions in 1870

Structure of the Economy in the 1870's. Perloff and his associates document that only 4,585,278 workers in the American labor force of 12,505,923 were located in employments of interest to us in 1870.[43] This subset of the labor force is our reference point, and it includes only eastern industrial employment and midwestern employment in both industry and agriculture. That is, we explicitly exclude all regions outside the Northeast and Midwest, and ignore employment in services, mining, forestry and fishing. How was this labor force distributed in 1870? The Perloff figures are presented in Table B.1 and this is one key facet of the 1870 industrial structure assumed for the initial period of the simulation. Almost 65 per cent of our labor force is located in the West and agriculture accounts for 49 per cent of the employment in the two regional economies taken together.

The implied 1870 distribution of total value added and value added of commodity output is also reported in Table

Table B.1

The Distribution of the Labor Force and Gross National Product Assumed in 1870

Sector or Region	Labor Force		Value of Output		Value of Commodity Output	
	Level	Share	Level	Share	Level	Share
Western Agriculture	49.3	.493	110.572	.358	110.572	.433
Eastern Industry	35.1	.351	100.195	.325	100.195	.393
Western Industry	15.6	.156	44.531	.144	44.531	.174
Transport	-	-	53.354	.173	-	-
Total	100.0	1.000	308.652	1.000	255.298	1.000

B.1. These output figures, although they appear reasonable enough, are difficult to document given the limited data available on a sectoral and regional basis for the 1870's. First, compare our assumed share of transport value added (revenue) in total value of output with Kuznets' estimated share of transport and communications in United States net national product 1869-79. For the 1870's as a whole, Kuznets estimates the share as 18.4 per cent, while for 1870 our model implies a comparable figure of 17.3 per cent.[44] Second, compare the regional output distribution implied by the model for 1870 with Easterlin's "income originating" estimates for 1880.[45] Excluding eastern agriculture, midwestern agriculture in 1880 accounted for 31.5 per cent of total output in the Northeast and Midwest, a figure very much in conformity with our 35.8 per cent share for 1870. Furthermore, Easterlin finds in 1880 that 34.4 per cent of non-agricultural income was generated by the midwestern states, while we assume that share to be 30.7 per cent in 1870. Since the Midwest underwent significant industrialization during the 1870's, these two figures appear to be roughly comparable. Finally, we note that average labor productivities implied by the model in 1870 and by Easterlin's 1880 figures are of the same magnitude. The ratio of agricultural to non-agricultural labor productivity is estimated as .58 in 1870 while Easterlin's data suggest a figure of .54.

Input Prices in the 1870's. The appropriate measure of the interest rate facing Midwest farmers is the *real* rate on farm mortgages. Bowman reports the *nominal* interest rate on farm mortgages in Illinois, Wisconsin, Iowa and Nebraska in 1870 to be, respectively, 9.6, 8.0, 9.5 and 10.5 per cent. The real farm mortgage rate was far higher, however, since the late 1860's were years of rapid decline in all prices. When these adjustments are made, the real farm mortgage rate in these four midwestern states was 17.0, 15.4, 16.9 and 17.9 per cent.[46] We take 16 per cent as a representative farm mortgage rate facing midwestern farmers in 1870.

Recent research on Wisconsin banking suggests that farm mortgage rates offered by country banks were from 25 to 30 per cent higher than the investment rates prevailing in Milwaukee.[47] On the basis of this and other evidence, 12.8 per cent is taken as the relevant real interest rate facing urban manufacturing in the Midwest.

Finally, Lance Davis' research on the American capital market documents a 25 per cent differential in interest rates on comparable assets quoted in western and eastern markets.[48] It follows that the real interest rate prevailing in eastern financial markets was approximately 10.2 per cent. Given the depreciation rates and capital goods' prices presented in Appendix C, the gross rates of return can be readily derived. Both the interest rates and the gross rental rates are reported in Table B.2.

Table B.2

Gross Rates of Return and Real Rates of Interest
by Sector, 1870

Variable	Eastern Industry	Western Agriculture	Western Industry
i_{ij}	0.102	0.160	0.218
δ	0.030	0.030	0.030
P_{Ij}	1.000	1.250	1.250
$r_{ij} = (i_{ij} + \delta)P_{Ij}$	0.132	0.197	0.237

Source: The i_{ij} estimates are discussed in the text. The price and depreciation parameters can be found in Appendix C.

Regional wages have been documented by Lebergott. In 1869, the average daily earnings of common laborers—a relatively homogeneous unskilled labor input—were the following:[49] New England, $1.56; Middle Atlantic, $1.58; East North Central, $1.58; and West North Central, $1.55.

Given this evidence, it certainly seems justified to assume in 1870 money wage equalization across regions. Since we can define our monetary units in any way we wish without influencing the analysis, we take Lebergott's daily wage as representing annual income per member of the 1870 labor force regardless of employment location. In Appendix C, the regional commodity price differentials are presented in detail. These output price data imply a *real* wage in the West almost half again larger than that prevailing in the East. Obviously, money wage equalization was fully consistent with the continued massive westward migration in the 1870's.

Capital Intensity and Factor Productivity in the 1870's. Since we have chosen arbitrary units in measuring both wage income and labor inputs, absolute levels of output, per capita income, and capital-labor ratios have little meaning. We can, of course, compare capital-output and land value-output assumed in the model with those estimated for the 1870's since these are pure numbers, independent of the monetary unit. Furthermore, the *relative* factor intensities and average factor productivities across regions and sectors should conform with the 1870 evidence.

First, consider midwestern agriculture. Tostlebe reports gross farm income in current prices in 1869, the current 1870 value of buildings, implements, and machinery, and the current 1870 value for land. In terms of our notation, these three series represent the value of midwestern farm output, the value of farm capital, and land, respectively. Furthermore, Tostlebe constructs these estimates separately for the Great Plains, the Lake States and the Corn Belt: these three regional groupings in fact aggregate to our Midwest. The series imply for the Midwest a capital-output ratio (in value terms) of 1.053 and a land-output ratio of 8.792.[50] These ratios are utilized in the analysis and are displayed in Table B.3.

337

is fully consistent with the available fragments of historical data for the 1870's. That is, the implied sectoral wage shares are consistent with Budd's data;[53] the share of transport income in national product is consistent with Kuznet's data; and the regional distribution of income conforms fairly closely with Easterlin's 1880 estimates.

Our prime concern in this section is the implied 1870 patterns of demand. Table B.5 reports the composition of gross national product assumed in 1870. Note first that the share of gross savings in gross national product is 18 per cent. Davis and Gallman estimate that gross capital formation (excluding inventories and agricultural clearing) was 18 per cent of gross national product during the decade 1869-78.[54] The model assumes a uniform savings rate of 18 per cent for all income groups in 1870. Depreciation amounts to approximately 34 per cent of gross investment. This figure is reasonably close to Kuznet's calculation for the year 1870: Kuznets' finds the share to be 38 per cent.[55]

The remainder of income represents consumption expenditures. The share of expenditures on foodstuffs may vary across regions: indeed, our model assumes for 1870 that 55.4 per cent of expenditures are devoted to foodstuffs in the East and 46.7 per cent in the West. The former figure is almost identical to that reported for Massachusetts

Table B.5

Gross National Product Composition, 1870

Variable	Value
Net Investment	38.013
Depreciation	17.544
Current Account Balance in Foreign Sector	0
Consumption	253.095
Gross National Product	308.652

workers in 1875.[56] On the basis of Fishlow's research, the figure for the West is taken to be 46.7 per cent.[57]

To complete our specification of the 1870 initial conditions an estimate of export values is required. The ratio of the value of farm exports to gross farm product is needed. This ratio averaged approximately 16.8 per cent in the early 1870's,[58] while it assumes a value of 16.6 per cent in our 1870 economy. The share of export receipts in gross commodity output implied by our model is 6.1 per cent in 1870. This figure is far lower than the 11.5 per cent share of exports in commodity output calculated from Kuznets' data for 1871.[59] The difference reflects our exclusion of the South from our regional economy.

APPENDIX C

Summary of Initial Conditions (1870)

Physical Outputs

$Q_{IE} = 100.195$
$Q_{IW} = 35.625$
$Q_{AW} = 110.573$

Output Prices

$P_{IW} = 1.250$
$P_{AW} = 1.000$
$P_{IE} = 1.000$
$P_{AE} = 2.000$

Income

$Y_E = 132.100$
$Y_W = 176.552$
$T = 53.354$

Savings and Demand

$$S_W = 31.748$$
$$S_E = 23.778$$
$$D_{AW} = 70.647$$
$$D_{IW} = 59.326$$
$$D_{AE} = 30.749$$
$$D_{IE} = 46.825$$

Inputs

$$K_{IE} = 341.572$$
$$K_{IW} = 101.463$$
$$K_{AW} = 93.114$$
$$L_{IE} = 35.100$$
$$L_{IW} = 15.600$$
$$L_{AW} = 49.300$$
$$R = 972.157$$

Input Prices

$$i_{AW} = 0.160$$
$$i_{IW} = 0.128$$
$$i_E = 0.102$$
$$r_E = 0.132$$
$$r_{AW} = 0.237$$
$$r_{IW} = 0.197$$
$$w_E = 1.570$$
$$w_{IW} = 1.570$$
$$w_{AW} = 1.570$$

Foreign Trade

$$EX = 9.178$$
$$IM = 18.355$$
$$EXVAL = IMVAL = 18.355$$

342

Parameter Estimates

The parameter estimates are discussed in detail elsewhere.[60] In order to conserve space, we present here only a summary of the empirical results.

Production Conditions:

$\alpha_K = 0.45$ $\beta_K = 0.20$
$\alpha_L = 0.55$ $\beta_L = 0.70$
                  $\beta_R = 0.10$

Capital Accumulation Parameters:

$\delta = 0.03$ 1870-1889: $s = 0.18$
              1890-1894: $s = 0.19$
              1895-1910: $s = 0.20$

Consumer Demand Parameters:

$d_2 = 0.80$
$d_3 = -0.80$

Labor Migration Parameters

$\varphi_{WE} = 0.007 = \varphi_{EW}$ $b = 0.33$
$\varphi_{IA} = 0.070 = \varphi_{AI}$

Capital Market Parameters:

$\mu = 4.00$ $(1-\epsilon) = 0.33$

343

Transport Service Sector:
$\gamma = 0.50$

t	$Z_A(t)$	$Z_I(t)$	t	$Z_A(t)$	$Z_I(t)$	t	$Z_A(t)$	$Z_I(t)$
1870	2.00	1.25	1884	1.60	1.24	1897	1.41	1.34
1871	1.62	1.22	1885	1.67	1.26	1898	1.43	1.33
1872	1.69	1.18	1886	1.69	1.29	1899	1.49	1.31
1873	1.89	1.19	1887	1.63	1.28	1900	1.45	1.29
1874	1.75	1.22	1888	1.56	1.26	1901	1.50	1.29
1875	1.79	1.21	1889	1.48	1.28	1902	1.33	1.27
1876	1.84	1.20	1890	1.40	1.29	1903	1.56	1.27
1877	1.64	1.27	1891	1.37	1.29	1904	1.53	1.27
1878	1.68	1.28	1892	1.45	1.31	1905	1.44	1.27
1879	1.74	1.21	1893	1.63	1.30	1906	1.38	1.26
1880	1.48	1.23	1894	1.42	1.34	1907	1.41	1.25
1881	1.40	1.22	1895	1.38	1.33	1908	1.32	1.25
1882	1.43	1.20	1896	1.48	1.34	1909	1.35	1.24
1883	1.70	1.23				1910	1.21	1.23

Total Factor Productivity Growth:

t	B(t)	A(t)	A'(t)	t	B(t)	A(t)	A'(t)
1870	1.466	1.025	.983	1891	1.726	1.377	1.320
1871	1.486	1.035	.992	1892	1.733	1.392	1.335
1872	1.507	1.044	1.001	1893	1.739	1.407	1.350
1873	1.528	1.053	1.010	1894	1.746	1.423	1.364
1874	1.550	1.063	1.019	1895	1.753	1.438	1.379
1875	1.571	1.072	1.028	1896	1.760	1.454	1.395
1876	1.593	1.082	1.038	1897	1.767	1.470	1.410
1877	1.616	1.092	1.047	1898	1.775	1.480	1.420
1878	1.624	1.112	1.067	1899	1.782	1.491	1.430
1879	1.632	1.134	1.087	1900	1.789	1.501	1.440
1880	1.640	1.155	1.108	1901	1.796	1.512	1.450
1881	1.648	1.177	1.129	1902	1.803	1.522	1.460
1882	1.656	1.199	1.150	1903	1.810	1.533	1.470
1883	1.665	1.222	1.172	1904	1.818	1.544	1.480
1884	1.673	1.245	1.194	1905	1.825	1.554	1.490
1885	1.681	1.269	1.217	1906	1.832	1.565	1.501
1886	1.690	1.293	1.240	1907	1.839	1.576	1.512
1887	1.698	1.318	1.264	1908	1.847	1.587	1.522
1888	1.705	1.332	1.278	1909	1.854	1.598	1.533
1889	1.712	1.347	1.292	1910	1.862	1.610	1.544
1890	1.719	1.362	1.306				

Labor Force Growth Parameters:

t	$M(t)$	$n_E(t)$	$n_W(t)$	t	$M(t)$	$n_E(t)$	$n_W(t)$
1870	.846	1.022	1.025				
1871	.846	1.022	1.025	1891	1.154	1.009	1.015
1872	1.038	1.020	1.024	1892	1.346	1.010	1.014
1873	1.077	1.018	1.024	1893	.923	1.010	1.014
1874	.500	1.017	1.023	1894	.077	1.010	1.014
1875	.077	1.015	1.023	1895	-.154	1.010	1.013
1876	-.077	1.014	1.022	1896	.154	1.010	1.013
1877	-.231	1.014	1.021	1897	-.154	1.009	1.013
1878	-.154	1.014	1.021	1898	-.154	1.009	1.013
1879	.077	1.013	1.020	1899	.192	1.009	1.013
1880	1.038	1.012	1.020	1900	.731	1.009	1.012
1881	1.885	1.012	1.019	1901	.269	1.009	1.012
1882	2.154	1.011	1.019	1902	.692	1.009	1.012
1883	1.577	1.011	1.018	1903	1.154	1.009	1.012
1884	1.115	1.010	1.018	1904	1.269	1.009	1.012
1885	.385	1.010	1.017	1905	1.692	1.009	1.011
1886	.269	1.010	1.017	1906	2.269	1.009	1.011
1887	.769	1.009	1.016	1907	1.962	1.009	1.011
1888	.808	1.009	1.016	1908	.192	1.009	1.011
1889	.385	1.009	1.015	1909	1.192	1.009	1.011
1890	.462	1.009	1.015	1910	0	1.009	1.011

Exogenous World Prices: $P_{AW}(t) = 1.00$

t	$P_{AE}(t)$	t	$P_{AE}(t)$	t	$P_{AE}(t)$
1870	2.00	1884	1.60	1897	1.41
1871	1.62	1885	1.67	1898	1.43
1872	1.69	1886	1.69	1899	1.49
1873	1.89	1887	1.63	1900	1.45
1874	1.75	1888	1.56	1901	1.50
1875	1.79	1889	1.48	1902	1.33
1876	1.84	1890	1.40	1903	1.56
1877	1.64	1891	1.37	1904	1.53
1878	1.68	1892	1.45	1905	1.44
1879	1.74	1893	1.63	1906	1.38
1880	1.48	1894	1.42	1907	1.41
1881	1.40	1895	1.38	1908	1.32
1882	1.43	1896	1.48	1909	1.35
1883	1.70			1910	1.21

t	$P_{IE}(t)$	t	$P_{IE}(t)$	t	$P_{IE}(t)$
1870	1.00	1884	.92	1898	.82
1871	1.13	1885	.93	1899	.90
1872	1.30	1886	.93	1900	.95
1873	1.29	1887	.91	1901	.96
1874	1.08	1888	.81	1902	.75
1875	.96	1889	.99	1903	.89
1876	.95	1890	.95	1904	.93
1877	.88	1891	.68	1905	.91
1878	1.03	1892	.80	1906	.93
1879	1.01	1893	.97	1907	.84
1880	.93	1894	.99	1908	.68
1881	.73	1895	.91	1909	.63
1882	.76	1896	1.03	1910	.61
1883	.90	1897	.84		

Exogenous Land Stock:

Year	R(t)	% Increase	Year	R(t)	% Increase
1870	972.157	.000	1891	1780.393	.019
1871	1017.848	.047	1892	1813.330	.018
1872	1063.651	.045	1893	1845.970	.018
1873	1109.388	.043	1894	1878.274	.017
1874	1154.873	.041	1895	1911.144	.017
1875	1200.259	.039	1896	1944.589	.017
1876	1244.669	.037	1897	1977.647	.017
1877	1288.232	.035	1898	2010.278	.016
1878	1330.744	.033	1899	2042.443	.016
1879	1373.328	.032	1900	2074.100	.015
1880	1414.528	.030	1901	2102.101	.013
1881	1452.720	.027	1902	2126.275	.011
1882	1487.585	.024	1903	2146.474	.009
1883	1518.824	.021	1904	2162.573	.007
1884	1556.795	.025	1905	2174.467	.005
1885	1587.931	.020	1906	2184.252	.004
1886	1618.895	.019	1907	2192.989	.004
1887	1650.464	.019	1908	2201.761	.004
1888	1682.648	.019	1909	2210.568	.004
1889	1714.618	.019	1910	2219.410	.004
1890	1747.196	.019			

Note: The research underlying this paper was supported by a grant from the National Science Foundation. I am grateful for the critical comments offered, but often ignored, by Leo DeBever, John Bowman, Bob Brito, Stanley Engerman, Donald Hester, and Donald McCloskey. In addition, the comments of the participants in the Madison MSSB Seminar on the Application of General Equilibrium Models to Economic History (Summer, 1972) are happily acknowledged; in particular, my thanks to Michael Mussa and Ronald Jones. This essay draws heavily upon chapter 9 of my *Late Nineteenth-Century American Development: A General Equilibrium History* Cambridge: Cambridge University Press, 1974).

1. A. Fishlow, *American Railroads and the Transformation of the Ante-Bellum Economy* (Cambridge, Mass.: Harvard University Press, 1965).

2. R. W. Fogel, *Railroads and American Economic Growth: Essays in Econometric History* (Baltimore: The Johns Hopkins Press, 1964); *The Union Pacific Railroad: A Case in Premature Enterprise* (Baltimore: The Johns Hopkins Press, 1960).

3. The best critical evaluation, from this writer's point of view, can be found in Fishlow's, *American Railroads and the Transformation of the Ante-Bellum Economy*, Chapter II. See also: M. Nerlove, "Railroads and American Economic Growth," *Journal of Economic History* (March 1966), 107-15; S. Lebergott, "United States Transport Advance and Externalities," *Journal of Economic History*

(December 1966), 437-61. Much of the remainder of this section relies heavily on Fishlow's critique.

4. Fishlow, *American Railroads and the Transformation of the Ante-Bellum Economy*, p. 27.

5. *Ibid.*, p. 30.

6. Professor Fogel himself has suggested a linear approximation to the approach taken in this paper. He argues that a linear programming model would be an attractive method for attacking the problem but never utilizes the approach. Fogel, *Railroads and American Economic Growth*, pp. 26-27. In any case, we have rejected linearization of our system as inappropriate for long term historical analysis.

7. R. Higgs, "Railroad Rates and the Populist Uprising," *Agricultural History*, XLIV (July 1970) and *The Transformation of the American Economy, 1865-1914: An Essay in Interpretation* (New York: John Wiley and Sons, 1971), pp. 87-90.

8. A detailed discussion of these points can be found in the Appendix to Chapter III in my *Late Nineteenth-Century American Development: A General Equilibrium History* and in W. Z. Ripley, *Railroads: Rates and Regulations* (New York: Longmans and Green, 1912), Chps. II-VIII; F. A. Shannon, *The Farmer's Last Frontier: Agriculture, 1860-1897* (New York: Harper, 1968), pp. 173-79 and pp. 295-303; C. C. McCain, *The Diminishing Purchasing Power of Railway Earnings* (New York: 1909).

9. J. G. Williamson, *Late Nineteenth-Century American Development*, Appendix A.

10. Fishlow has documented a 50 per cent increase in total factor productivity in the rails from 1870 to 1890. The equivalent decline in Z_A over the same period hardly seems a coincidence given our constant (short run) cost characterization of the transport sector! A. Fishlow, "Productivity and Technological Change in the Railroad Sector, 1840-1910," in *Output, Employment, and Productivity in the United States After 1800* (New York: Columbia University Press, 1966), p. 626.

11. Fishlow adopts this view in *American Railroads and the Transformation of the Ante-Bellum Economy*, p. 45:

> Changed regional terms of trade over this [ante-bellum] period largely reflect improved transport conditions: western farmers far from the market received relatively more for their output than eastern farmers closer in. Calculation of the effect upon income of the more favorable later terms of trade then will approximate the change due to better transportation.

12. R. Jones, "The Structure of Simple General Equilibrium Models," *The Journal of Political Economy*, vol. LXXIII, No. 6 (December 1965), 557-72; R. Jones "General Equilibrium with Three Factors of Production," (unpublished paper, University of Rochester); G. Hueckel, "The Napoleonic Wars and Factor Returns Within the English Economy," paper presented to the Madison Cliometric Conference, Madison, Wisconsin (April 27-29, 1972).

13. Presumably, Ames and Rosenberg would object and insist we allow agricultural goods to be utilized as intermediate inputs to manufacturing activities as well. See E. Ames and N. Rosenberg, "The Enfield Arsenal in Theory and History," *Economic Journal*, LXXVII (December 1968), 827-42, and D. L.

Brito and J. G. Williamson, "Skilled Labor and Nineteenth Century Anglo-American Managerial Behavior," *Explorations in Economic History*, (spring 1973), 235-52.

14. The reader interested in the derivation of these equations is advised to examine the papers by Jones and Hueckel where they are treated in detail.

15. F. J. Turner's views can be found in *The Frontier in American History* (New York: 1920); *The Significance of Sections in American History* (New York: 1932); *The Rise of the New West, 1811-1829* (New York: 1906); and *The United States 1830-1850* (New York: 1935). H. J. Habakkuk, *American and British Technology in the Nineteenth Century* (Cambridge: Cambridge University Press, 1962).

16. In addition to the papers cited, there have been some recent applications of general equilibrium analysis to antebellum United States. They include the following papers read at the 1970 Cliometrics Conference (Madison, Wisconsin: April 30-May 2): C. Pope, "The Effect of the Ante-bellum Tariff on Income Distribution"; P. Passell and M. Schmundt, "Pre-Civil War Land Policy and the Growth of Manufacturing"; and J. Green, "The Effect of the Iron Tariff in the United States, 1847-1859: The Estimation of a General Equilibrium System with Non-Traded Goods."

17. This section is taken from my *Late Nineteenth-Century American Development* Chapter III where a much longer defense of the historical relevance of the model is developed. See also J. A. Swanson and J. G. Williamson, "Explanations and Issues: A Prospectus for Quantitative Economic History," *Journal of Economic History*, (March 1971), 43-57.

18. Z. Griliches, "Production Functions in Manufacturing: Some Preliminary Results," *The Theory and Empirical Analysis of Production*, Studies in Income and Wealth, Vol. 31 (NBER: 1967), 275-321; and P. Zarembka, "On the Empirical Relevance of the CES Production Function," *Review of Economics and Statistics*, (February 1970), 47-53.

19. This would hardly be a relevant assumption for cotton exports in the antebellum period. An inelastic foreign demand for cotton becomes a critical element in Professor Pope's analysis of ante-bellum tariffs in his general equilibrium framework. See C. Pope, "The Effect of the Antebellum Tariff on Income Distribution."

20. G. Borts, "Returns Equalization and Regional Growth," *American Economic Review*, (June 1960), 319-47.

21. This is hardly a completely realistic characterization of the location of intermediaries, especially after the 1880's. The assumption is not critical, however, since our results do not prove to be sensitive to it. In any case, we shall see below that *intra*regional Western intermediation is assumed to be performed by Western cities and returns to such intermediation accrue to Western "industrialists". See L. Davis, "The Investment Market, 1870-1914: The Evolution of a National Market," *Journal of Economic History*, (September 1965), 355-99; A. Bogue, *Money at Interest* (Ithaca, N.Y.: Cornell University Press, 1955); H. F. Williamson and O. A. Smalley, *Northwestern Mutual Life: A Century of Trusteeship* (Evanston, Ill.: Northwestern University Press, 1957).

22. M. L. Primack, "Land Clearning Under Nineteenth-Century Techniques: Some Preliminary Calculations," *Journal of Economic History*, XXII (December 1962), 484-87; Primack, "Farm Construction as a Use of Farm Labor, 1850-1910," *Journal of Economic History*, XXV (March 1965), 114-25; Primack, "Farm Capital Formation as a Use of Farm Labor, 1850-1910," *Journal of Economic History*, XXVI (September 1966), 348-62. Capital formation in land clearing, farm building, fencing, drainage, and irrigation were very large components of capital formation in agriculture, although the main input was farm labor. As late as 1869-78, a little less than 10 per cent of United States capital formation was in this form. R. E. Gallman and L. Davis, "The Share of Savings and Investment in Gross National Product During the 19th Century, The United States of America," Stanford Research Center in Economic Growth, Memorandum No. 63 (July 1968), p. 3.

23. P. Kenen, "Nature, Capital, and Trade," *Journal of Political Economy*, LXXIII (October 1965), 437-60.

24. R. Gallman and L. Davis, "The Share of Savings and Investment in Gross National Product," Tables 1 and 2. Although our model is open to foreign trade, we exclude foreign capital inflows. Are we justified in ignoring external sources of finance from abroad following 1869? Were not foreign capital inflows critical determinants of the gross domestic capital formation ratio? Surely they were during *peak* decades of capital inflow used to finance the expanding railroad network, but Gallman shows that they were negligible over longer periods. R. Gallman, "Gross National Product in the United States, 1834-1909," *Output, Employment, and Productivity in the United States After 1800* (New York: Columbia University Press, 1966), pp. 3-75. See also J. G. Williamson, *American Growth and the Balance of Payments, 1820-1913* (Chapel Hill: University of North Carolina Press, 1964).

25. P. Temin, "General-Equilibrium Models in Economic History," *Journal of Economic History* (March 1971), 72-74.

26. The financial intermediation thesis is explored at length in my *Late Nineteenth-Century American Development*, Chapters 3 and 6.

27. In fact the so-called "Great Depression" during the late nineteenth century can be readily explained by such a framework. See my *Late Nineteenth-Century American Development*, Chapter 5 and "Late Nineteenth Century American Retardation: A Neoclassical Analysis," *The Journal of Economic History*, (September 1973), 581-607.

28. Unless otherwise noted, for the remainder of this paper we shall refer to our Midwest and Northeast as the American economy.

29. R. W. Fogel, "The Specification Problem in Economic History," *Journal of Economic History*, XXVII (September 1967), 297-98.

30. A more detailed analysis of the results contained in this section can be found in my *Late Nineteenth-Century American Development*, Chapter 4.

31. The causes and consequences of this retardation in American late nineteenth century growth can be found in my "Late Nineteenth Century American Retardation."

32. Let the Gallman series be denoted by A(t), and the simulated series by P(t). Estimation of the simple regression

$$P(t) = -6.540 + 1.042 \, A(t)$$
$$(2.721) \quad (0.141)$$

yields $R^2 = 0.891$. Significance tests indicate that the slope coefficient is *not* significantly different than unity. Judged by the conventional forecasting literature, these results speak well of the plausibility of the model.

33. Let the Lebergott series be denoted by $A_W(t)$ and the predicted $w_E(t)$ series by $P_W(t)$. A regression between these two variables has been estimated as

$$P_W(t) = -0.039 + 1.066 \, A_W(t), \ R^2 = 0.59.$$
$$(0.300) \quad (0.139)$$

A "perfect" forecast would have the estimated slope coefficient equal to unity and the intercept equal to zero. The regression results show in fact that the slope coefficient is insignificantly different from unity and the intercept insignificantly different from zero. This "goodness-of-fit" test bodes well for the model. Although only half of the variance in $P_W(t)$ is explained by $A_W(t)$, the short run movements are of little concern to us and the R^2 could be easily raised by smoothing devices.

34. In addition, of course, the relative price of farm equipment also falls during the period giving further impetus to farm mechanization. We shall have more to say about this in section 5.

35. W. N. Parker and J. Klein, "Productivity Growth in Grain Production in the United States, 1840-60 and 1900-10," in *Output, Employment and Productivity in the United States after 1800* (New York: Columbia University Press, 1966), Tables 10 and 11, pp. 542-3.

36. R. Fogel and J. Rutner, "The Efficiency Effects of Federal Land Policy, 1850-1900: A Report of Some Provisional Findings," University of Chicago, Center for Mathematical Studies in Business and Economics, Report 7027 (June 1970), Table 3, 12. Fogel and Rutner use the wholesale price index as a deflator. The regional income estimates are constructed by applying Easterlin's state relatives to Gallman's value added per worker.

37. C. R. Chambers, "Farm Land Income and Farm Land Values," *American Economic Review*, XV (December 1924).

38. J. G. Williamson, *American Growth and the Balance of Payments*, pp. 138-39.

39. W. W. Rostow, *The Process of Economic Growth* (Oxford: Clarendon Press, 1950) and *The Stages of Economic Growth* (Cambridge: Cambridge University Press, 1960).

40. R. W. Fogel, *Railroads and American Economic Growth*, Chaps. IV-VI.

41. That is, we continue to assume that the terms of trade in the East is determined by world market conditions. Interregional transport cost changes have an impact only on midwestern relative prices under those assumptions.

42. The author is presently exploring two promising revisions. The first involves a departure from the convenient "small country" assumption and attempts to determine commodity prices endogenously. The second introduces an endogenous explanation of foreign immigration.

43. H. S. Perloff, E. S. Dunn, E. E. Lampard and R. F. Muth, *Regions, Resources and Economic Growth* (Baltimore: Johns Hopkins Press, 1970), Chapter 12.

44. Calculated from S. Kuznets, *Modern Economic Growth: Rate, Structure, and Spread* (New Haven, Conn.: Yale University Press, 1966), Tables 3.1 and 3.5, pp. 88-93, 131-32.

45. Easterlin's estimates are based on income originating in commodity production and distribution. His industry category includes mining, construction, manufacturing, transportation and public utilities. R. A. Easterlin, "Interregional Differences in Per Capita Income, Population, and Total Income, 1840-1950," in *Trends in the American Economy in the Nineteenth Century* (New York: National Bureau of Economic Research, 1960), Appendix A, pp. 97-104.

46. The nominal rates are taken from J. Bowman, "Trends in Midwestern Farm Land Values, 1860-1900," (unpublished doctoral dissertation, Yale University, 1964), Table II, Chapter III, III-14. The real rates include the influence of the observed rate of price change where the preceding five years are utilized as an average. The price changes are based on the Warren-Pearson all commodity index.

47. R. H. Keehn, "Nineteenth Century Wisconsin Banking," (unpublished doctoral dissertation, University of Wisconsin, 1971), Chapter IV, Tables 1-3.

48. This differential prevailed in 1880 and is based on regional mortgage rate differences. L. Davis, "The Investment Market, 1870-1914: The Evolution of a National Market," *Journal of Economic History* (September 1965), Table 7, p. 375. Other evidence presented in Davis' article implies that this differential was roughly the same in the early 1870's.

49. S. Lebergott, *Manpower in Economic Growth: The American Record Since 1800* (New York: McGraw-Hill Book Company, 1964), Table A-25, p. 541.

50. Calculated from A. S. Tostlebe, *Capital in Agriculture: Its Formation and Financing Since 1870* (New York: National Bureau of Economic Research, 1957), Tables 7 and H-3, pp. 54-57, 214-16.

51. S. Kuznets, *Capital in the American Economy: Its Formation and Financing* (New York: National Bureau of Economic Research, 1961), Table 27, pp. 198-99.

52. Industry is defined broadly in Table B.3 to include all urban oriented nonagricultural activities.

53. E. C. Budd, "Factor Shares, 1850-1910," in *Trends in the American Economy in the Nineteenth Century*, pp. 365-98.

54. R. E. Gallman and L. E. Davis, "The Share of Savings and Investment in Gross National Product During the 19th Century, The United States of America," Stanford Research Center in Economic Growth, Memorandum No. 63 (July 1968), Table 1, 2.

55. S. Kuznets, *Capital in the American Economy: Its Formation and Financing*, Table 2, p. 56.

56. In the Massachusetts urban workers sample, 55.5 per cent was spent on food in 1875. J. G. Williamson, "Consumer Behavior in the Nineteenth Century: Carroll D. Wright's Massachusetts Workers in 1875," *Explorations in Entrepreneurial History*, 2nd Series, IV (Winter 1967), Table 4, p. 116.

57. A. Fishlow, "Consumption Patterns and the Extent of the Market: Nineteenth Century United States, France and Britain," presented to the Conference on Micro Aspects of Development, Chicago Circle, Chicago, Illinois (November 19-21, 1970).

58. R. Lipsey, *Price and Quantity Trends in the Foreign Trade of the United States* (New York: National Bureau of Economic Research, 1963), Table G-14, p. 436. The figure is an average over 1870-74.

59. S. Kuznets, *Capital in the American Economy*, Tables R-21 and R-27, pp. 553, 565. The figures are in current prices and the "Variant I" estimate excludes services.

60. J. G. Williamson, *Late Nineteenth-Century American Development: A General Equilibrium History*, Appendix A.

352

Index

Adams, D., 127
Agriculture: (see also Midwest)
  fencing costs, 122
  implements, 122
  income per state, 103-104, 110
  income per worker, 84-85, 105, 110
  investment outlays, 119-126
  labor costs, 127-128
  labor force, 111-122
  land, 9-10, 20, 43-47, 57-65, 118-137,
    145-157, 170-171, 198, 234-235, 283
  availability, and fertility, 145-157
  availability, and wages, 283
  crop yields, 126-127
  loans on, 234-235
  ownership, 9-10
  prices, 122, 198
  productivity, 43-47, 57-65
  profitability, 131-133
  settlement patterns, 201, 133-134
  speculation, 118-137, 234-235
Albany, 247
Astor, J. J., 21

Baltimore, 248
Bank: (see also State Bank)
  of Detroit, 209
  of Illinois (Shawneetown), 213, 218,
    236-237
  of Michigan, 212, 218
  of the United States (First), 209, 219
  of the United States (Second), 212-
    214, 219, 226-288
Banks: (see also Old Northwest)
  Old Northwest, 208-245
  Social savings of, 239-240
Barton, C. R., 47, 65-67
Berry, R., 124, 126, 230
Blodget, S., 57-59
Borts, G., 289
Boston, 206
Bowman, J., 307, 309, 335
Brodell, A. P., 47, 65-67

Budd, E. G., 340
Buffalo, 247

Calender, G., 87
Cameron, R., 208, 221, 242
Canals: (see also Indiana, Ohio, and Old
  Northwest)
  Chesapeake and Ohio, 248
  and economic rent, 252-254
  Erie, 129, 247-250, 254-255, 258-259,
    261, 263
  Mainline, 248-249
  in Old Northwest, 246-268
Chambers, C. R., 310
Child-woman ratio, 140-144, 175
Clinton, D., 247
Cobb-Douglas production function,
  287, 309
Cole, A. H., 124
Cooper, M. R., 47, 65-67

Danhof, C., 122
David, P., 36, 38-41, 49, 87-90
Davis, L., 240, 294-295, 336, 340
DeBow, J., 58
Denison, E., 40, 46, 68-69
Deposit Act of 1836, 214-215
Distribution Act, 215-217
Douglas, S. A., 217

East (North-Eastern States), 3-5, 17
Easterlin, R., 197, 286, 335
Economic Growth:
  railroads and midwestern, 298-300,
    314-316
  rate in nineteenth century, 54-57
  in United States, 35-76
  and wealth growth, 192-204
Engerman, S., 239

Fertility:
  and economic stress, 146-152
  and urbanization, 152-155

353